Adjudicating Campus Sexual Misconduct and Assault

Adjudicating Campus Sexual Misconduct and Assault

Controversies and Challenges

Claire M. Renzetti and
Diane R. Follingstad, Editors

Cognella Series on Family and Gender-Based Violence

Claire M. Renzetti, Series Editor

cognella®
SAN DIEGO

Bassim Hamadeh, CEO and Publisher
Amy Smith, Project Editor
Jeanine Rees, Production Editor
Jess Estrella, Senior Graphic Designer
Stephanie Kohl, Licensing Coordinator
Natalie Piccotti, Director of Marketing
Kassie Graves, Vice President of Editorial
Jamie Giganti, Director of Academic Publishing

9781516577934

cognella® | ACADEMIC PUBLISHING
3970 Sorrento Valley Blvd., Ste. 500, San Diego, CA 92121

Brief Contents

Detailed Contents

Preface

Claire M. Renzetti and Diane R. Follingstad

The announcement came at lunchtime during the Center for Research on Violence Against Women's first national Title IX conference in Lexington, Kentucky on September 22, 2017. The conference attendees—attorneys, researchers, Title IX officers, university administrators and student life personnel, victim advocates, students, and survivors—stopped eating and chatting and turned their attention to the big screen in the conference venue as U.S. Secretary of Education Betsy DeVos rescinded what she described as "much criticized" Obama-era guidance to universities regarding the investigation and adjudication of campus sexual assault cases. DeVos promised new guidance following a period of public notice and comment. She also announced interim guidance—a Q&A document—that would "help schools as they work to combat sexual misconduct and w[ould] treat all students fairly" (U.S. Department of Education, 2017). DeVos stated that universities must respond to "these horrific crimes and behaviors," that they must stop "sweeping them under the rug," but at the same time, the investigation and adjudication process must be "fair and impartial" (U.S. Department of Education, 2017).

It is difficult to capture with a single adjective the mood in the room that day following DeVos's announcement. Conference participants—most with many years of experience in responding to campus sexual misconduct and assault cases—expressed a mixture of concern, frustration, and anger. One word that definitely did not characterize the conference participants was silent. At the close of DeVos's announcement, the room erupted into discussion about the potential consequences of the rescission and what might be expected from the U.S. Department of Education in the months to come. To be sure, there had been plenty of heated debate regarding the 2011 and 2014 Title IX guidance from the U.S. Department of Education's Office for Civil Rights. But the individuals in the room that day, along with many of their colleagues throughout the country, had been working diligently to ensure that their institutions addressed campus sexual misconduct and assault "head-on," as DeVos was urging them to do, while also balancing the rights of complainants and the accused and ensuring just outcomes. There was—and remains—plenty of room for improvement, but the conference attendees clearly had little confidence that the current Trump Administration's perspective on campus sexual misconduct and assault would result in equity and justice for all parties.

For us, the editors of this volume, the time appeared ripe for a broad but deep assessment of Title IX's impact on the investigation and adjudication of campus sexual misconduct and assault cases, and for strategic reflection on how to continue to make progressive change despite the constraints that may be imposed by the federal government yielding to a conservative backlash. Consequently, we invited some of the most respected legal and social analysts and practitioners in the country to discuss what may arguably be considered the most controversial and perplexing dimensions of campus sexual misconduct adjudication (e.g., the issue of consent, mandatory reporting, confidentiality, the role of attorneys, and, of course, standards of proof). We also asked contributors to discuss such issues as how campus adjudication processes differ from those of the criminal justice system; the advantages and disadvantages of various models of investigation and adjudication, including alternative models such as restorative justice; and the advantages and disadvantages of various types of sanctions. We also sought to include views of adjudication and sanctions from the perspectives of the accused ("respondents") and from college students more broadly. These are the topics that are the focus of the chapters in this volume, which concludes with a thoughtful discussion of best practices and recommendations for continuing progress.

As the contributors to this volume were writing their chapters, the Center for Research on Violence Against Women convened a second national Title IX conference (University of Kentucky, n.d.), with this one focused on "navigating change at the Department of Education." Based on the presentations and discussions at the 2018 conference, we became even more strongly convinced of the need for this book. The 2018 conference participants continued to express concern about the direction the U.S. Department of Education's Title IX guidance might take; a variety of potential scenarios and what-ifs were discussed and debated. Our goals for this book, therefore, are to provide a thorough and honest assessment of options for adjudication of campus sexual misconduct and assault cases, to promote dialogue among those involved in these cases on how to improve responses while not losing sight of the importance of prevention, to increase collaboration, and to address the challenges that arise both within our institutions and externally.

We wish to take this opportunity to thank the host of individuals who helped us bring this book to fruition. We are grateful to University of Kentucky President Eli Capilouto and his staff for their generous support of the Title IX conferences as well as their commitment to preventing and effectively addressing campus sexual misconduct and assault. We also thank our colleagues and staff in the Center for Research on Violence Against Women, especially Jaspreet Chahal and Brandon Bell, for their hard work on the two national conferences. And, of course, we are deeply grateful to the chapter authors, not only for their contributions to the book, but for their dedication to ensuring fairness and justice on and off our nation's campuses.

References

University of Kentucky. (n.d.). *2018 national conference*. Retrieved from www.uky.edu/crvaw/2018-national-conference

U.S. Department of Education. (2017, September 22). *Department of Education issues new interim guidance on campus sexual misconduct* (Press release). Retrieved from https://www.ed.gov/news/press-releases/department-education-issues-new-interim-guidance-campus-sexual-misconduct

I Setting the Stage

CHAPTER ONE

Sexual Misconduct and Assault Cases on Campus and in the Justice System

A Comparison

Callie Marie Rennison

Title IX was passed in 1972 to end sex discrimination in educational institutions receiving federal funds. Yet it is only relatively recently that educational institutions have established policies, procedures, and offices to comply with this law. By doing so, institutions attempt to ensure that students, staff, faculty, and other affiliates of the institutions do not engage in sex discrimination and that they work or matriculate in an environment free from sex discrimination. A part of this work includes adjudication of Title IX complaints.

Establishing robust Title IX offices, policies, and procedures to deal with sex discrimination is critical. Why? First, it is the right thing to do to ensure that all people have an opportunity for education and/or employment in a setting free from sex discrimination. Ensuring those who experience sex discrimination have the support and resources they need and educating and sanctioning those who engage in sex discrimination are necessary to end this behavior. Merely ignoring the actions of a perpetrator, or moving a perpetrator from one setting to another where the behavior continues, solves nothing. Appropriate adjudication is key. Second, failure to facilitate an environment free from sex discrimination can and has resulted in massive financial fines from lawsuits or settlements against educational institutions (e.g., Michigan State University in 2019). Third, failure to address the requirements of Title IX can lead to the loss of federal funding for these institutions. Fourth, with increased media awareness of Title IX issues, failure to address sex discrimination—and in some cases encourage, perpetuate, and fail to adjudicate it—has led to negative public relations, a loss of enrollment, and deservedly poor reputations.

How did these Title IX policies, procedures, and offices come to be? How did educational campuses become the adjudicators of Title IX cases? The purpose of this chapter is to answer these questions by presenting the foundational history, as well as describing *how* and *why* Title IX processes are not miniature versions of the criminal legal system's process of punishing criminal sexual acts. This chapter should make clear that university Title IX processes are not intended to be a system of punishment for wrongdoing at all.

The chapter first presents a brief history of Title IX, and it describes crucial court cases that continue to define Title IX offices, policies, and procedures. Next, the chapter identifies how and why Title IX proceedings are not scaled-down versions of the criminal legal system. This is accomplished by presenting significant differences in the processes, goals, and outcomes of the criminal legal and educational systems. In doing this, the chapter identifies similarities and differences between the types of cases handled by the criminal legal and university systems.

Foundational Elements of Title IX

Title IX as we know it today is rooted in several legislative acts, executive orders, lawsuits, complaints, and the hard work of many. Some of the greatest influences of Title IX come from shortcomings in several laws. Consider the **Civil Rights Act of 1964**, which was designed to end discrimination in employment and public accommodations based on race, color, religion, sex, or national origin. **Title VII** of the Civil Rights Act specifically prohibits discrimination in federally funded private and public entities due to race, color, and national origin, but unfortunately Title VII did not prohibit discrimination based on sex at educational institutions receiving federal funds, which was crucially needed.

Bernice Sandler was a major force behind the ultimate passage of Title IX. While working as a part-time lecturer at the University of Maryland, and as a senior scholar in residence at the National Association for Women in Education, Sandler discovered an amendment to a 1965 Executive Order (EO 11246) signed by President Lyndon Johnson that prohibited federal contractors from discriminating on a variety of characteristics. Like Title VII, EO 11246 failed to include sex as a protected characteristic. However, Sandler found an amendment to EO 11246 that was signed in 1967 (EO 11375), which specifically included the prohibition of sex discrimination by federal contractors. This executive order allowed Sandler and the groups she worked with to file complaints and lawsuits in an effort to end sex discrimination. Harvard University has the dubious distinction of being the first university to have a contract compliance investigation involving sex discrimination against it.

Using EO 11375 as a foundation, Sandler filed 269 lawsuits against universities alleging sex discrimination.

As a result of this work, Sandler became a member of U.S. House Representative Edith Green's Subcommittee on Higher Education of the Education and Labor Committee. In hearings focused on women's issues in employment and equal opportunity, Sandler and representative Green first proposed the idea of Title IX. Representative Patsy Mink, with the assistance of representative Green, drafted the initial Title IX legislation. It was this robust body of work that earned Bernice Sandler the moniker of **godmother of Title IX** (e.g., see Seelye, 2019).

Title IX Becomes Law

Title IX is not a part of nor an amendment to the Civil Rights Act of 1964. Rather, it is a stand-alone civil rights law that was passed in June of 1972 to address the limitations of earlier legislation by prohibiting sex discrimination for all federally funded entities. Title IX was passed as a part of the **Education Amendments of 1972** and, in 2002, was renamed the **Patsy T. Mink Equal Opportunity in Education Act** after one of the coauthors and sponsors. Title IX begins,

> *No person in the United States shall, on the basis of sex, be excluded from participation in, be denied the benefits of, or be subjected to discrimination under any education program or activity receiving Federal financial assistance. (U.S. Department of Labor, n.d.)*

Title IX applies to all educational institutions including K–12 and public and private institutions as long as they receive federal funds. This includes more than 16,000 local school districts, 7,000 postsecondary institutions, as well as charter schools, for-profit schools, libraries, museums, vocational rehabilitation agencies, and educational agencies in the United States, its territories, and its possessions.

Although Title IX makes no specific mention of athletics, historically it has been most widely known for its impact on athletics. Still, Title IX applies to every aspect of education including athletics, recruitment, financial aid, admissions, course offerings, counseling, housing, sexual harassment, and employment (to name only a few). Another misconception is that Title IX only applies to women; in fact, Title IX applies equally to men and women. Others erroneously believe that Title IX applies only to students, but it protects students, employees, applicants for admission and employment, and other affiliated persons from all forms of sex discrimination. The law requires that polices, practices, and programs in place in educational institutions do not discriminate against *anyone* on the basis of sex. The ultimate goal of Title IX is to create environments in which all students are afforded the opportunity to learn, and employees, applicants, and affiliates are afforded the opportunity to succeed in employment without regard to their sex.

The Department of Health, Education, and Welfare (HEW) initially oversaw Title IX and in this capacity released the first set of regulations in 1975 (U.S. Department of Education, n.d), which required that educational institutions designate at least one employee as Title IX coordinator, who was charged with overseeing compliance efforts and investigating allegations of sex discrimination. They also required that all students be notified of their Title IX coordinator's name and contact information and that grievance procedures and nondiscrimination policies be made public. In addition, they required educational institutions to conduct a one-time self-evaluation and to modify any practices that were not Title IX compliant. And, finally, the 1975 regulations required educational institutions to take remedial and affirmative steps to increase the participation of students in programs or activities where bias was present. Of note is that nothing in the regulations dictated adjudicative practices. Rather, adjudicative practices were developed independently across institutions using federal government guidance and court findings. As a result, even today the policies and procedures used differ across institutions.

What Is Sex Discrimination?

Title IX prohibits sex discrimination, also described as sex discrimination-harassment and sex-based harassment. Title IX sex discrimination encompasses three broad sets of behaviors, according to the U.S. Department of Education's Office for Civil Rights (OCR): sex harassment, gender-based harassment, and sexual violence. While the Title IX policies and procedures of educational institutions are rooted in OCR guidance, additional guidance comes from other sources focused on Title VII. For example, the regulations and guidance provided by the Equal Employment Opportunity Commission (EEOC) are rooted in Title VII, and educational institutions must adhere to these requirements as well. These overlapping sources of sex discrimination law and guidance are why it is challenging to separate Title IX from Title VII in practice. The EEOC finds that discrimination occurs if a person is treated differently based on gender identity, transgender status, and sexual orientation. Court rulings as well as administrative regulations demonstrate that even a single action can constitute sex discrimination under certain conditions. Sex discrimination definitions and the behaviors they include as per the OCR and the EEOC are presented in Table 1.1.

TABLE 1.1 Sex Discrimination

1. OCR Sex Discrimination and Sex-Based Harassment		
Sex Harassment	**Gender-Based Harassment**	**Sexual Violence**
Defined: Unwelcome conduct of a sexual nature. It includes unwelcome sexual advances, requests for sexual favors, and other verbal, nonverbal, or physical conduct of a sexual nature.	**Defined**: Unwelcome conduct based on a student's actual or perceived sex. It includes slurs, taunts, stereotypes, or name-calling, as well as gender-motivated physical threats, attacks, or other hateful conduct.	**Defined**: Physical sexual acts perpetrated against a person's will or where a person is incapable of giving consent (e.g., due to the student's age or use of drugs or alcohol, or because an intellectual or other disability prevents the student from having the capacity to give consent). A number of different acts fall into the category of sexual violence, including rape, sexual assault, sexual battery, sexual abuse, and sexual coercion.
2. EEOC Sex Discrimination and Sex-Based Harassment		
Defined: Treating someone unfavorably because of that person's sex, which includes unwelcome sexual advances, requests for sexual favors, and other verbal or physical harassment of a sexual nature. Harassment does not have to be of a sexual nature, however, and can include offensive remarks about a person's sex including making offensive comments about a group of people.		

While Title IX and Title VII both prohibit sex discrimination, it is important to note that some of the prohibited behaviors constitute criminal actions, while others do not. Rape, sexual assault, stalking, sexual exploitation, and interpersonal and domestic violence are criminal in nature and there are both criminal code and administrative policies that prohibit them. In contrast, sex discrimination/harassment, including creating a hostile environment by telling sexually explicit jokes, hiring a man over a woman because of his sex, failing to hire someone based on their LGBTQ status, or paying a woman less than a man because of her sex, are examples of administrative, but not criminal violations. While legislation has greatly influenced the Title IX space, additional influence stems from significant court cases. These are discussed next.

Crucial Court Cases

Although Title IX has been law for almost 50 years, it is only relatively recently that educational institutions have seriously addressed sex discrimination. Much of this recent attention comes from court case outcomes that cost educational institutions huge financial losses, equally large settlements, and negative press. Institutions that have historically failed to take sex discrimination seriously are finding greater motivation to address it. An important legal precedent came from ***Franklin v. Gwinnett*** (1992), which established that monetary awards for damages under Title IX can be awarded to victims and be paid by educational institutions. High school student Franklin was enrolled in the Gwinnett County Public School District and was subjected to continual sexual harassment and abuse by Mr. Hill, who was a teacher/sports coach. Hill engaged Franklin in sexually explicit conversations, forced kissing, and coercive intercourse on school grounds. Franklin claimed that teachers and administrators were aware of the harassment and did nothing to stop it. Further, Franklin said that teachers and administrators discouraged her from bringing charges against Hill. Ultimately, Franklin sued for monetary damages under Title IX. Although a federal trial court in Georgia and the Eleventh Circuit rejected Franklin's claims, the U.S. Supreme Court ultimately ruled in her favor. *Franklin v. Gwinnett* (1992) is important because the Supreme Court found that educational institutions can be liable for individuals in the institution who are discriminating on the basis of sex. Further, it was the first case wherein the Supreme Court upheld an award of monetary damages under Title IX.

Additional cases focused on the **deliberate indifference standard**, which is the conscious or reckless disregard of the consequences of one's acts or omissions. Under Title IX, this means that universities can be held accountable if they demonstrate deliberate indifference to sex discrimination. An early case is ***Gebser v. Lago Vista*** (1998). Gebser was a ninth-grade student in the Lago Vista Independent School District in Texas. Waldrop, one of Gebser's teachers, made sexually suggestive comments to her and ultimately initiated sexual contact with her at her home. For almost 6 months, the two engaged in a sexual relationship and were ultimately discovered by the police. Waldrop was terminated, and Gebser and her mother sued the school board for monetary damages under Title IX. Both a federal trial court in Texas and the Fifth Circuit ruled in favor of the school board. Ultimately, on review, the U.S. Supreme Court affirmed this finding by a 5-to-4 margin, stating that a school board that receives federal funds cannot be liable for damages for sexual harassment unless officials with the authority to correct the harassment had actual notice of, and were deliberately indifferent to, the actions of the harasser. *Gebser v. Lago Vista* (1998) is an important case in that it indicated that *any* action taken by the school board is enough to demonstrate it did not engage in deliberate indifference. This finding indicated that the courts were unconcerned whether the actions taken by the school board were reasonable, but only that the school board did not fail to act.

The indifference standard established by *Gebser v. Lago Vista* (1998) changed 6 years later in ***Davis v. Monroe*** (1999). Fifth-grader Davis experienced ongoing sexual harassment, including repeated, completed, and attempted fondling and routine offensive and sexualized language by a schoolmate, referred to as G.F. Davis and her mother reported these incidents to teachers and the principal, but their requests for Davis's protection were ignored. In response, Davis and her mother filed a Title IX lawsuit against the Board of Education. Both the federal trial court in Georgia and the Eleventh Circuit Court of Appeals initially rejected Davis's claims. Ultimately, in 1999, the U.S. Supreme Court ruled in favor of Davis. The outcome of *Davis v. Monroe* (1999) means that educational institutions can be held liable when they are deliberately indifferent to sexual harassment about which they have knowledge, and the sexual harassment is so severe, pervasive, and objectively offensive that it deprives the victim of equal access to education. The court also found that the definition of deliberate indifference includes when an institution fails to train for risks, such as sexual harassment. *Davis v. Monroe* (1999) also established that deliberate indifference exists if an institution fails to provide adequate and obviously necessary training. This ruling is in part responsible for the mandated training found at educational institutions today. In contrast to *Gebser v. Lago Vista* (1998), under *Davis v. Monroe* (1999) the court ruled that there must be actual notice of sexual harassment to the institution and there must be an institutional failure to act to control or eliminate the harassment. *Davis v. Monroe* (1999) showed that simply failing to act is not enough to establish deliberate indifference; the nature of the action taken matters.

An Avalanche of Deliberate Indifference

Justice Kennedy who dissented in the *Davis v. Monroe* (1999) case argued that the ruling would lead to an avalanche of litigation. In fact, since *Davis v. Monroe* (1999), there have been many cases filed that focused in part on deliberate indifference. As a result, millions of dollars have been awarded to victims of sex discrimination. However, it is unclear if the number of cases filed since *Davis v. Monroe* (1999) stem from the court findings or instead from educational institutions that continue to act with deliberate indifference to sex discrimination.

One does not have to look far to find Title IX cases brought for deliberate indifference with devastating (and deserved) consequences to educational institutions. In 2007, a federal appeals court ruled against the University of

Georgia for recruiting, admitting, and neglecting to supervise a student athlete named Cole, whom university administrators *knew* had been removed from other educational institutions for harassing and sexually assaulting women. ***Williams v. Board of Regents of University System of Georgia*** (2007) involved a case in which Tony Cole, a student athlete, participated in the gang rape of fellow student, Tiffany Williams. On the day of the rape, Tiffany engaged in consensual sex in Cole's dorm room. Unknown to Tiffany, student athlete Brandon Williams (no relation to Tiffany) had been hiding in Cole's closet. After Cole left the room, B. Williams emerged from the closet and attempted to sexually assault Tiffany. Meanwhile, Cole called two other athletes to join in. A third student, Steven Thomas, came to the room and raped Tiffany. After the incident, Tiffany Williams filed charges and a formal complaint with the university police against the perpetrators and withdrew from the university. The university treated this incident as a disciplinary matter and Cole, B. Williams, and Thomas were charged with disorderly conduct. Each was suspended from their sports team. It was not until almost a year later that a university hearing was held that resulted in no sanctions for the perpetrators. The point was moot as none of the student athletes attended the university any longer. Tiffany Williams sued the University of Georgia for Title IX violations, and the university ultimately settled the case before a court verdict was reached given the ugly facts of the case. This case is particularly important because it demonstrated that a university can be found to have engaged in deliberate indifference by recruiting a known sexual offender. In doing so, the university had early notice of a high-risk student and still failed to implement prevention, response, and disciplinary procedures to minimize the risk to other students at the university.

Concurrently in 2007, a federal appeals court found in ***Simpson v. University of Colorado Boulder*** (2007) that the university could be sued for multiple rapes associated with their football recruiting program. This finding stemmed from an ill-conceived ambassador program used to recruit football players. Ambassadors were usually females who were paired with visiting recruits and charged with entertaining them during their campus visit. Two female students, Simpson and Gilmore, were at Simpson's apartment when a football team representative asked if four football players could come over. Twenty football players arrived, at least some having the understanding that they were there for sex. As the night went on, Simpson went to her locked room to sleep and woke up while being raped by recruits and players. At the same time, Gilmore was being raped in her room, and three other women at the apartment were sexually harassed by players. Another female student was raped by two players after she left the apartment. Simpson and Gilmore filed a Title IX lawsuit alleging that the athletic department was not only aware of these attacks, but that the department created this known risk due to deliberate indifference.

The court found that the university demonstrated deliberate indifference by creating an environment that posed a risk to students and that the evidence indicated that the risk of rape during recruiting visits was so obvious that by ignoring this risk, the University of Colorado Boulder violated Title IX. Like *Williams v. Board of Regents of University System of Georgia* (2007), the grim facts of the *Simpson v. University of Colorado Boulder* (2007) case prompted a multimillion-dollar settlement by the university.

The Office for Civil Rights

As these court cases demonstrate, the landscape of Title IX is always changing. Not only are educational institutions under Title IX required to understand and respond to the changing landscape due to court findings, they are also required to follow guidance and regulations provided by the **Office for Civil Rights (OCR)**, which is a part of the U.S. Department of Education. The U.S. Department of Education was formed in 1979 out of HEW and was given oversight of Title IX, where it remains today. OCR is responsible for enforcing Title IX, meaning it has the authority to develop related policy on the regulations, including the evaluation, investigation, and resolution of allegations of sex discrimination. In addition, OCR conducts compliance reviews to investigate potential systemic violations learned about outside a formal complaint. OCR is also a source for technical assistance and guidance to those entities required to comply with Title IX.

Over time, a series of OCR guidance documents have been released to assist institutions in addressing sex discrimination. For example, guidance was released in 1997 and 2001 and was reiterated in 2006. Updated OCR guidance reflects changing understanding about sex discrimination, clarified and/or defined key terms, and court precedent. Since 1998, OCR has disseminated guidance using **Dear Colleague Letters (DCL)** (U.S. Department of Education, n.d.). Perhaps the most well-known DCL was released in 2011 and has become known as *the* Dear Colleague Letter (many mistakenly believe it is the first and only DCL). The 2011 DCL differs from past guidance because it specified procedures that educational institutions were required to use in Title IX cases. This was a departure because until the 2011 DCL educational institutions developed their own policies and procedures using the guidance set forth by OCR. A new policy was put forth in the 2011 DCL that required institutions to use a preponderance of the evidence standard. Before then, educational institutions used varying evidentiary standards, although most used **preponderance of the evidence**, which requires the evidence to show that a policy violation was more likely to have occurred than not to have occurred. It is also referred to as "50% plus a feather," or *more probable than not* that the violation occurred. This is the same level of evidence used in civil courts, as well as cheating, plagiarism, and other student conduct violations at educational institutions. Prior to the 2011 DCL, some educational institutions used the more stringent **clear and convincing** standard, which means the evidence must show that the policy violation is highly and substantially more probable to have happened than not, reflecting more of a 75% certainty.

Another requirement in the 2011 DCL is that educational institutions must allow **complainants** (i.e., those who allege they were victims of sex discrimination) to appeal no-policy-violation findings. The ability to appeal a no-policy-violation finding provides an additional, and important, layer of due process. **Due process** rights are found in the Fifth and 14th Amendments to the U.S. Constitution and act to prevent individuals from the arbitrary denial of life, liberty, or property by the government. Appeal provides the complainant a mechanism to challenge findings not in his or her favor. It follows, though, that **respondents** (i.e., those accused of sex discrimination) should also be allowed an appeal for those instances when there is a finding of a policy violation against them, but the 2011 DCL does not require this. Another change recommended in the 2011 DCL was to use a more victim-centered approach by discouraging the cross-examination of complainants. A **victim-centered approach** (also frequently referred to as trauma informed) prioritizes the complainant's wishes, safety, and well-being during a proceeding. Using a victim-centered approach is not mandated by any national-level policy but is identified by some professionals as the recommended practice or approach in cases of sexual violence in dealing with complainants. Finally, the 2011 DCL recommended that institutions limit formal investigations to 60 days. While these requirements resulted in major changes for some institutions, for others it had no effect. In reality, it is unknown how much impact the 2011 DCL has had on the day-to-day operations in Title IX offices across the nation.

Since the 2011 DCL was released, many have argued that the guidance resulted in an unfair system where respondents are deprived of due process. In particular, some argue that respondents have not been given fair hearings (in those institutions that use hearing models), access to an attorney (although many institutions do allow both the complainant and respondent to have an attorney or other representative/advisor present during Title IX proceedings), or the ability to directly question the complainant. Because educational institutions are responsible for crafting their own policies and procedures, there are instances in which these criticisms are warranted, and due process claims have been accepted by the courts. For example, in 2017, a federal panel blocked the 1-year suspension of a University of Cincinnati student, stating his constitutional rights were denied because he was not given the opportunity to question the student who accused him of sexual assault. Due process grievances have led some to describe Title IX processes as "kangaroo courts," suggesting they ignore recognized standards of law or the justice system.

The problem with suggesting that Title IX gives rise to kangaroo courts is that Title IX is an administrative process and not a criminal process. It does not pretend to be a court system that identifies criminal misconduct, but rather a system designed to identify Title IX policy violations. However, this may change in the future. Just as there was a time when the courts allowed suits by complainants surrounding Title IX (e.g., *Davis v. Monroe* [1999]; *Gebser v. Lago Vista* [1998]), and institutions changed their policies and procedures to reflect these outcomes, we are now seeing the impact of those institutional reactions. These newer claims, generally brought by respondents, are primarily focused on a lack of due process and the fact that education has long been considered a property right. In ***Goss v. Lopez*****,** (1975)**,** the Supreme Court ruled that the 14th Amendment due process clause of the U.S. Constitution means that public school students possess liberty and property interests in their education. This means that principles of due process (notice and a hearing) apply to educational officials considering suspension of a student. Given the constitutional right to due process, the expectation is that these due process claims will be considered by school officials.

In part because of pressures applied by those representing respondents, OCR rescinded the 2011 DCL in 2017. Secretary of Education DeVos's stated purpose of recension was to treat all students fairly and to stop what was considered the federal government's unwarranted requirements that educational institutions use specific procedures (such as the mandate that educational institutions use preponderance of the evidence only and disallow mediation in rape and sexual assault allegations) for Title IX claims. An important influence has come from institutions that find the 2011 DCL requirements burdensome. Another argument made in the recension of the 2011 DCL is that the regulations it imposed were burdensome and were enacted without offering notice and the opportunity for the public to comment.

OCR stated new guidance was forthcoming, but as of late 2018, no new guidance had been released (although weekly rumors suggested that new guidance was imminent and leaked copies were freely shared). To date, all that is available is an OCR Q&A document released in 2017 (Office for Civil Rights, 2017). The Q&A document indicates little expected change due to the 2011 DCL recension, except for one clear change that removes the requirement that institutions use preponderance of the evidence as the standard of proof for hearings. Instead, institutions were given the choice to use either the clear and convincing standard or the preponderance of the evidence standard.

Title IX v. The Criminal Justice System

Title IX offices have never intended to serve as a scaled-down version of the criminal justice system. Rather, the goals of Title IX offices are to protect those in an educational institution from sex discrimination, to educate those associated with educational institutions about sex discrimination, to offer resources and accommodations to both complainants and respondents, to adjudicate (some) allegations of sex discrimination, and to sanction (if appropriate) those found to have engaged in sex discrimination.[1] In contrast, the goals of the criminal justice system are to define what constitutes criminal behavior, to investigate alleged crimes, and to punish criminals who have been found to have committed criminal acts. Title IX does not seek to replace the criminal justice system, and, in fact, the two entities frequently work together in a complementary fashion. Title IX offices establish MOUs (memoranda of understanding) with local law enforcement agencies to facilitate their collaboration when appropriate.

The dissimilarities between Title IX and the criminal justice system should not be surprising because each system has a different purpose (i.e., addressing policy violations versus criminal behavior, respectively), covers (mostly) different behaviors, and leads to different outcomes. While different, it is also true that both serve important, albeit imperfect, roles. Historically, as demonstrated by court cases, too many educational institutions have ignored, or even actively encouraged and condoned, a culture and atmosphere that allowed sexual misconduct to thrive. And it is no secret that the criminal justice system has too often failed to deal appropriately with criminal sexual behavior.

Table 1.2 identifies the differences between the two systems, which, in part, reflect that Title IX proceedings are designed to be educational rather than punitive. Officials at educational institutions may gather evidence, take testimony, and make factual findings in regard to a Title IX allegation, but they cannot and do not convict or incarcerate anyone. No one loses their liberty or life as a result of a Title IX finding. Title IX may result in **sanctions** against a respondent who has been found to violate policy. The goal of sanctions is to increase a respondent's chances of educational or employment success in the future. For example, if a respondent tackles a drug or alcohol abuse issue through counseling, or learns better coping skills when angered through counseling, he or she is more likely to succeed in the future. Because Title IX proceedings are not criminal court proceedings, many argue that those accused of Title IX violations are not entitled to the protections guaranteed in a criminal court case. However, as noted previously, education is considered a property right and depriving one of his or her educational rights at a particular institution can occur if a serious Title IX policy violation is found. How this tension will be resolved remains to be seen, as some courts have ruled in favor of respondents who were not afforded sufficient due process.

TABLE 1.2 Comparing Title IX and the Criminal Justice System

Topic	Title IX System	Criminal Justice System
Intention	Ensure educational institutions receiving federal funds are free from sex discrimination. Determine if there has been a university policy violation regarding sex discrimination. Some types of sex discrimination are criminal in nature (e.g., sexual assault and rape), while others are illegal but not criminal in nature (e.g., sexual harassment). Educate the educational institution's community about Title IX, sex discrimination, how to report, resources, etc. Provide remedies and accommodations to those involved in alleged sex discrimination.	Focused on criminal law. Determine what criminal acts are, investigate alleged criminal acts, apprehend alleged criminals, conduct trials, punish and/or incarcerate those found guilty.
Types of behaviors considered	Sex discrimination includes unwelcome conduct of a sexual nature. Specifically, this includes unwelcome sexual advances, requests for sexual favors, and unwanted verbal and nonverbal or physical conduct of a sexual nature. In addition, it includes unwelcome conduct based on a person's perceived sex, gender-motivated physical attacks, rape, sexual assault, sexual battery, sexual abuse, sexual coercion, domestic violence, and stalking.	Any alleged criminal activity can be investigated and adjudicated by the criminal justice system.
Reporting requirements	Responsible employees in educational institutions are required to report sexual misconduct to the Title IX coordinator (or representative) regardless of the victim's wishes. Only confidential resources are not mandatory reporters. Who confidential resources are depends on each university's policy and generally include licensed therapists or counselors and university health employees acting in their professional capacity only.	N/A. There is no requirement to report criminal sexual behavior to the police except in specific situations (e.g., sexual abuse of children).

(Continued)

Topic	Title IX System	Criminal Justice System
Names of participants	The person allegedly experiencing sexual misconduct is the complainant. The person allegedly perpetrating the sexual misconduct is the respondent.	The person allegedly experiencing criminal sexual conduct is the victim/survivor. The person allegedly perpetrating the criminal sexual conduct is the offender, perpetrator, or criminal.
Right to counsel	Because Title IX is an administrative process and not a legal proceeding, there is no right to counsel. However, the ability to have a support person in the form of an advocate, friend, professor, or attorney (or anyone) during Title IX proceedings (interviews, meetings, hearings [if applicable]) and the role he or she plays depends on the institution's policies and procedures.	One has a constitutional right to counsel. In particular, the Sixth Amendment to the Constitution guarantees this for criminal proceedings.
Who conducts the investigation	Investigations are conducted by university officials required to receive training on sexual misconduct including sex discrimination, sexual harassment, stalking, dating violence, sexual assault, and rape.	Investigations are conducted by members of the criminal justice system (e.g., detectives) as well as professionals representing attorneys. The findings of the investigation are presented by lawyers in an adversarial system.
Duration of investigation	Suggested length of a formal investigation is 60 days (2011 DCL), with consideration of case complexity, requests from law enforcement conducting criminal investigations, witness response time, translation services, university vacations, and access to documentation.	Length of investigations vary. Investigations can occur over the span of multiple years or never be concluded.
Nature of hearings	The use of a hearing depends on each educational institution's policies and procedures. Some institutions may use hearings, but many do not. Some use standing review panels; others have a single or dual investigator model in which the investigation determines whether a policy violation occurred.	The Sixth Amendment guarantees public hearings/trials for criminal cases. Criminal trials can be held before a jury or can be a bench trial (before a judge only).

(*Continued*)

Topic	Title IX System	Criminal Justice System
Cross-examination practices	Per the 2011 Dear Colleague Letter, institutions were discouraged from allowing the respondent to directly question or cross-examine the complainant or witnesses.	The alleged offender is constitutionally able to directly cross-examine witnesses and alleged victims, which is generally accomplished using attorneys.
Assessment of facts	University officials assess facts within the confines of university policies and federal legislation. The goal is to determine if the facts point to a violation of university policy.	A jury or judge assesses the evidence presented in the trial to determine if criminal law has been violated.
Evidence standard used	The evidentiary standard varies across educational institutions. Under the 2011 DCL, all institutions were required to use preponderance of the evidence. After the 2017 recension, institutions can choose between preponderance or clear and convincing evidence.	Beyond a reasonable doubt is the evidentiary standard used in the criminal justice system. This means the evidence must make one believe the crime occurred "beyond a doubt."
Outcome	Outcome is either a policy violation or no policy violation. Those found to have committed a policy violation can receive a range of sanctions that are determined by university official(s) and differ based on each university's policy and by the facts of the case. Sanctions can include temporary or permanent removal from campus, written reprimands, mandatory class or program attendance, housing reassignment, university probation, suspension, exclusion from portions of university property, or recommendation for revocation of degree.	Outcome is either guilty or not guilty. Those found to be guilty of a criminal act can receive a range of punishments that are based on the particular facts of the case. Sanctions can include payment of restitution, suspension of the sentence, probation, community corrections, incarceration, registering as a sex offender, or the death penalty.
Right of appeal	The right to, and nature of, appeals is contingent on the educational institution's particular policies and procedures. The 2011 DCL required the complainant be allowed to appeal a no-policy violation.	In criminal cases, a convicted offender has a right to appeal the verdict based on procedural errors only.

(Continued)

Topic	Title IX System	Criminal Justice System
Lasting implications	If found responsible of a policy violation, the respondent's records are not released to the public or the university community. If expelled, removed, or terminated, the individual is still able to apply to enroll at other universities outside of the university system from which he or she was removed.	Individuals charged and sentenced have public criminal records and may remain incarcerated and/or be required to register as a sex offender.

Source: U.S. Department of Education (n.d.) and U.S. Equal Employment Opportunity Commision (n.d.).

Conclusion

Although Title IX is almost 50 years old, much work remains. Sex discrimination continues to exist in educational institutions, and how institutions adjudicate it changes based on court rulings and shifting guidance. What has remained unchanged is an educational institution's responsibility to offer an environment free from sex discrimination. Honoring that responsibility and navigating the realities of managing Title IX cases, especially in light of continually changing legal and guidance landscapes, is challenging. Time will tell if the adjudication system found in institutions will become more or less regulated and more similar to the criminal justice system.

KEY TERMS

2011 Dear Colleague Letter (DCL): Controversial guidance provided by OCR that dictated specific procedures that educational institutions had to use when dealing with sexual misconduct claims.

Civil Rights Act of 1964: Act that prohibits discrimination in employment and public accommodations based on race, color, religion, or national origin. It failed to include sex as a protected category.

Clear and convincing: Standard of evidence suggesting the policy violation is highly and substantially more probable to have happened than not.

Complainant: The person who allegedly experienced the sex discrimination.

***Davis v. Monroe County Board of Education* 526 U.S. 629 (1999):** This case established that deliberate indifference was present, and institutions can be held liable when they are deliberately indifferent to sexual harassment about which they have knowledge and when the sexual harassment is so severe, pervasive, and objectively offensive that it deprives the victim of equal access to his or her education. It also found that deliberate indifference includes the failure to train for risks such as sex harassment.

Dear Colleague Letter (DCL): Format of OCR guidance regarding Title IX since 1998.

Deliberate indifference: A legal standard that refers to the conscious or reckless disregard of the consequences of one's acts or omissions. Related to Title IX, this means that universities can be held accountable if they demonstrate deliberate indifference to sex discrimination.

Department of Education: The Federal department where the Office for Civil Rights, which oversees Title IX, is housed.

Due process: Rights constituting due process found in the Fifth and 14th Amendments to the U.S. Constitution, which act as protections from arbitrary denial of life, liberty, or property by the government.

Education Amendments Act of 1972: Formal name of the legislation under which Title IX was passed.

***Franklin v. Gwinnett County Public Schools* 503 U.S. 60 (1992):** Case in which the Supreme Court found that educational institutions can be liable for individuals in the institution who are discriminating on the basis of sex. It is also the first case in which the Supreme Court upheld an award of monetary damages under Title IX.

***Gebser v. Lago Vista Independent School District* 524 U.S. 274 (1998):** Case that established that deliberate indifference was present only when an institution failed to act. This precedent was changed in *Davis v. Monroe* (1999).

Godmother of Title IX: Nickname given to Bernice Sandler for her work in introducing Title IX and the ultimate passage of it.

***Goss v. Lopez* 419 U.S. 565 (1975):** A case heard by the Supreme Court of the United States that concluded that education is a property right, which indicates that public school students have a right to due process when it comes to issues related to student conduct.

Office for Civil Rights (OCR): An office in the U.S. Department of Education that is tasked with enforcing Title IX.

Patsy T. Mink Equal Opportunity in Education Act (2002): The renamed Education Amendments Act of 1972, which included Title IX. Mink was an initial drafter of Title IX.

Policy violation: A finding based on evidence that a respondent violated the Title IX policy at an institution. It is not a criminal finding, but rather an administrative finding.

Preponderance of the evidence: A standard of evidence mandated in the 2011 DCL that required the finding of a policy violation if the sex discrimination alleged to have occurred was more likely than not.

Respondent: The individual accused of engaging in sex discrimination.

Sanctions: Outcomes of Title IX proceedings resulting in a policy violation. The nature of sanctions depends on several characteristics of the sex discrimination.

Sandler, Bernice: A major force behind the passage of Title IX who brought complaints and/or sued 269 universities for sex discrimination.

Sex discrimination: The prohibition against treating *anyone* differently on the basis of sex. Definitions come from both OCR and the EEOC.

Sexual harassment: A type of sex discrimination as per OCR that includes unwelcome conduct of a sexual nature including unwelcome sexual advances, requests for sexual favors, and other verbal, nonverbal, or physical conduct of a sexual nature. The EEOC defines sexual harassment as treating someone unfavorably because of that person's sex, which includes unwelcome sexual advances, requests for sexual favors, and other verbal or physical harassment of a sexual nature. Sex harassment can include offensive remarks about a person's sex including making offensive comments about a group of people (e.g., individual who identifies as LGBTQ).

Sexual misconduct: Phrase widely used to describe the behaviors prohibited by Title IX, some of which are criminal in nature (e.g., rape, sexual assault), and others which are illegal, but not criminal in nature (e.g., discrimination).

***Simpson v. University of Colorado Boulder*, 500 F.3d 1170 (10th Cir. 2007):** Like *Williams v. Board of Regents of University System of Georgia*, (2007), this case established that a university can be shown to demonstrate deliberate indifference by failing to act on a known risk on campus and failing to mitigate that risk.

Title VII: A part of the 1964 Civil Rights Act that prohibits discrimination in federally funded private and public entities due to race, color, and national origin. It failed to call out sex as a protected category.

Title IX of the Education Amendments Act of 1972: Legislation signed into law by President Richard Nixon that prohibits sex discrimination in educational institutions that receive federal funds. This stand-alone legislation fills in the gaps found in Title VII of the Civil Rights Act of 1964 and other legal documents.

Victim-centered approach: Prioritizes the complainant's wishes, safety and well-being during a proceeding.

***Williams v. Board of Regents of University System of Georgia*, 477 F.3d 1282 (11th Cir. 2007):** Case that established that deliberate indifference can be demonstrated when an educational institution has notice of a high-risk student and fails to protect others from this harm.

DISCUSSION QUESTIONS

1. Title IX is a stand-alone law, yet it is related to Title VII and other governmental acts. There have been suggestions by some that Title IX proceedings should be removed from educational institutions and handled by independent entities. Given what you know about Title IX and Title

VII and the overlap between the two, is that feasible? Or, will utilizing a third-party to handle only Title IX reports give rise to two concurrent administrative processes where the independent group considers Title IX claims and the institution considers related Title VII claims? Would having two concurrent administrative processes become burdensome to all involved parties? Would it make the process better? What would you do if you were a policy maker and tasked with this decision?

2. As the Title IX coordinator, you are contacted by the police about a case in which a student was alleged to have raped another student in a remote part of the campus library. The incident was recorded on video. You are aware of this respondent because he was involved in two previous Title IX cases where he was accused of trying to sexually assault two other students. In those cases, there were no witnesses, no video, and no police contacted, resulting in "he-said-she-said" situations. As a result, there was no investigation, findings, or sanctions. With this new case, you must decide whether to remove this person from campus during the investigation to ensure the safety of others on campus. However, by removing him, you know there is a strong chance that the respondent will file a lawsuit claiming his due process rights were not honored. If you let the respondent remain on campus while the Title IX investigation takes place, you recognize the strong chance that the university will be sued by the complainant because the university is failing to ensure the safety of her and others by allowing a student on campus who is a known risk. How do you balance the needs of the complainant, respondent, others on campus, and the university? What decision would you make and why?
3. According to the 2011 DCL, Title IX proceedings should be victim centered. Is being victim centered the best approach? What are advantages and disadvantages of using this approach? What are other options you see as better? Why?
4. Educational institutions are required to deal with sexual misconduct even if one of the parties involved is unaffiliated with the institution, and even if the event takes place away from institutional property. Imagine that one of your staff members has reported that her partner (who is unaffiliated) has been physically abusing her. Do you think that addressing this Title IX case is the appropriate role of the university, or is it a private and personal matter? What if the abuse affected her work productivity and attendance? What do you think is the appropriate response by the educational institution? Why?
5. You are a student and you begin sharing with a trusted professor that you were sexually assaulted at a party the previous week. Before you

can tell the story, the professor stops you and informs you that, as a mandatory reporter, he is required to share any sexual misconduct with the Title IX office. What do you do? Do you finish telling your story, or do you keep it to yourself? How do you think this reporting responsibility affects the professor? What would you do if you were the professor? What are the advantages and disadvantages of each choice?

Note

1 Some are surprised to learn that both the respondent and the complainant benefit from resources and accommodations to the extent that they are available. For example, there are often counseling services that are free to respondents (employee respondents are likely have access to EAP-type services; student respondents may have access to counseling through a student counseling center). When appropriate, both complainant and respondent are directed toward specific counseling such as anger management, healthy relationships, and alcohol/drug treatment available outside formal channels. (These may come at a personal financial cost.) In addition, universities work with professors to alter paper deadlines, test dates, and other class-related events to accommodate both the complainant and respondent navigating this process.

References

Davis v. Monroe County Board of Education 526 U.S. 629 (1999)

Franklin v. Gwinnett County Public Schools 503 U.S. 60 (1992)

Gebser v. Lago Vista Independent School District 524 U.S. 274 (1998)

Goss v. Lopez, 419 U.S. 565 (1975)

Office for Civil Rights. (2017, September). *Q&A on campus sexual misconduct*. Retrieved from https://www2.ed.gov/about/offices/list/ocr/docs/qa-title-ix-201709.pdf

Seelye, K. Q. (January 8, 2019). Bernice Sandler, "godmother of Title IX," dies at 90. Retrieved from https://www.nytimes.com/2019/01/08/obituaries/bernice-sandler-dead.html

Simpson v. University of Colorado Boulder, 500 F.3d 1170 (10th Cir. 2007)

U.S. Department of Education. (n.d.). *Title 34 education*. Retrieved from https://www2.ed.gov/policy/rights/reg/ocr/edlite-34cfr106.html

U.S. Department of Labor. (n.d.). Retrieved from https://www2.ed.gov/about/offices/list/ocr/frontpage/faq/rr/policyguidance/index.html.

U.S. Equal Employment Opportunity Commission. (n.d.). *Sex-based discrimination*. Retrieved from https://www.eeoc.gov/laws/types/sex.cfm

Williams v. Board of Regents of University System of Georgia, 477 F.3d 1282 (11th Cir. 2007)

II | Concepts Affecting Whether Cases Are Adjudicated

CHAPTER TWO

The Complexity of College Consent

Aya Gruber

Introduction

Teachers, parents, and administrators tell students that **consent** is "simple." To be sure, the directive to have only consensual sex appears straightforward and easy to comply with. Every day, millions of people follow this directive with great success and have mutually wanted, unproblematic sex. Law and policy, however, rarely intervene in easy cases. The cases with which lawyers, teachers, and college administrators struggle do not involve clearly desired sex or clearly forced sex. Consent standards intervene in the hard cases. When college bureaucrats formulate sexual consent policies, they delineate when sex between two competent adults of equal status, without force or threat, is a punishable offense. They determine what should happen when the accuser feels harmed but the accused believes he or she has not committed harm. They weigh in on default views of sex—whether people generally desire, are ambivalent toward, or fear sex. They guide decision makers on whom to believe in "he-said-she-said" cases. In short, consent is far from simple.

The requirement of sexual consent gained traction during the **second wave of feminism,** roughly from the early 1970s to the 1990s. Feminists successfully lobbied to reform rape laws they saw as manifestly sexist and retrogressive. They objected that rape statutes prohibited only forcible rape and thus gave a pass to men who used more subtle coercive tactics to impose sex on unwilling women (e.g., MacKinnon, 1989; Remick, 1993). Feminists' reform efforts were remarkably successful, and by the millennium, most states criminalized sex without consent, regardless of force (American Law Institute, 2014).

Consent is a central issue in many sexual assault cases, both on and off campus. The consent inquiry is two-fold: (1) Was the complainant in fact unwilling to have sex? and (2) If so, did the defendant know (or would a reasonable person know) the complainant was unwilling? At trial, defense attorneys often asked jurors to focus on the behavior of the complainant, before, during, and after the sexual encounter, to determine whether the complainant consented or whether the defendant reasonably believed he or she did. This phenomenon of "putting the victim on trial" spurred additional feminist reforms. In the 1980s, reformers convinced state and federal legislatures to pass **rape shield laws**, which prohibited the defense from introducing the complainant's past sexual history to prove consent. In the 1990s, feminist activists pushed even further, asserting that consent should not be a question of complainants' state of mind but one of their *expression*. The law, they maintained, should require **affirmative consent** to sex—a clear communication of consent. Without it, sex would be rape, regardless of whether the defendant honestly and reasonably believed the complainant was willing, or indeed, the complainant was willing. Reformers contended that like a doctor performing surgery, a person desirous of sex must obtain an unequivocal and "affirmative" expression of willingness (Bryden, 2000).

Today, the affirmative consent standard, often referred to somewhat inaccurately as "yes means yes," is regarded as *the* standard for enlightened sexual relations. However, feminists' 1990s efforts to embed the standard in criminal practice generally failed. At that moment in time, society largely wrote off affirmative consent as radical feminists' imposition of a "sex contract" to be ridiculed, if not reviled (Baker, 1999; Gruber, 2009). The criminal law's concept of consent remained contextual: A person could divine consent from the totality of the circumstances, including subtle cues.

Fast-forward to 2011. The federal government issued a clarion call to colleges throughout the nation to take a stronger stand against sexual assault on campus. In 2010, National Public Radio released an explosive report on the hidden epidemic of campus rape that was being insufficiently handled by the federal government (Shapiro, 2010). In response, the U.S. Department of Education's Office for Civil Rights issued a **Dear Colleague Letter (DCL),** a form of federal administrative guidance (Ali, 2011), that made clear that institutions of higher learning must take strong measures to prevent, address, and remedy campus sexual assault, and failure to do so constituted gender discrimination in violation of **Title IX** of the 1972 Education Amendments Act. During this time, the campus rape issue was increasingly occupying public attention, with significant press coverage of egregious campus rapes, statistics on its prevalence, and student protests.

As a result, many schools engaged in wholesale revisions of their sexual misconduct policies. As the pressure mounted to counteract a perceived plague of rape, many colleges adopted affirmative consent standards far more sex regulatory than even the feminist proposals of the 1990s. College codes accordingly defined sexual assault in a manner unheard of in criminal law. By 2014, over 800 institutions of higher learning had adopted the requirement of affirmative consent to sex (New, 2014). Today, the body of college regulations regarding sexual consent are a patchwork of doctrines that vary in their meanings, applications, and disciplinary strength.

Most university policies require "affirmative" and "clear" consent (e.g., Brown University, 2016; Columbia University, 2018; Dartmouth College, 2014; Northwestern University, 2018; University of Colorado, 2018). Several require a "'yes,' verbal or otherwise" (e.g., Allegheny College, 2017; Johns Hopkins University, 2017; Yale University, 2019). A good number of codes forbid sex without "ongoing" or "continuous" affirmative consent (e.g., Brown University, 2016; Johns Hopkins University, 2017; Northwestern University, 2018). When pressed on these requirements, some policymakers rationalize them through an "I know it when I see it"-type analysis, holding that it will be obvious when someone is "into it" or not (Helwick, 2014). It is no wonder that people come to wholly different conclusions about how ordinary and affirmative consent standards impact legal decisions and human behavior.

Some say that sexual consent is present whenever the parties mentally agree to sex (e.g., Ferzan, 2016). However, it is not altogether clear what mental agreement is. Does "giving in" because you are tired count? Does sex have to be hotly desired? According to other commentators, consent is not about what the parties think, but about how they act (e.g., Schulhofer, 1998). Then again, opinions differ wildly on what a consent "act" looks like. At one extreme, there are still some people who believe that everything short of a kick in the face, including frozen passivity and weak protest, is consent. At the other extreme are those who insist that consent invariably requires an ask-and-answer-type dialogue that produces a thoughtful, wise, and enthusiastic endorsement. Most views fall somewhere in between. In the end, the rapid proliferation of consent law, policy, and scholarship has produced a legal terrain marked by uncertainty, contradiction, and hidden value judgments.

This chapter unpacks the complex concept of consent in college codes. Its aim is taxonomical and explanatory: to categorize various consent formulations and clarify how they regulate behavior and resolve disputes. The first part of the chapter is a brief history of "ordinary" and affirmative consent standards in criminal law. The second turns to the concept of consent itself. There, I explore what it means to say that a sexual transaction between two people is consensual and whether consent relates to a state of mind, communication, or both. The third part examines the various formulations of consent in college codes, placing them on a scale from most to least regulatory. Finally, I discuss the complicated costs and benefits of affirmative consent.

A Brief History of Sexual Consent

In 19th-century America, rape laws accompanied **fornication and adultery statutes** to confine lawful sex to marriage and to make all marital sex lawful. When it came to nonmarital rape, "proper" middle-class women found some success claiming rape either as victims or as a defense against adultery. However, this privilege did not extend to classes of women considered unchaste, including women of color, servant girls, and prostitutes or other women of "ill repute" (Larson, 1997). Rape laws had other regulatory designs and played a distinct and reprehensible role in maintaining White supremacy and justifying racial terror in the post-Civil War South. During this era, rape law and policy envisioned the rapist as a predatory stranger—a "bestial" Black man—waiting for the opportunity to ravish a chaste White woman (Giddings, 2009; Gruber, 2009; Harris, 1990; Wells-Barnett, 1892).

Owing to these paradigms, the South witnessed an "epidemic" of rape-based lynching of Black men, which gave way to racist capital prosecutions after World War II. Historian Danielle McGuire (2010) observes that "Black activists in the post-World War II period often joked that 'the closer a black man got to a ballot box, the more he looked like a rapist'" (p. 54). Given this history, some of the earliest liberal objections to rape law involved its *overenforcement*. In 1977, civil rights lawyer Ruth Bader Ginsburg filed an ACLU amicus brief in *Coker v. Georgia*, the case that struck down capital punishment for rape of an adult woman. Ginsburg characterized the feminist position as one *against* overly punitive rape laws, noting that "a large segment of the women's legal community … oppose the death penalty for rape as a vestige of an ancient, patriarchal view of women as the property of men" (ACLU Brief, *Coker v. Georgia*, 1977).

American rape law policed women's chastity through several peculiar doctrines imported from British law, including the requirements of **resistance** "to the utmost," a **fresh complaint** (requiring that the victim made a relatively contemporaneous report of the rape), and **corroboration**. Because there are rarely eyewitnesses to rape, independent corroboration usually came in the form of serious injury, effectively rendering noninjurious rapes lawful. Evidence of a woman's unchaste nature was also formal legal grounds to discredit her testimony (Anderson, 2002; Gruber, 2009). These sexist doctrines remained a solid facet of rape law well into the latter 20th century when feminists championed their elimination. Feminists also objected to laws that defined rape in terms of physical **force** and required proof that the defendant compelled sex through violence or threat of imminent violence. Feminists pointed to cases where strict interpretations of force exonerated defendants who compelled victims to have sex by using subtle intimidation, ignoring their refusals, "pinning," isolation, or sudden penetration.

One case that particularly outraged feminists was *Commonwealth v. Berkowitz* (1992), which involved a 1988 campus rape and continues to be taught in law schools throughout the nation. The parties, sophomores, were acquaintances with a somewhat flirtatious relationship. On the night in question, the victim, Lisa, entered Berkowitz's room to leave a note for his roommate. Berkowitz awoke from his slumber and invited Lisa to "hang out." Lisa testified that he then "kind of pushed [her] back with his body. It wasn't a shove, it was just kind of a leaning-type of thing." Lisa demurred that she had to go meet her boyfriend. Eventually, Berkowitz walked over to the door, locked it, and put Lisa on the bed. "It wasn't slow like a romantic kind of thing, but it wasn't a fast shove either. It was kind of in the middle," Lisa explained. During the sexual intercourse, Lisa said "no" several times but, she acknowledged, "softly in a moaning kind of way … because it was just so scary." Berkowitz conceded that Lisa had said "no" several times, but he claimed that she "whisper[ed]" it, while "amorously … passionately" moaning and eagerly returning his kisses. Berkowitz said he locked the door for privacy, after which Lisa helped him undress and they had sex. His defense was that he honestly understood Lisa's protests as playing "coy." The jury heard all the evidence and convicted Berkowitz of rape, a first-degree felony, and indecent assault, a serious misdemeanor (*Commonwealth. v. Berkowitz*, 1992).

The Pennsylvania Supreme Court reversed the rape conviction, holding that the prosecution had not proven the statutory requirement of "forcible compulsion." It upheld the conviction for indecent assault, defined as sex without "consent." The Court opined that "forcible compulsion" meant physical force beyond the contact inherent in sexual activity and that Berkowitz's coercive acts, even as described by the victim, did not meet that threshold (*Commonwealth. v. Berkowitz*, 1994). The case produced a public outcry. From the Pennsylvania press to the *New York Times*, *Berkowitz* became known as the "'no' is not enough" case (Cattabiani, 1994; Lewin, 1994). The legislature amended the rape definition to specify that "forcible compulsion" includes "intellectual, moral, emotional or psychological force, either express or implied" (18 Pa. Stat. § 3101 2014) and made nonconsensual sex a serious felony carrying a ten-year jail term (18 Pa. Stat. § 3124.1 2014).

Other states followed similar patterns, replacing force with non-consent, and soon consent was considered the gold standard of rape law (Estrich, 1986). Feminists further argued that providing a defense to defendants whenever they honestly thought there was consent served to exonerate men who believe that everything short of physical resistance is consent (e.g., Estrich, 1986; Taslitz, 2007). Many states responded by requiring that the defendant's belief that the complainant consented be *reasonable* (American Law Institute, 2014; e.g. *State v. Jackson*, 1996). Within a decade, the crime of rape transformed from knowingly forcing sex on a person to unreasonably interpreting another's sexual signals.

Still, activists worried that sexist jurors could find it reasonable to believe that "no means yes." Further, sexist jurors might focus on whether the complainant was a "slut" who "always" wants sex, rather than whether there was consent on the particular occasion. Feminists thus advocated for affirmative consent standards to focus the jury away from whether the victim "really" wanted the sex and toward what he or she actually communicated during the particular incident. Affirmative consent is either a total revolution or a nonstarter, depending on *which* communications count as consent. In the 1990s, affirmative consent opponents characterized the standard as revolutionary—and ridiculous—because it required a contract-like "yes" at every stage of a sexual encounter (Baker, 1999; Gruber, 2009). However, affirmative consent laws never did spawn a sex police making sure that everyone engages in a rigid consent performance. Nevertheless, critics continue to warn of affirmative consent's potential to outlaw desirable, everyday sex that does not follow a specific script.

Affirmative consent proponents rejoin that the "sex contract" caricature is no more than right-wing hysteria characteristic of "rape culture." And yet, in 2018, the exclusive Phillips Academy boarding school, in the wake of media reports that teachers had sexually abused students for decades, required "each student ... to sign a document agreeing to obtain 'unambiguous' verbal consent at every stage of a sexual encounter" (Hartocollis & Goldstein, 2018). Still, affirmative consent proponents insist that the standard merely reflects typical sexual practices. It counts *any* words or conduct that, in context, convey agreement. But given that "moaned" "no's" are words, and passivity while being undressed is conduct, this broad interpretation of affirmative consent hardly solves the no-means-yes and character problems for which it was formulated.

Consent v. Affirmative Consent

Substantial confusion results from affirmative consent proponents' vacillation between touting the standard as a sex-norm-changing revolution and defending it as merely reflecting the heterodox ways people communicate about sex. Does affirmative consent change everything or nothing? How do I know if a communication is mere consent or *affirmative* consent? Do I need a contract just to be safe?

To begin to sort through the thicket, let us start by thinking about the mental and communicative aspects of consenting to sexual activity. A sexual consent transaction between two people, A and B, consists of a

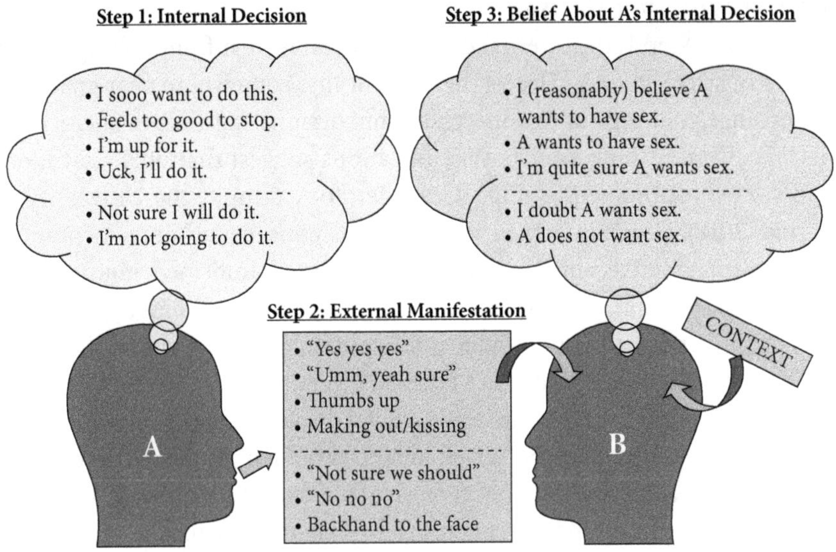

FIGURE 2.1 The Consent Transaction

three-step process. Step 1: A forms a mental state regarding the sexual activity. Step 2: A displays external manifestations of that mental state. Step 3: Based on A's external manifestations and the context, B forms a belief about A's mental state. For the sex to be unquestionably consensual, A's mental state must be sufficiently willing; A must sufficiently communicate that willingness; and B must sufficiently conclude that A was willing, and vice versa. That process is illustrated in Figure 2.1.

Figure 2.1 assumes that B is the "sex proponent," the person seeking sex, and A is the "sex acceptor," the person with the power to accept or reject the advances. Indeed, many consent standards in college codes require the person desiring sex to "obtain" or "ensure" the other's consent, presuming that sexual willingness is preternaturally asymmetrical (e.g., Cal. Educ. Code § 67386 2016; Wesleyan Policy, 2017). It is the "May I have this dance?" model of sexual communication. Northwestern University's (2018) misconduct code, for example, states, "It is always the requirement of the individual initiating sexual contact … to ensure that consent is present before acting and that consent is ongoing during sexual activity." Other campus codes, in their earnest attempts at gender neutrality, specify that *each* party must go through this ritual (e.g., Amherst University, n.d.; Duke University, n.d.; University of California, 2016). Thus, after I agree to dance with you, I must follow up with, "Now may *I* have this dance?" Only then can we dance.

Step 1: A's Internal Decision

Let us turn to Step 1, the internal decision. A can have infinite feelings about B's offer of sex. Figure 2.1 draws the consent line somewhere near grudging acquiescence, making desire unnecessary but designating ambivalence a nonconsensual state. Some university publications suggest that only a far more impassioned attitude will suffice. Consider, for example, the University of Georgia (2018), which informed students that "consensual" agreement must be "sober, imaginative, enthusiastic, creative, wanted, informed, mutual [and] honest." It is true that such strict, if not impossible, requirements appear more often in university student service publications on how to have "healthy" relationships than in misconduct codes. Nevertheless, some colleges have incorporated these concepts into their official disciplinary definitions of consent. Colleges incorporated the "sober, imaginative," language in their federally required **Clery Act** security reports on sexual assault (Gersen & Suk, 2016).

Consequently, the apparently simple proposition that one must mentally consent to sex is really the outcome of a struggle between various value judgments, such as whether sex can be instrumental rather than hedonistic and whether it is no big deal or a life decision of grave importance. College directives instill the notion that intimate activity must be carnally desired and engaged in for its own sake. But for university students and others, the motivations behind sex are not always so simple. Studies find that college students, female and male, widely agree to "unwanted sex," meaning sex that is not physically desired, for a variety of reasons, such as status and relationship intimacy (Impett & Peplau, 2003; Muehlenhard & Cook, 1988; Sprecher, Hatfield, Cortese, Potapova, & Levitskaya, 1994). Surprisingly, this unwanted sex can produce positive outcomes (O'Sullivan & Allegeier, 1998).

Step 2: A's External Communications

Let us turn to Step 2, the external manifestations. There is little controversy when internal mental states and communicative performances correspond. When a person is averse to sex and says no, subsequent intercourse is clearly nonconsensual. Controversy arises, however, when there is a mismatch between internal states and external manifestations. A sex acceptor can express intentions in various ways. An enthusiastic A might say "Yes, yes, yes," but also might say, "OK, I guess," or nothing at all. And although such is anathema to activists, research reveals that A might even moan "no" (Muehlenhard, 2011; Muehlenhard & Hollabaugh, 1988; Sprecher et al., 1994). Sometimes, a person hotly desires sex but acts reticent so that the other takes the lead. Sometimes a person eagerly agrees to sex he or she does not really want, colloquially known as "faking it." As noted, this might be for various reasons, like making a partner happy. Faking it, it turns out, also runs contrary to some universities' requirement that consent be "honest" and "sincere" (Gersen & Suk, 2016; e.g., Northwestern University, 2018).

The cues that indicate mental willingness or unwillingness are infinitely variable. In October 2017, the student health portal, CampusWell, published the article, "What Enthusiastic Consent Actually Looks Like—and Why You Should Hold Out for It," which was distributed by college health offices throughout the nation. In attempting to prove that consent is "not complicated," the article ironically endorsed conflicting accounts of which manifestations indicate consent. First, the article quotes the director of Yale's Office of Gender and Campus Culture: "We aren't just looking for the 'yes' of consent—we're looking for the 'YES!' of enthusiasm." Here, consent is a statement made with alacrity. The article then quotes blogger Rachel Kramer Bussel: "You can gauge [consent] in the way their eyelids flutter (or close), the way their breathing gets heavier, the way their body squirms as they answer your questions" (Chamoniz, 2017). Here, consent is divined from body language, even physiological response, which feminists generally reject. Indeed, the University of Chicago's (2018) code, in direct contrast to Bussel's sentiments, opines that "heavy breathing … can be a sign of distress."

The upshot of the CampusWell article is that "we use the same everyday signals—both verbal and nonverbal—to communicate interest in sexual situations as we do in everyday life" (Chamoniz, 2017). But there are millions of "verbal and nonverbal" signals people use in "everyday life," hardly rendering consent "not complicated." Luckily, people are generally quite good at divining the meaning of subtle sexual signals (Hickman & Muehlenhard, 1999), and most sex goes off without a hitch. Indeed, the CampusWell article described a 2010 study where young adults "reported easily being able to understand their partner's subtle, nonverbal forms of agreement and refusal during casual sexual encounters" (Chamoniz, 2017).

Step 3: B's Understanding of A's Internal Decision

This leaves Step 3, the sex proponent's state of mind. Under ordinary consent laws, B is innocent so long as B believes, or reasonably believes, that A had a sufficiently consensual mental state. In the easy situation, B correctly interprets A's intentions, but things get more difficult when there is a discrepancy between B's belief and A's actual state of mind. Some criminal law theorists argue that because punishment is about defendants' moral culpability, the test should be whether the defendant *honestly* believed there was agreement. By contrast, feminist reformers, loath to give a pass to chauvinist or clueless men, were successful in getting rape statutes to incorporate reasonableness (American Law Institute, 2014). Under these statutes, defendants are guilty even though they truly believed there was consent, so long as the jury finds their

FIGURE 2.2 Consent Manifestations and Affirmative Consent

interpretation unreasonable. Most other criminal prohibitions require a defendant to *know*—or at least heavily suspect—that he or she has engaged in the prohibited conduct.

In a typical **contested consent case**, A (the complainant) will argue that his or her mental state was one of unwillingness; B (the respondent) will defend that A was in fact willing or that B honestly and reasonably believed A was; and the factfinder will decide who has the better claim by looking at all of A's external manifestations in context. Affirmative consent changes things. First, it makes A's mental state irrelevant; it eliminates Step 1. B can no longer argue that regardless of what A said or did, A mentally agreed. B instead must argue that A performed (or B reasonably believed A performed) "affirmative consent." As the Amherst (n.d.) code puts it, "In the absence of an outward demonstration, consent does not exist."

This is not much of a change if *any* verbal or nonverbal signal can count as an "outward demonstration." The affirmative consent standard changes things dramatically, however, when it narrows the world of external manifestations that count as "affirmative" consent. Recall that to reduce the taint of factfinder prejudice or mistake, reformers pushed for laws declaring that only certain, preapproved performances could express consent. Figure 2.2 illustrates this narrowing move.

The Consent Scale

University publications create affirmative consent circles of varying circumferences. The circle is bigger or smaller depending on the school's regulatory designs. Figure 2.3 places affirmative consent formulations on a scale from narrow to broad, from most to least sex regulatory. I should note that this is not the only scale relevant to consent in college codes. As mentioned, there are numerous constructions of the consensual state of mind, from ambivalent acceptance to enthusiastic passion. Codes also engage in varying treatments of **incapacitation** and **coercion** that undermine consent. Finally, there are differing rules regarding which promises, deceptions, and power differentials invalidate consent. But each of these scales merits its own discussion, so I will

More Regulatory

- A continuous and enthusiastic expression of consent.
- A "yes."
- Words or conduct that clearly convey consent, with categorical exclusion (i.e. of foreplay, playful "no's," passive acceptance).
- Words or conduct that clearly convey consent, with limits on context.
- Words or conduct that, under the totality of the circumstances, reasonably convey consent.

Less Regulatory

FIGURE 2.3 The Affirmative Consent Scale

confine my cartographic efforts to some common formulations of college consent.

Criticisms of colleges' overly aggressive sex regulation generally focus on yes means yes. However, the requirement of "continuous" or "ongoing" affirmative consent is actually more regulatory. "Yes" is theoretically possible to comply with. Indeed, reformers' argument is that once people know the yes rule, they will obtain a "yes." By contrast, the requirement that sex proponents ensure that sex acceptors communicate "active, present and ongoing" agreement throughout the encounter (Northwestern University, 2018) is virtually impossible to conceptualize, let alone follow. Continuous internal consent is epistemologically problematic. There is no way to guarantee a person will not have a fleeting second thought or wandering mind. The requirement of an "ongoing" external "affirmative act or statement" (Stanford University, 2016) is even more confounding. What exactly does a "continuous" statement of consent look, or sound, like? Perhaps the "ongoing" requirement means there must be consent for each distinct intimate sex act and that consent can be withdrawn. However, those requirements *also* appear in policies, leading to the unfortunate conclusion that "continuous" is an additional, and impossible, requirement. Moreover, "continuous-ongoing" formulations are as common as they are troubling.

Most codes also require consent to be "clear." This unquivocability requirement is subject to varying interpretations. It is possible, although unlikely, that the codes merely require that consent be clear to the sex proponent. More likely, the external manifestations must meet some objective standard of clarity. But what is this standard? Must the external manifestations convince an extremely risk-averse, sexually conservative person? One is left to speculate about the size and contents of the Venn-diagram circle of manifestations that unambiguously dispel any doubts as to agreement. Even a yes, depending on how it is said, can be ambiguous.

The "yes" directive is easier to follow than the "continuous" affirmative consent standard. Codes specify that students must obtain a "yes, verbal or otherwise" (e.g., Allegheny College, 2017; Johns Hopkins University, 2017; Yale University, 2019). At the most basic level, this requires the sex proponent, at some point, to stop what he or she is doing, make a request for sexual activity, and receive a verbal "yes," "cool," or "let's go," or a nonverbal thumbs-up, immediate undressing, or extra-heated engagement. The Duke University (n.d.) policy adds guidance that specifies "[i]t is essential that each participant stops and clarifies, verbally, willingness to continue." Presumably, answers like "I guess," "Why not?," and "If you want to," or actions like continuing foreplay, shrugging with a smile, and staying still while being undressed do not count as "clear" authorizations. Moreover, if this requisite ask-and-answer performance must precede literally "each act," the yes-means-yes standard makes consensual sex as impossible as the "continuous" standard. Perhaps codes intend consent to apply to "critical" acts, roughly corresponding to the baseball-metaphor "bases" in teenage vernacular. In this model, initial kissing, above-the-waist touching of private parts, below-the-waist touching, oral sex, and sexual intercourse each require a distinct "yes." Of course, this leaves infinite other sexual activities (e.g., disrobing oneself, undressing another, lying on someone, touching non-private parts) in limbo.

Even if it only applies to "bases," the yes requirement is a departure from sexual communication norms. There is an obvious disconnect between policy and practice when university codes require strict affirmative consent for "any intentional sexual touching, however slight," which includes kissing, hand-holding, hugging, and caressing (e.g., University of Colorado, 2018). These policies make a person a sexual offender for giving a hug at the end of a pleasant date, just because he or she did not ask, "Can I hug you?" Even for intimate activities like intercourse, consent communication is often nonverbal and subtle. Given this, critics reason, the top-down imposition of a "yes" requirement outlaws much of the ordinary, mutually desired sexual interactions people have every day.

Affirmative consent proponents rejoin that, even if a "yes" at every critical stage of the sexual proceedings is not the current norm, it is "easy" to obtain (e.g., Kuschmider, 2015). Once students are made to chant the yes-means-yes slogan during orientation, they are on notice to get a yes and can be held responsible for failing to do so (Anderson, 2005). However, even if students knew which activities require the "yes" script and which words are included in it, it is not so easy for relatively sexually inexperienced, insecure, rejection-fearing, status-conscious young people to perform the script. Studies show that people of both sexes have strong incentives to eschew direct expression of sexual desire to "save face" in the event of rejection (Humphreys & Brousseau, 2010). Women doubly feel the pressure *not* to speak forthrightly about wanting sex. The terrain they must navigate involves simultaneously communicating their actual desires and ensuring that they portray an image in line with still-existing gendered expectations and chastity norms (Hickman & Muehlenhard, 1999; Johnson & Hoover, 2015). Because sex proponents bear all the burdens of the yes standard, sex acceptors will have *no* incentive to comply with the directive that their external communications be "honest."

Slightly less regulatory than yes-means-yes is the formulation that affirmative consent can be words and actions that convey consent, but with delineated exceptions. Under this standard, the factfinder may look at some, but not all, "words and actions" to determine consent. For example, codes exclude kissing, foreplay, and prior and current relationships from the range of consent manifestations, categorically proclaiming that they "do not imply" consent (e.g., Brown University, 2016; Columbia University, 2018; Massachusetts Institute of Technology, 2018; Northwestern University, 2018). These restrictions declare that increasingly intimate, mutually orchestrated sexual contact that culminates in intercourse constitutes sexual assault, unless there is some independent communication. For example, if kissing and heavy petting cannot be considered consent to digital penetration ("fingering"), it means that the sex proponent must stop and perform the ask-and-answer script before that intimate contact.

In a similar vein, codes specify that silence and passivity are not within the world of "actions" that convey consent (e.g., Northwestern University, 2018; University of Chicago, 2018). This effectively outlaws the "allowing oneself to be undressed" and "passively receiving sexual attention" that researchers identify as a typical consent communication (Humphreys & Brousseau, 2010). Many people outside the antirape activist world would find the following scenario acceptable, if not ideal: The man says, "If anything I do makes you uncomfortable let me know and I'll stop immediately." The woman then is silent while the man takes the lead, culminating in passionate and mutually desirable sexual activity. The college codes adopting anti-passivity, anti-silence rules make this scenario a violation. To be sure, it is a reasonable ideological stance to hold that in a fully equal world, men would not be the pursuers and women would often take the lead. However, this feminist critique of desire as dominance runs up against the reality that sexual desire is highly culturally ordered and deeply gendered. College codes' ideal of constant and equal communication conflicts with the way many students do, and like to, have sex.

Some activists recognize that escalating intimacy and subtle signals can indicate agreement, but nevertheless worry that sex proponents and factfinders will assume that initial foreplay makes everything "fair game." Some codes compromise by specifying that initial contact, early agreement, or silence does not "necessarily" or "in itself" establish consent to sex (e.g., Cornell University, n.d.; Johns Hopkins University, 2017; Princeton University, 2018). This preserves the possibility that escalating intimacy and passive acceptance can be affirmative consent, under certain circumstances, while maintaining the strong message that kissing does not authorize sexual intercourse.

Codes also commonly restrict the type of information that sex proponents can rely on to contextualize the sex acceptor's external manifestations. Limiting the time frame of information to the interaction immediately preceding sex is a very popular move. In determining consent, proponents may not consider past sexual experiences with the person, the fact that they are in a current relationship, or the person's behaviors and communications earlier in the night. Columbia University's (2018) policy, for example, states that the definition of consent is not affected by "relationship status." The University of Colorado's (2018) policy similarly specifies, "Previous sexual relationships or the existence of a current relationship do not imply consent." The upshot of these policies is that sex proponents can contextualize external manifestations with very recent occurrences (i.e., the sex acceptor said, "You take the lead."). They may not, however, contextualize manifestations with past evidence (e.g., on ten previous occasions increasingly intimate foreplay led to sex). Such policies require that in *every* sexual interaction, even with a long-time partner, the sex acceptor's external manifestations must be so clear that they would convey sexual willingness to a total stranger.

Of course, people do not view communications in a vacuum. People in long-term relationships communicate with less formality than people who have just met. Old married couples express consent differently than tentative first daters (Humphreys & Brousseau, 2010). Administrators worry that sex proponents and factfinders will overemphasize past sex and relationship status in determining present consent. Again, the more moderate approach is to caution that past sex and current relationships do not *in themselves* constitute consent, versus the more radical approach of dismissing such information as irrelevant.

In sum, many of the formulations of consent in university policies are far more regulatory than the consent applied in criminal laws. In the criminal arena, the jury must find beyond a reasonable doubt that the defendant knew or should have known, based on the totality of the circumstances, that the victim did not want the sex. In the college arena, accused students are guilty when the factfinder concludes that it is more likely than not that the complainant's consent performance was deficient, regardless of whether the accused reasonably believed there was consent; indeed, regardless of whether there *was* consent. Under a "yes" policy, parties engaging in increasingly intimate foreplay that culminates in desired sex are *both* violators subject to expulsion. Some affirmative consent proponents applaud the standard's deliberate overbreadth. One opined, "The 'Yes Means Yes' laws create an equilibrium where too much counts as sexual assault. Bad as it is, that's a necessary change" (Klein, 2014).

Aspirations and Distributions

Feminists of the 1990s reasoned that focusing on affirmative communication would prevent sexist juries from imposing their retrograde notions of consent. However, the factfinders in Title IX offices and university administrations are hardly sexists who believe that no generally means yes or unchaste women deserve to be raped. Administrators are perfectly capable of examining the totality of the circumstances and deciding whether the respondent reasonably believed the complainant agreed to sex. Thus, university codes embrace affirmative consent for a different reason altogether. They impose strict performative requirements not just to control sexist factfinders who mishandle the ordinary consent analysis, but to send a message to students about how sexual consent *should* occur.

Student health publications on how to have healthy sex substantially overlap with the conduct codes intended to prescribe the minimum standards for lawful (non-expellable) behavior. There is little sunlight between college administrators' notion of ideal, respectful, hedonistic consent and the consent that disciplinary codes require for continued matriculation at the college—or frankly any college, given that a violation equates to branding as a rapist. To be sure, affirmative consent critics regard the notion of university administrators imposing their visions of ideal sex on students, on pain of expulsion, as more Orwellian than utopian. For **sex radical** theorists, the idea of bureaucratic imposition of a sex script involving sober negotiation, analytic deliberation, unequivocal assent, and frequent double-checking is dystopian—and not altogether compatible with "enthusiastic passion" (e.g., Franke, 2001).

Nevertheless, commentators on both sides of the affirmative consent issue generally agree that the current cultural standard, which designates men as aggressors and women as gatekeepers and requires women to navigate the chastity-desirability double bind is highly problematic. Most thoughtful analysts agree that universities should encourage students to adopt better sexual practices, including being open about sex, less afraid of stigma and rejection, and concerned about the feelings of their sexual partners. Men should certainly abandon the notion that sex, under most conditions, is a boon. At the same time, schools need to be careful not to counsel women that sex, under most conditions, is a life-destroying trauma. There is some question whether consent messaging changes behavior at all, given that people interpret "consent" so variably (Johnson & Hoover, 2015). Universities' affirmative consent efforts lead students to parrot, but not necessarily practice, "yes means yes" (Bedera, 2017; Beres, 2014; Curtis & Burnett, 2017). In any case, the main controversy is whether schools' efforts to change sexual norms should include disciplining students for participating in the prevailing, if far-from-ideal, sexual culture.

It will be a long time, if ever, before the larger sexual culture is one where young people get a "yes" before "each act." I submit that people in relationships will never follow the strict communicative dictates of many college codes. Thus, on any given day, thousands of students have sex in violation of the "yes," "ongoing," and unequivocal requirements. They are expellable and only saved by the fact that no one reports the violation whether because both parties enjoyed the code-defying sex, or the Title IX administrator weeded out de minimis or "gray zone" cases. If the latter, then the administrator is imposing a de facto ordinary consent standard, despite the code's strict performative requirements.

For some affirmative consent defenders, this is an ideal situation. Misconduct policies "send the message" to students that mere consent will not suffice in the absence of a passionate, well-considered, unequivocal "yes." At the same time, schools do not actually sanction individuals for failing to get a yes when the sex otherwise appears consensual, despite codes' formal strictures. Sanctions, this argument goes, are still reserved for unambiguous cases involving respondents who use force, ignore protests, or otherwise believe sex is unwanted (Tuerkheimer, 2016). This defense of affirmative consent—that it will not end up punishing sex without a yes—is somewhat strange in that it upholds the standard because it will *not* be followed. It justifies affirmative consent by the fact that it will be honored in the breach. Of course, if most violations of yes means yes are not sanctioned, discipline holds little promise of larger cultural transformation.

It is worth asking whether administrators in fact confine their broadened regulatory power to the "worst" cases or whether the power distributes in less palatable ways. There are at least some reports filed where the respondent is innocent under force or ordinary consent standards but in violation of strict affirmative consent standards. To be sure, affirmative consent proponents tout the standard for encouraging more women to understand their sexual experiences as reportable assault. Thereafter, whether any given sex without a yes reaches a Title IX office can be quite path dependent. Imagine the following scenario:

> **A:** *"Last night I had sex with B. I played along with B, but I wasn't into it. I didn't say to stop, so B probably thinks everything was fine. But it just doesn't feel right."*
>
> **A's Friend:** *"I know the misconduct policy at this school. B did not stop and ask for permission. You did not say yes. That is rape, and you should report it. Don't let B do it to someone else."*

By the time an official complaint is filed, A may be quite resolute and insist on an investigation and adjudication (Paul, Zinzow, McCauley, Kilpatrick, & Resnick, 2013). Not all such complaints will be "weeded out" by cautious administrators. Within this subset of cases involving failure to get a yes to arguably consensual sex, one might wonder which complaints are pursued and which respondents end up expelled. There is no empirical answer, but we can theorize about the parties in this subset of on-the-line cases where affirmative consent (versus ordinary consent) makes all the difference.

Administrators may pursue gray zone complaints when they instinctively view the respondent as a "bad guy" or the complainant as a "good girl" or "true victim." These instinctual and discretionary decisions might meaningfully overlap with guilt and culpability, but they might not. Administrators' views of respondents' predatory nature could be influenced by race, low socioeconomic status, high status (like fraternity membership), or other rule-breaking and deviant behavior. Similarly, assessments of complainants' credibility may depend on their race, class, conformity with gender norms, eloquence, or typical "traumatized" appearance. Administrators may be inclined to pursue on-the-line cases when the victim is particularly vehement or appears in emotional turmoil, neither of which necessarily match up with the quality of the defendant's conduct (Bryden, 2000). Once administrators make the decision to move forward with a case, respondents are at higher risk of severe sanction if they cannot afford private representation (Halley, 2016).

Another possibility is that the strict affirmative consent standards will serve a difference-splitting function in fraught he-said-she-said disputes. For example, there could be a case where A says that A was in an advanced drunken state when B physically forced sex. B, by contrast, says A eagerly engaged in escalating foreplay and sexual intercourse. Let us assume that there is reason to discredit A's account. There are several witnesses who attest that A was not in fact drunk and that A's early accounts of the incident did not mention force but just that A was "not into it." The university process requires adjudicators to find by a preponderance of the evidence—and in some codes, by clear and convincing evidence—that assault occurred. In this case, the administrator should find A not credible and conclude that B did not force a drunk person to have sex. At the same time, the administrator could reason that B must have done *something* to make A upset enough to file a complaint. To resolve the conundrum, the administrator can sanction B for violating the affirmative consent requirement, despite B's superior credibility, because B's story of mutually desired sex still did not involve a "yes" or "continuous" consent to "each act" (*State in the Interests of M.T.S.* 1991).[1]

Conclusion

Affirmative consent as articulated in college and university codes is far narrower than sexual consent in criminal law and in the real world. Given the gap between this aspirational notion of consent and actual sexual practice, codes outlaw the typical, non-criminal sexual behavior in which students often engage. In practice, misconduct policies are often not applied to the letter. However, there will inevitably be a residuum of cases where administrators sanction sex accompanied by ordinary but not affirmative consent (i.e., mutually wanted sex without a yes). Such cases may arise when there are particularly vehement or privileged complainants and particularly disempowered or disfavored student respondents. This is a steep price to pay for the purported expressive benefit of placing aspirational standards into misconduct codes.

Punishing a randomly obtained and small subset of those who have sex without a yes will hardly incentivize the larger student population to abandon culturally entrenched and emotionally ingrained sexual practices. That said, changing the default of sexual communication from nonverbal subtle signaling to open and unequivocal communication is possible. Universities can, and arguably should, play a role in such a cultural shift, but the evidence is that they lack the power to do more than nudge it along. Schools can use evidence-informed educational campaigns to help change the negative aspects of student sexual culture, but this should be separate from disciplinary law. Universities should use their limited investigative and adjudicative resources to discipline the students who violate *current* norms by imposing sex on unwilling people, not to send messages about how to have ideal sex.

KEY TERMS

Adultery statutes: Statutes that made it a crime to engage in extramarital sexual intercourse.

Affirmative consent: Lack of affirmative consent is an element of certain laws and policies defining sexual assault. In these laws and policies, lack of affirmative consent makes sexual activity between competent adults unlawful. Affirmative consent has differing meanings, but it commonly signifies that each participant has communicated that he or she is willing to engage in the relevant sexual activity and such communication meets certain requirements set forth by the law or policy (e.g., it must be "ongoing," "clear," or a "yes, verbal or otherwise").

Clery Act: The Jeanne Clery Disclosure of Campus Security Policy and Campus Crime Statistics Act, 20 U.S.C.A. § 1092(f), mandates that colleges and universities track, record, publicize, and report campus crime incidents to the federal government.

Coercion: Words or conduct on the part of the defendant/respondent that are sufficiently compulsive, forcible, or threatening to render consent invalid. Definitions of coercion vary.

Consent: Lack of consent is an element of certain laws and policies defining sexual assault. In these laws and policies, lack of consent makes sexual activity between competent adults unlawful. Consent has differing meanings, but it most commonly signifies that each participant is mentally willing to engage in the relevant sexual activity and expresses that willingness in a manner sufficient to make the other participant, or a reasonable person, believe, under the totality of the circumstances, that he or she is willing.

Contested consent case: A case where the complainant claims he or she did not consent and the defendant/respondent claims the complainant did consent or that he or she reasonably believed the complainant consented.

Corroboration requirement: The requirement in certain rape statutes and cases that the prosecution must present independent evidence corroborating the complainant's testimony.

Dear Colleague Letter (DCL): Format of OCR guidance regarding Title IX since 1998.

Force: Force is an element of certain laws and policies defining sexual assault. In these laws and policies, physical force, unless clearly consented to, makes sexual activity between competent adults unlawful. Force has differing meanings, but most statutes define it as compulsion or violence beyond the physical contact inherent in the sexual activity. Others define any nonconsensual sexual touching as a forcible encounter.

Fornication statutes: Statutes that made it a crime to engage in nonmarital sexual intercourse.

Fresh complaint requirement: The requirement in certain criminal rape statutes and cases that the prosecution must prove the complainant reported the rape to an authority shortly after the rape.

Gray zone cases: Cases in which the sex appears consensual under an ordinary consent standard but will likely be found unlawful under a strict affirmative consent standard.

Incapacitation: A person's state of temporary or permanent physical or mental impairment sufficient to make sexual activity with that person unlawful. Incapacitation definitions vary.

Rape shield laws: State and federal evidence rules that bar from the trial certain information about the rape complaint, typically including past sexual behavior and sexual reputation, from the trial.

Resistance requirement: The requirement in certain rape statutes and cases that the prosecution prove the complainant resisted the rape to the utmost.

Second wave of feminism: A juris-generative period of feminist activism, organizing, and lawmaking stemming from the 1970s to the 1990s.

Sex radical: A theoretical position that sexual activity is a good; the harms of sex are overstated; sex has been overregulated; sexual regulation has reinforced unfair hierarchies; and sex restriction holds little promise for liberation and anti-subordination.

Title IX of the Education Amendments Act of 1972: Legislation signed into law by President Richard Nixon that prohibits sex discrimination in educational institutions that receive federal funds. This stand-alone legislation fills in the gaps found in Title VII of the Civil Rights Act of 1964 and other legal documents.

DISCUSSION QUESTIONS

1. Imagine you are a university administrator overseeing the revision of the student sexual misconduct code. Among other things, you are tasked with determining when sexual activity between two competent adult students is a violation of the code. You intend to prohibit sex without consent, but you are struggling to articulate exactly what "sex without consent" is. Do you require an affirmative expression of willingness or a verbal expression? Do you add that there must be consent to "every act" or that consent be ongoing "throughout"? Do you specify who is responsible for obtaining consent (i.e., the "sexual pursuer")? How do you determine whom that party is?
2. Studies reveal that people are socialized to be vague, indirect, and nonverbal regarding sexual consent and to adhere to gender roles in sexual communications. Students thus need to be educated about asking for and expressing consent. However, research shows that most college consent education programs fail to displace the ingrained cultural sexual norms. Efforts to embed sexuality and sexual consent education in elementary and secondary school curricula face political backlash

and parental protest. Given this, is requiring students to ask for and give a "yes," with the potential penalty of expulsion, a fair and effective way to create cultural change? If it is not, then where should anti-rape activists invest their efforts?

3. In many universities, both parties to the sexual transaction must "ensure" the "affirmative consent" of the other. This means that every sexually active student is required to make sure that his or her partner has affirmatively consented to sex to avoid school discipline. How should students understand this directive? Are female students entitled to presume that male students who make the "first move" have affirmatively consented? Are male students allowed to presume that female students who initiate sex affirmatively consent? Do all people—women, men, cis, trans, hetero, LGBTQ—have the obligation to verbally double-check with their partners, even when the partner appears to be the sex proponent?
4. In a similar vein, if every student must obtain "affirmative consent" to each (relevant) sex act, it becomes very important to know the parameters of "affirmative consent." Can affirmative consent be nonverbal? Does increasingly intimate foreplay and petting count as affirmative consent? Should the quality of the expression of consent depend on the nature of the sexual contact (for example, kissing does not require verbal consent, but penetration does)? Should college codes give examples of what types of performances do and do not count as affirmative consent?
5. Affirmative consent is intended to aid factfinders (juries, college administrators) in deciding "he-said-she-said" cases where the complainant alleges the sex was nonconsensual and the respondent maintains that it was consensual. Instead of focusing on whether the complainant was willing to have sex or whether the respondent reasonably believed the complainant was willing, affirmative consent directs us to focus on whether the complainant sufficiently expressed consent. On its face, the standard punishes people who honestly and even reasonably believe sex was consensual, if the other person's consent expression was deficient. Why punish people for having sex with a person they reasonably believed consented? Is it because factfinders are too eager to believe that it was reasonable for the accused to think there was consent? Is there any way to make sure that rape law and policy cover enough cases of wrongdoing, without policing "ordinary" sex? Can you think of alternatives to affirmative consent that strike the right balance between harm regulation and sexual freedom?

Note

1 In the famous 1991 case, *State in the Interests of M.T.S.*, which established an affirmative consent standard in New Jersey, the complainant claimed that she was in a "deep sleep" when the defendant penetrated her. The defendant said that after "kissing and all," he consensually penetrated her. The juvenile court judge discredited the complainant's testimony that she was asleep at the time of the sex. Nevertheless, the judge convicted the defendant because in his testimony there was no evidence that the complainant *affirmatively* consented.

References

18 Pa. Stat. § 3101 (1984)

18 Pa. Stat. § 3124.1 (1984)

Ackerman, J. (1994, June 7). Two protests by NOW take judges to task on rape ruling. *Pittsburgh Post-Gazette*. Available at 1994 WLNR 2265884.

Ali, R. (2011, April 4). *Dear colleague letter.* Washington, DC: U.S. Department of Education, Office for Civil Rights.

Allegheny College. (2017, July). *2017–18 Policy against discriminatory and sexual harassment.* Retrieved from https://sites.allegheny.edu/titleix/2017-18-policy-against-discriminatory-and-sexual-harassment-including-sexual-assault-and-other-forms-of-sexual-violence-dating-violence-domestic-violence-and-stalking/

American Law Institute. (2014, April 30). *Model penal code: Sexual assault and related offenses* (Tentative draft No. 1). Philadelphia, PA: Author.

Amherst College. (n.d.). *College sexual misconduct policy.* Retrieved from https://www.amherst.edu/offices/student-affairs/community-standards/college-standards/examples-of-sexual-misconduct

Anderson, M. J. (2002). From chastity requirement to sexuality license: Sexual consent and a new rape shield law. *George Washington Law Review, 70*(1), 51–162.

Anderson, M. J. (2005). Negotiating sex. *University of Southern California Law Review, 78*(6), 1401–1438.

Baker, K. K. (1999). Sex, rape, and shame. *Boston University Law Review, 79*(3), 663–716.

Bedera, N. (2017). Moaning and eye contact: College men's negotiations of sexual consent in theory and in practice (unpublished doctoral disseration). University of Michigan, Ann Arbor, MI, USA. Retrieved from https://osf.io/preprints/socarxiv/eqfya/

Beres, M.A. (2014). Rethinking the concept of consent for anti-sexual violence activism and education. *Feminism and Psychology 24*(3), 373–389.

Brief of the ACLU et. al. as Amici Curiae, *Coker v. Georgia*, 433 U.S. 584 (1977), 1976 WL 181482 (U.S.) (1976)

Brown University. (2016, September 2). *Sexual and gender-based harassment, sexual violence, relationship and interpersonal violence and stalking policy.* Retrieved from https://www.brown.edu/about/administration/title-ix/sites/brown.edu.about.administration.title-ix/files/uploads/2016-09-02_Policy_2.pdf

Bryden, D. P. (2000). Redefining rape. *Buffalo Criminal Law Review, 3*(2), 317–512.

Cal. Educ. Code § 67386 (2016)

Cattabiani, M. F. (1994). Berkowitz surrender delayed, ESU student in "no is not enough" case gets extension to Aug. 1. *Morning Call.* Retrieved from http://articles.mcall.com/1994-07-19/news/2996047_1_berkowitz-conviction-superior-court

Chamoniz, A. P. (2017, October 1). *What enthusiastic consent looks like—and why you should hold out for it.* Retrieved from https://www.campuswell.com/what-enthusiastic-consent-looks-like/

Columbia University. (2018, August 24). *Gender-based misconduct policy and procedures for students.* Retrieved from http://www.columbia.edu/cu/studentconduct/documents/GBMPolicyandProceduresforStudents.pdf

Commonwealth v. Berkowitz, 609 A.2d 1138 (Pa. Sup. Ct. 1992), order aff'd in part, vacated in part, 641 A.2d 1161 (1994)

Commonwealth v. Berkowitz, 641 A.2d 1161 (Pa. 1994)

Cornell University. (n.d.). *Prohibited student conduct: Sexual assault.* Retrieved from http://titleix.cornell.edu/prohibited-conduct/sexual-assault/

Curtis, J.N. & Burnett, S. (2017). Affirmative consent: What do college student leaders think about "yes means yes" as the standard for sexual behavior? *American Journal of Sexuality Education, 12*(3), 201–214.

Dartmouth College. (2014, June 8). *Unified disciplinary procedures for sexual assault.* Retrieved from https://sexual-respect.dartmouth.edu/policy/unified-disciplinary-procedures-sexual-assault

Duke University. (n.d.). *Student sexual misconduct policy and procedures: Duke's commitment to Title IX.* Retrieved from https://studentaffairs.duke.edu/conduct/z-policies/student-sexual-misconduct-policy-dukes-commitment-title-ix

Estrich, S. (1986). Rape. *Yale Law Journal, 95*(6), 1087–1184.

Ferzan, K. (2016). Consent, culpability, and the law of rape. *Ohio State Journal of Criminal Law, 13*(2), 397–440.

Franke, K. M. (2001). Theorizing yes: An essay on feminism, law, and desire. *Columbia Law Review, 101*(1), 181–208.

Gersen, J., & Suk, J. (2016). The sex bureaucracy. *California Law Review, 104*(4), 881–948.

Giddings, P. J. (2009). *Ida: A sword among lions: Ida B. Wells and the campaign against lynching,* New York, NY: HarperCollins.

Gruber, A. (2009). Rape, feminism, and the war on crime. *Washington Law Review, 84*(4), 581–660.

Halley, J. (2016). The move towards affirmative consent. *Signs: Journal of Women in Culture and Society, 42*(1), 247–279.

Harris, A. (1990). Race and essentialism in feminist legal theory. *Stanford Law Review, 42*(3), 581–616.

Hartocollis, A. & Goldstein, D. (2018, September 2). Schools are tackling 'Bro' culture. The Kavanaugh case shows why that's hard to do. *New York Times.* Retrieved from https://www.nytimes.com/2018/09/28/us/kavanaugh-fraternities-prep-school.html

Helwick, C. (2014, October 23). Affirmative consent, the new standard. *Inside Higher Education.* Retrieved from https://www.insidehighered.com/views/2014/10/23/campuses-must-wrestle-affirmative-consent-standard-sexual-assault-essay

Hickman, S. E., & Muehlenhard, C. L. (1999). By the semi-mystical appearance of a condom: How young women and men communicate sexual consent in heterosexual situations. *Journal of Sex Research, 36*(3), 258–272.

Humphreys, T. P., & Brousseau, M. M. (2010). The sexual consent scale—revised: Development, reliability, and preliminary validity. *Journal of Sex Research, 47*(5), 420–428.

Impett, E. A., & Peplau, L. A. (2003). Sexual compliance: Gender, motivational, and relationship perspectives. *Journal of Sex Research, 40*(1), 87–100.

Johns Hopkins University. (2017, July 17). *Sexual misconduct policy and procedures.* Retrieved from https://sexualassault.jhu.edu/policies-laws/index.html#Section%20II%20-%20Prohibited%20Conduct

Johnson, A. M., & Hoover, S. M. (2015). The potential of sexual consent interventions on college campuses: A literature review on the barriers to establishing affirmative sexual consent. *PURE Insights,* 4(1), n.p.

Klein, E. (2014, October 13). "Yes means yes" is a terrible law, and I completely support it. *Vox.* Retrieved from http://www.vox.com/2014/10/13/6966847/yes-means-yes-is-a-terrible-bill-and-i-completely-support-it

Kuschmider, R. (2015, October 29). Ask a feminist: Affirmative consent. What is it? *Huffington Post.* Retrieved from http://www.huffingtonpost.com/ravishly/ask-a-feminist-affirmative-consent-what-is-it_b_8153606.html

Larson, J.E. 1 (1997) Even a worm will turn at last: Rape reform in late nineteenth-century America. *Yale Journal of Law and the Humanities* 9(1), 1–72.

Lewin, T. (1994, June 3). Courts struggle over how much force it takes to be a rape. *New York Times.* Retrieved from https://www.nytimes.com/1994/06/03/us/courts-struggle-over-how-much-force-it-takes-to-be-a-rape.html

MacKinnon, C. A. (1989). *Toward a feminist theory of the state.* Cambridge, MA: Harvard University Press.

McGuire, D. L. (2010). *At the dark end of the street: Black women, rape, and resistance: A new history of the Civil Rights Movement from Rosa Parks to the rise of Black power.* New York, NY: Random House.

Massachusetts Institute of Technology. (2018, February 6). *Policies and definitions for students.* Retrieved from https://titleix.mit.edu/sites/default/files/documents/PDF%20-%20Policies%20-%20Students%202_12_18.pdf

Muehlenhard, C. L. (2011). Examining stereotypes about token resistance to sex. *Psychology of Women Quarterly, 35*(4), 676–683.

Muehlenhard, C. L., & Cook, S. W. (1988). Men's self-reports of unwanted sexual activity. *Journal of Sex Research, 24*(1), 58–72.

Muehlenhard, C. L., & Hollabaugh, L. C. (1988). Do women sometimes say no when they mean yes? *Journal of Personality and Social Psychology, 54*(5), 872–879.

New, J. (2014, October 7). The "yes means yes" world. *Inside Higher Education.* Retrieved from https://www.insidehighered.com/news/2014/10/17/colleges-across-country-adopting-affirmative-consent-sexual-assault-policies

Northwestern University. (2018, September 10). *Comprehensive policy on sexual misconduct.* Retrieved from https://www.northwestern.edu/sexual-misconduct/docs/sexual_misconduct_policy.pdf

O'Sullivan, L. F., & Allgeier, E. R. (1998). Feigning sexual desire: Consenting to unwanted sexual activity in heterosexual dating relationships. *Journal of Sex Research, 35*(3), 234–243.

Paul, L. A., Zinzow, H. M., McCauley, J. L., Kilpatrick, D. G., & Resnick, H. S. (2013). Does encouragement by others increase rape reporting? Findings from a national sample of women. *Psychology of Women Quarterly, 38*(2), 222–232.

Princeton University. (2018). Rights, rules, responsibilities. Retrieved from https://rrr.princeton.edu/university#comp133

Remick, L. A. (1993). Read her lips: An argument for a verbal consent standard in rape. *University of Pennsylvania Law Review, 141*(3), 1103–1152.

Schulhofer, S. J. (1998). *Unwanted sex: The culture of intimidation and the failure of law.* Cambridge, MA: Harvard University Press.

Shapiro, J. (2010, February 24). Campus rape victims: A struggle for justice. *NPR.* Retrieved from https://www.npr.org/templates/story/story.php?storyId=124001493

Sommers, C. H. (2015, January 23). The media is making college rape culture worse. *Daily Beast.* Retrieved from https://www.thedailybeast.com/the-media-is-making-college-rape-culture-worse

Sprecher, S., Hatfield, E. Cortese, A., Potapova, E., & Levitskaya, A. (1994). Token resistance to sexual intercourse and consent to unwanted sexual intercourse: College students' dating experiences in three countries. *Journal of Sex Research, 31*(2), 125–132.

Stanford University. (2016, March 11). *Prohibited sexual conduct: Sexual misconduct, sexual assault, stalking, relationship violence, violation of university or court directives, student-on-student sexual harassment and retaliation.* Retrieved from https://adminguide.stanford.edu/chapter-1/subchapter-7/policy-1-7-3#anchor-24463

State v. Hunt, 135 N.W.2d 475 (Neb. 1965)

State in the Interest of M.T.S., 609 A.2d 1266, 1276 (N.J. Super. Ct. App. Div. 1992)

State v. Jackson, 679 A.2d 572 (N.H. 1996)
Taslitz, A. E. (2007). Forgetting Freud: The courts' fear of the subconscious in date rape (and other) cases. *Boston University Public International Law Journal, 16*(2), 145–194.
Tuerkheimer, D. (2016). Affirmative consent. *Ohio State Journal of Criminal Law, 13*(2), 441–468.
University of California. (2016, January 1). *Sexual violence and sexual harassment.* Retrieved from https://policy.ucop.edu/doc/4000385/SVSH
University of Chicago. (2018). *Policy on harassment, discrimination, and sexual misconduct.* Retrieved from https://harassmentpolicy.uchicago.edu/policy/#VII.%20Important%20 Principles
University of Colorado. (2018, October 1). *Administrative policy statement: Sexual misconduct, intimate partner abuse and stalking.* Retrieved from https://www.cu.edu/sites/default/files/5014.pdf
University of Georgia. (n.d.). *Dawgs get consent.* Retrieved from https://www.uhs.uga.edu/rsvp/consent
Wells-Barnett, I. B. (1892). *Southern horrors: Lynch law in all its phases.* New York, NY: New York Age Print.
Wesleyan College. (2017). *Policy prohibiting discriminatory harassment & sexual misconduct.* Retrieved from https://www.wesleyan.edu/inclusion/dc/2017ONE-POLICY%20Definitions.pdf
Woods, P. B. (1994, June 14). Comment: Lock up rapists longer. *Allentown Morning Call.* Retrieved from 1994 WLNR 1956414.
Yale University. (2019, July 25). *Yale sexual misconduct policies and related definitions.* Retrieved from https://smr.yale.edu/find-policies-information/yale-sexual-misconduct-policies-and-related-definitions

Credits

Fig 2.1: Aya Gruber, The Consent Transaction, from "Consent Confusion," Cardozo Law Review, vol. 38, no. 2, pp. 424. Copyright © 2017 by Cardozo School of Law.
Fig 2.2: Aya Gruber, Narrow Affirmative Consent, from "Not Affirmative Consent," The University of the Pacific Law Review, vol. 47, pp. 689. Copyright © 2017 by McGeorge Law Review.
Fig 2.3: Aya Gruber, The Affirmative Consent Scale, from "Consent Confusion," Cardozo Law Review, vol. 38, no. 2, pp. 431. Copyright © 2017 by Cardozo School of Law.

CHAPTER THREE

Mandatory Reporting in Context

Development, Concerns, and Best Practices

Christina Mancini

Introduction

Concern about campus crime has led to efforts designed to increase reporting (Heldman, Ackerman, & Breckenridge-Jackson, 2018). Illustrative of this focus was the implementation of the Jeanne Clery Disclosure of Campus Security Policy and Crime Statistics Act (or **Clery Act**), which requires institutions to record officially reported/known crime statistics and safety policies and to publicize them (Engle, 2015). Even so, scholarship demonstrates that sexual victimization among college students remains underreported (Rennison & Addington, 2018; Rennison, Dragiewicz, & DeKeseredy, 2013; Renzetti, Edleson, & Bergen, 2010), as only 20% disclose assaults to law enforcement (Cantor et al., 2017 Sinozich & Langton, 2014). Institutional investigations into sexual assault allegations (which may or may not involve police) also do not appear to capture the full extent of the problem (Richards, 2018). This realization has led to the development of **mandated reporting (MR)**, or compelled disclosure[1] in the college setting. Such reporting policies require that individuals in roles in which students might divulge information about sexual assault or harassment report disclosures to a designated authority.

Virtually no scholarship has documented the national extent of MR or, importantly, variation in MR practices (e.g., who must report, the process, whether law enforcement is contacted). There appears to be wide variability concerning the "design" of MR across institutions. With that context in mind, what follows in this chapter is an overview of the evolution of MR, how MR functions in practice, a discussion of concerns about its use, and proposals for improving outcomes associated with reporting policies.

Development of Mandatory Reporting in the College Context

Mandated reporting is not a new legal concept. In the 1960s and 1970s, spurred by attention to unreported child abuse, the federal government and states enacted legislation that requires individuals in certain professions to report suspicions of abuse of children (Brown & Gallagher, 2013). By the 1990s, states extended that practice to other populations, such as the elderly and individuals with disabilities, as well as those abused by intimate partners, who also may be at increased risk of experiencing mistreatment while not being in a position to report it (Hyman, Schillinger, & Lo, 1995; Sachs, Peek, Baraff, & Hasselblad, 1998).

Perhaps motivated by these movements, increasing accounts of campus crime, and perceived ineffective responses from academic institutions, some states started to consider legislation that would mandate reporting in instances of sexual assault involving college students (Richards & Kafonek, 2016). This extension of MR is more controversial than past policies because of its intended population. College students are distinct from children, victims of intimate partner abuse, and the elderly. MR has traditionally focused on these subsets of "vulnerable victims," who by dint of age, declining health, and/or having experienced trauma are viewed as being incapable of either recognizing or reporting abuse.

Despite the controversy, MR policies are being increasingly implemented across college campuses. As previously noted, the Clery Act mandates that postsecondary institutions provide information about known or reported violent and serious property crimes occurring on or near campus, such as homicide, sex crimes, and burglary (U.S. Department of Education, 2016). Institutions are required to make this information easily accessible to faculty, students, staff, and the public. To advance this goal, Clery identifies campus security authorities (generally campus police/security officers) as individuals who must report aggregate information about sex crimes (e.g., location, date of assault) disclosed to them in their official role. The role of a responsible employee is in direct contrast to **confidential reporters (CRs)**, which include pastoral and professional counselors; CRs can keep allegations in confidence.

In 2014, the **Violence Against Women Act (VAWA)**, a seminal piece of federal legislation designed to improve policy responses to sexual assault and other gender-based crime, was reauthorized to include an emphasis on addressing gender-based violence in institutions of higher learning (Cantalupo, 2014). Specifically, the amendments, known as the **Campus Sexual Violence Elimination Act (SaVE)**, require that postsecondary institutions promote greater transparency, accountability, and educational training in responding to the threat of sexual victimization. While several provisions are outlined, a few are notable for understanding how MR policies have been influenced over time. First, institutions must now publicize statistics on the extent of other forms of crimes that often co-occur within the context of sexual assault, such as dating violence and stalking. SaVE also mandates new provisions designed to improve fairness and promote greater accountability during the disciplinary review hearing process. Those campus personnel who are responsible for determining policy violations (or not), and those sanctioning (if appropriate), are required to be trained in understanding the dynamics of sexual violence (e.g., victim-offender relationship, trauma and its role in delayed reporting response) in a way that "promotes accountability" and "protects the safety of victims." As a final emphasis, postsecondary institutions must make victims aware of on- and off-campus resources and provide educational resources that promote awareness of sexual assault (Marshall, 2014). Hence, Clery and SaVE are complementary efforts that share the objective of improving detection and investigation of sexual violence. However, neither piece of federal guidance compels institutions to designate all or most employees as mandated reporters. This ambiguity has led to institutional discretion in determining the types of mandated reporters (e.g., all faculty and staff versus only certain classes of employees) and the specific procedures governing the process of MR (e.g., the content of what must be reported, how those allegations are investigated by the university, whether police involvement occurs).

Another piece of federal legislation, Title IX, enacted in 1972, stipulates other responsibilities for institutions. Unlike Clery (and SaVE), it is not geared to exclusively address campus safety, but rather to ensure there is gender equity and equal opportunity in educational settings. It is relevant to a discussion about reporting because it requires postsecondary institutions to establish clear and fair procedures for responding to sexually hostile educational environments. Indeed, in a Dear Colleague Letter (DCL) (U.S. Department of Education, 2011, p. 4) the federal government clearly established the "known or should have known standard" that universities are legally obligated to conduct meaningful investigations and ensure that procedures exist to detect sexual assault, particularly of unreported offenses. Even so, similar to Clery, this federal guidance permits discretion in how universities implement their procedures to compel disclosure, particularly regarding the decision to forward allegations to police (Savino, 2015). Title IX directs institutions to determine which employees will constitute another class of reporters[2] or "**responsible employees**" **(REs)**. Typically, these personnel are theorized to be in contact with students and so presumably could learn about crimes committed against them. Title IX stops short, though, of classifying all or most employees meeting this criterion (e.g., faculty) as required reporters (American Association of University Professors [AAUP], 2012).

Occurring at the same time as this legislative activity have been a number of high-profile cases involving perceived university "cover-ups" of allegations of sexual violence. One which began the discussion of MR in the college context was the 2011 Pennsylvania State University scandal involving former assistant football coach Jerry Sandusky. Following inaction, administrators were convicted of crimes involving endangerment of children (Dowler, Cuomo, & Laliberte, 2014). Although Sandusky's crimes did not involve university students, the failure to report abuse sparked a national discussion concerning the value of requiring university personnel to report knowledge of sex assault allegations (Mancini, Pickett, Call, McDougle, Brubaker, & Brownstein, 2017). By 2018, some states had adopted legislation regarding compelled disclosure to law enforcement, and many institutions implemented their own policies (Holland, Cortina, and Freyd, 2018). Next, this chapter further explores compelled disclosure as currently implemented in higher education.

Mandatory Reporting in Practice

There is no nationally endorsed model requiring colleges and universities receiving federal aid to incorporate MR policies (AAUP, 2012; C.M. Rennison, March 12, 2019, personal communication; T. N. Richards, February 26, 2019, personal communication; Weiss & Lasky, 2017). Recall that Clery's primary objective is to inform the community about the extent of crime at postsecondary institutions. While it does provide a general basis for determining REs, it gives institutions substantial latitude in designating reporters in addition to campus security officials (Holland & Cortina, 2017). Compelled disclosure policies are also distinct from Title IX provisions in that the latter law generally encourages institutions to conduct fair fact-finding *institutional* investigations when allegations surface. In contrast, the broader version of compelled disclosure policies, those that designate most or nearly all employees as mandated reporters (whether law enforcement is involved or not) appears to go further by providing a pathway for better detection of offenses that otherwise would not surface. To illustrate, professors and advisors are in unique positions to observe and interact with students (Richards, Branch, & Hayes, 2013). Through those contacts, students might be more willing to disclose to such individuals than to law enforcement or an institutional official.

MR policy is unique in that, unlike other sexual assault reforms (e.g., sex offender registration and notification), its recent proliferation was not the result of federal policymaking. Instead, compelled disclosure policies have been the result of piecemeal state-level and institutional-level efforts. It is important to emphasize that state-sponsored MR has occurred in only a handful of jurisdictions (Mancini et al., 2017). With this point in mind, we turn now to identifying the types of compelled disclosure systems that currently exist nationally. That conversation starts with identifying classifications of reporters.

Defining Responsible Employees

Both the Clery Act and Title IX provide *general* standards for determination of reporters. While there may be some overlap, persons considered to be campus security authorities for Clery Act reporting are not necessarily the same as those defined as "responsible employees" for Title IX (U.S. Department of Justice, 2016). This ambiguity led to the publication of a clarification document issued by the federal government. The guidance explained that a RE is any individual "who has the authority to take action and redress sexual violence … or whom the student could reasonably believe has this authority or duty" (Lhamon, 2014, p. 15). Thus, although Clery and Title IX (and corresponding clarification documents) may have sought to establish a national model of reporting standards, the language therein remains vague enough to permit discretion in designating others as mandated reporters among institutions (Lhamon, 2014, p. 15).

In one of the only reviews of policies regarding MR, Holland and colleagues (2018) analyzed a random sample of 150 universities and colleges and found a very small number of universities (4%) named "few employees" as mandatory reporters, "limiting this [reporting] role [only] to faculty and staff who are in top leadership positions and/or have significant responsibility for student safety and wellbeing" (Holland et al., 2018, p. 258). In contrast, nearly 70% of universities/colleges have adopted the "universal reporting" approach (Weiner, 2017, p. 72), identifying *all* faculty and staff (that is, per Holland et al., 2018, "all faculty, staff, volunteers, vendors and agents are required to report any incidents of sexual misconduct … to the Title IX Coordinator or a Title IX Deputy Coordinator," p. 260).[3]

What to Report?

The answer to the question concerning what acts REs must report is complicated (Engel, 2015). Because no federal law outlines a standardized reporting practice, variation exists in the content of reporting procedures (T. N. Richards, February 26, 2019, personal communication; Weiner, 2017); in short, what to report (e.g., an in-person disclosure, a disclosure on a discussion board, incidents occurring at events off and/or unrelated to campus), the content of the report (e.g., types of criminal acts that are "reportable"), and the timing of the incident (e.g., occurs prior to enrollment, assault experienced in high school) depends on the specific institutional policy.

A 2018 investigative article in the *Chronicle of Higher Education* highlights this complexity. For example, the University of Oregon utilizes a "nuanced MR" model, where faculty and staff are required to report known allegations of assault or harassment in a timely manner to the Title IX coordinator *only if* the victim gives permission after disclosure. The article contrasts the University of Oregon's policy with other institutions; for example, a faculty member teaching at Pennsylvania State University must immediately disclose to the school's Title IX Office an allegation made in a term paper submitted by a student, with no discretion to withhold the report if the victim requested confidentiality (Brown, 2018). Per federal statutes, universities are required to have transparent reporting procedures; consequently, many now include definitions of acts that are reportable and outline the general process on their websites. Purdue University (2018), for example, lists seven categories of reportable acts (e.g., sexual violence, sexual assault). In addition, it specifies the process for reporting, instructing reporters to contact Title IX "immediately" and to record as much information as possible for the report. The protocol advises that overreporting is better than underreporting: "If in doubt as to whether an incident needs to be reported, report it. There is no such thing as over-reporting!"

Investigation Process

A natural next question is, "Under a typical mandatory reporting model, what occurs once an allegation or suspicion is disclosed to a university official or school?" This is another complicated issue given the overlapping federal legislation and the vagueness of the requirements for schools to ensure they have fully addressed possible hostile educational environments (Weiner, 2017). In posing this question to the lead author of one of the only investigations of mandated reporting nationally (K. Holland, February 26, 2019, personal communication), she stated that "there is no current/published research examining what happens in a Title IX Office in response to reports from mandatory reporters." For this reason, it is difficult to provide a systematic account of how third-party reports are investigated as compared to "direct" reports from a student-victim (see also, Richards, 2018, discussing the lack of research examining variation in investigations across institutions). To simplify matters, this section summarizes what is known *generally* about the processing of compelled disclosure reports.

As a first step, when a Title IX Office receives a report from a mandatory reporter, federal law indicates that action be taken in some way (Cantalupo, 2014). That likely involves initiating contact with the victim—for instance, through an official university e-mail address (K. Holland, personal communication, February 26, 2019; Lhamon, 2014). The purpose of that outreach is to provide information about the office, offer on- and off-campus resources, and invite the person to the office to discuss the incident further if he or she chooses. Generally, care is taken to ensure the outreach does not endanger the victim (e.g., in cases of intimate partner violence) (C. M. Rennison, personal communication, March 12, 2019).

After that outreach effort, coordinators may (a) continue to contact the victim in order to obtain a statement regarding the assault, or (b) discontinue contact with the victim if they receive no response (K. Holland, personal communication, February 26, 2019). When (or if) the Title IX Office receives a response from victims/survivors, there are many possible pathways. One practice is to ask victims/survivors if they would like to move forward with an investigation. If victims/survivors do not wish to do so, dependent on the specific policy, the office may respect that decision (K. Holland, personal communication, February 26, 2019). At a minimum, when this occurs, the Title IX Office typically offers informal mechanisms and support. In a personal communication (March 12, 2019), noted sexual violence expert and former Title IX Office Coordinator Dr. Callie M. Rennison shared that "[i]nformal resolutions are a huge part of the work done in these offices, and are often overlooked by external audiences." Such resolutions may include classroom accommodations, assistance with addressing off-campus living arrangements, and other resources. Alternatively, though, dependent on the specific institutional policy, the Title IX Office may unilaterally decide to move forward with a formal investigation if the allegation is deemed a serious ongoing threat or risk (e.g., named offender was previously reported for a similar act) to the university community (Lhamon, 2014).

With respect to this last point, some universities are required to take another step forward and involve law enforcement per state law. In Virginia, for example, public colleges and universities must use a committee model comprised of three individuals (the Title IX coordinator or designee, a representative of law enforcement, and a student affairs representative) to determine which allegations[4] should then be forwarded to law enforcement (Mancini, Picket, Call, & Roche, 2016). California recently enacted a similar law stipulating police involvement in the reporting process (Richards & Kaponef, 2016). These two states' efforts are unique as most compelled disclosure policies are not the result of a change in state law, but rather are the outcome of institutional policymaking (Holland et al., 2018).

Consequences for Failing to Report

Another question that has not received systematic attention but is pertinent for contextualizing MR is, "What happens if REs fail to report?" Here, again, the answer is "it depends" on the specific institutional policy. Generally, failing to abide by institutional policy can result in a plethora of disciplinary actions for faculty and staff, including placement on leave and termination of employment (Swan, 2015). It is unlikely the noncompliant employee would face criminal sanctioning in the absence of making a report when it was required. As mentioned, only a handful of states have enacted statewide MR procedures. Even if laws were enacted by most states, the language of the statutes appears to limit liability to the institution and not the individual employee (Richards & Kafonek, 2016). Still, REs may face civil liability or be required to testify in instances where others disclosed to them (AAUP, 2012).

What if the RE reports but the institution does not investigate the claim? Typically, failing to investigate allegations of assault could result in a successful claim of negligence or deliberate indifference (depending on the particulars of the case) by an aggrieved party (Cantalupo, 2014; Swan, 2015). The "known or should have known" standard articulated in the 2011 DCL means that institutions must take proactive measures to prevent hostile educational environments (Savino, 2015, p. 9). Institutions have frequently turned to universal or blanketed MR as a remedy to comport with this standard. However, having a MR policy in place does not seem to offer much protection (Savino, 2015) and could actually backfire, resulting in greater legal scrutiny. More about this issue is discussed in the next section as a concern of MR.

Mandatory Reporting Concerns

While the intent of compelled disclosure procedures (either involving law enforcement or simply university officials) was to assist victims of sexual assault through better detection of sexual assault, criticism and legal challenges have ensued. Three prominent concerns related to the wide variability across the policies in existence, the potential efficacy of MR, and the legal implications of compelled disclosures are discussed next.

Variation in Mandatory Policies

The extensive discretion across compelled disclosure procedures is problematic for two reasons. First, there is a lack of consensus on what to even call required reporting procedures. Much of the recent scholarship and news accounts of reporting policies (whether law enforcement is involved or not) do not distinguish between the type of MR procedure, whether it involves, for instance, reporting to just university officials or to law enforcement as well (Holland et al., 2018; Mancini et al., 2017). Thus, what might be termed "mandated reporting" in one university may or may not designate all faculty as mandated reporters and may or may not involve law enforcement (Holland et al., 2018). In turn, this makes generalizing across the different national versions of MR difficult.

Second, the wide discretion across institutions in their reporting policies means we do not know whether or how third-party reports (e.g., mandated disclosures) are investigated vis-à-vis a "direct" report by a complainant (Richards, 2018). For example, do institutions prioritize first-person accounts over "third-party" reports, as the former suggests a victim/survivor perhaps more willing to assist with an investigation? This is largely unknown given the variability across institutions and the difficulty in accessing data that provide incident-level characteristics of Title IX investigations (Richards, 2018). The absence of research describing and evaluating the many variants of MR and how investigations unfold is concerning. In turn, this research gap has implications for determining the impact of reporting procedures, a topic to which we turn now.

Efficacy

The lack of consensus concerning what MR actually is and how Title IX investigations unfold (whether involving third-party or direct reports, law enforcement or not) hinders our ability to predict how mandated reporting policies work in practice. At the core of any required reporting procedures (variation not withstanding) is the belief that increased capable guardianship reduces assaults and assists victims (Brubaker & Mancini, 2017). If authorities (either university officials and/or law enforcement) can intervene on behalf of a victim who may not be willing to report, better outcomes—such as increased reporting and investigation and victim care—might be expected.

Does MR actually accomplish those goals and, if so, which versions (i.e., those involving just college administrators or models emphasizing a criminal justice response) are most effective in generating these outcomes? A study of college students, those whom the laws seek to protect, suggests a tempered response (Mancini et al., 2017). While 60% of students supported a law that would require faculty to become mandated reporters in a model where law enforcement would be contacted (even if victims did not want police contact), over 60% also felt the laws could boomerang, resulting in fewer disclosures among their peers. Furthermore, most students anticipated negative impacts of the new procedures, believing that MR involving police could lead to wrongful arrests (69%), diminish help-seeking behavior among victims (57%), retraumatize victims (65%), and waste official/law enforcement resources (60%).

Another study examining student and instructor views about a Title IX-only policy found that over 50% of students were either unsure or not likely to disclose their own sexual victimization under this version of MR (Newins & White, 2018). In that same study, most faculty reported that they would comply with the university policy, but at least one-fifth were unsure or would not disclose, even if required to do so. Moreover, a separate examination of perceptions among resident assistants (RAs) found that MR (to university officials) might not lead to increased disclosures. Specifically, the reporting likelihood (to Title IX only) was dependent on the extent to which the RA was aware of reporting obligations and perceptions of the practice. RAs who felt conflicted about their role were not likely to report (Holland & Cortina, 2017).

Legal Issues of Mandatory Reporting

Although schools have seemingly adopted the broad practice of MR with the benevolent goal of protecting the university community (Moylan, 2017), a more cynical view suggests the procedures serve institutional interests by showing an attempt to comply with the "known or should have known" standard established in federal guidance (Savino, 2015, p. 9) in order to avoid liability claims. A 2017 legal analysis (Weiner), tracing the origins of compelled disclosure procedures highlights this rationale: "Well-known attorneys recommended these wide-net [mandatory] reporting policies to [university] general counsel … institutions likely adopted the wide-net reporting policies because it was easy to do so, no alternative approach was similarly touted, faculty were often not involved in the policy decisions, and administrators found comfort in following the crowd" (p. 81).

Notwithstanding the initial appeal of MR, some legal experts claim that any apparent benefits in protecting the institution from civil liability are "actually unquantifiable and potentially illusory" (Weiner, 2017, p. 156). Many experts identify situations in which the implementation of MR could *increase* institutional liability. For example, consider a situation in which a student discloses to an instructor whose institution has designated faculty as REs. The faculty member may be ethically conflicted by the duty to report and the student's wish to not have his or her experience reported to the university. If the faculty member acquiesces to the student's wish, the inaction violates institutional policy and thereby subjects the school to a claim of negligence, if, say, the same perpetrator then assaults another student. MR creates this situation and possibly leads to other tort suits filed by students who claim invasion of privacy by a MR, or deliberate indifference if the incident was not reported (Weiner, 2017). These issues lead to some recommended best practices, outlined in the next section.

Best Practices

What is first needed to determine if mandatory reporting reflects "evidence-based" practice sounds very simple but is critical: a national review documenting the nature of compelled disclosure policies. Without that, it is impossible to move toward generalizing across such efforts. It is striking that the last report that comes close to this focus, a federally funded report examining university procedures for investigating sexual assault allegations, is over 15 years old (Karjane, Fisher, & Cullen, 2002). A more recent and comprehensive national report could help shed light on the variability discussed earlier, specifically (a) the types of individuals who are required to report, (b) exemptions to the policy, (c) the content of what is reportable, (d) the process for making a report, (e) whether law enforcement is contacted, (f) whether a third-party report is treated differently, and (g) potential consequences mandated reporters/responsible employees incur for failing to disclose. Holland and colleagues' 2018 work is notable for providing one of the only national studies of compelled disclosure, but it is not exhaustive. It did not focus on the specific content of the reporting policy across schools and did not identify which policies compelled disclosure to law enforcement versus only to university officials.

With this review in hand, it is would then be necessary to evaluate the effects of MR (in all its various forms). This might involve conducting focus groups with diverse stakeholders: Title IX coordinators, investigators, and intake officers; law enforcement; faculty; student groups; victim advocates; and, possibly, victims/survivors who wish to participate. It remains unknown, beyond some limited accounts, how MR directly affects student-victims. For this reason, another recommendation would be to administer surveys to students to capture their perceptions of MR and their willingness to report under a compelled disclosure policy. Ideally, there would be questions that tap perceptions concerning the "varieties" of MR (e.g., MR involving only Title IX, or both Title IX and law enforcement). As reviewed earlier, one study of college students enrolled in a public university found overwhelming support for a mandated reporting policy that required law enforcement involvement. At the same time, students felt the laws were **paternalistic** and overrode victim autonomy (Mancini et al., 2016). This research is also salient for highlighting the potential for MR to backfire, as a large majority of students surveyed felt their peers would be *less* willing to report a sexual assault given the MR policy involving police. Subsequent research is needed to evaluate other views of MR. For example, given students' concern about victim autonomy, would students support hybrid or "blended" reporting options that require consent of the survivor? Because scholarship has only begun to scratch the surface of student views of MR, subsequent work is needed to determine these views.

In the absence of a strong knowledge base pointing to MR as "good" or "bad" practice, perhaps this "middle ground" or hybrid approach should be considered. At least one institution, the University of Oregon, has crafted a model that seems to strike that balance. After initially implementing a rigid, blanketed, compelled disclosure policy (giving victims no choice in how their disclosure was handled), the university appointed a task force of faculty and staff with knowledge of sexual crimes, which resulted in the university revising their MR policy to be victim directed. The new policy now cautions reporters (with the exception of some officials and other groups who must report under Clery) to "follow the student's wishes … if the student does not give consent to [the faculty member making] a connection to Title IX, then the faculty member shall not disclose the information" (University of Oregon, 2017, p. 11). Under this particular policy, only the Title IX Office is involved. Regardless of whether the student consents, the employee still has the obligation to provide the student with information about resources. This shift is innovative as it highlights how institutions can blend legal requirements with procedures that give victims autonomy during the reporting process.

Because broad compelled disclosure procedures emphasize "official bureaucratic structures" rather than "treating the whole person" (generally, Richards, Branch, Fleury-Steiner, & Kafonek, 2017), another technique, guided by a feminist perspective, may be to narrow the classification of mandatory reporters. Ideally, this targeting would net only willing instructors and, importantly, those most qualified to respond to disclosures of sexual assault (e.g., those who have received training, those with an expertise in teaching and researching sensitive topics). Extant scholarship, while underdeveloped, indicates that most faculty[5] struggle with how to respond to victimization disclosures (e.g., Richards et al., 2013). Among mandated reporters, many instructors feel conflicted about their institutional duty to report the assault (Newins & White, 2018). Not least, a large professional organization of faculty, the AAUP (2012, 2016), has criticized the practice on many fronts, most prominently concerning the lack of faculty governance in creation of the policy.

At least 14 institutions, such as the University of Michigan and New York University, apply the "narrowed net" approach, limiting who qualifies as a mandatory reporter (J. Freyd, personal communication, September 13, 2018). While variation exists across the content of these policies (e.g., whether police involvement occurs), institutions following this model designate only those individuals in leadership positions (e.g., dean, senior administrator) or those in charge of maintaining and monitoring the security of the institution as mandated reporters.

With the proliferation of procedures that require disclosure, it is critical that newly minted reporters are trained. The extent to which this occurs is unknown. The AAUP (2012), an organization of faculty members in higher education, cautions that professors are likely to have little training in the principles of investigation, trauma-centered care, and the law. Faculty with the duty to report should understand these legal and civil dimensions of policy, since they may face consequences for not reporting (Swan, 2015).[6] For this reason, education (beyond the typical once-a-year required training) and outreach (beyond the typical syllabus statement) might be needed (Brown, 2018).

Meaningful educational efforts might also include having the Title IX coordinator attend faculty meetings to provide faculty members with clear guidance on the process (e.g., what conduct is reportable, the timing of a report, and other intricacies, again, dependent on the specific institutional policy), offer tips for ensuring compliance with the procedure, and spell out the consequences of inaction (e.g., termination, other employee liability). Because faculty members who disclose often feel conflicted (Brown, 2018), procedures, such as offering a debriefing session to employees regarding the outcome and significance of their disclosure in helping the victim/survivor, may be useful. In this vein, the Title IX Office should extend outreach to students, explaining the MR process at that particular institution. This might involve coordinating in-class visits, targeting "high-disclosure" courses—those emphasizing victim studies, criminal justice, gender, and other classes where victimization and trauma issues might be discussed. The goals of such efforts would be to demystify the process (e.g., explain whether and when law enforcement is involved, if that is a provision of the specific policy), outline the aims of MR, and provide students with access to confidential reporting and victim services.

Alternatively, it may be that MR is not necessary to assist schools in detection and reporting of crime. Some scholars (Cantalupo, 2014) see promise in mandating climate surveys—designed to capture student, faculty, and staff experiences and attitudes toward sex crime and campus sex assault policy—rather than reporting procedures as a mechanism to more accurately address and respond to sexual violence. While no federal law mandates such surveys, some institutions have used them in an attempt to better estimate the true extent of sexual assault on campus so that it can be more effectively addressed. Still, the variation across these surveys, in their scope and design, and the prevalence of their administration nationally, is unclear (Moylan, Hatfield, & Randall, 2018).

Conclusion

As of now, it appears MR, in various forms, is used widely across universities and colleges in an attempt to respond to and prevent sexual victimization. The policies are controversial. For example, there are potential problems associated with their efficacy and some perceive the efforts as paternalistic in nature (Mancini et al., 2016). In the absence of federal guidance, institutions have had substantial discretion in modeling their reporting procedures. Ideally, such decisions will reflect best practices in responding to and addressing campus sexual assault. Such an assessment can only be determined by conducting careful and comprehensive investigations into how MR works in practice.

KEY TERMS

Campus Sexual Violence Elimination Act (SaVE): Amends the Clery Act to increase transparency requirements for colleges, guarantees rights for survivors, establishes disciplinary proceedings, and requires educational programs.

Clery Act: The Jeanne Clery Disclosure of Campus Security Policy and Campus Crime Statistics Act, 20 U.S.C.A. § 1092(f), mandates that colleges and universities track, record, publicize, and report campus crime incidents to the federal government.

Confidential reporters (CRs): Individuals who are exempt from the duty of reporting disclosures of sexual assault to the institution or police (e.g., counselors, clergy).

Mandated reporting (MR; also "compelled disclosure"): A legal or employer-based requirement that compels employees to disclose allegations of possible sexual victimization, including assault and harassment; can be "blanketed," covering all employees, or "nuanced," more narrowly defined policies.

Paternalistic: Having the tendency of usurping the autonomy of perceived vulnerable parties under the notion of protecting them.

Responsible employees (REs): A class of people designated by a postsecondary institution who must forward allegations of sexual assault or victimization to an administrative body and/or law enforcement.

Title IX of the Education Amendments Act of 1972: Legislation signed into law by President Richard Nixon that prohibits sex discrimination in educational institutions that receive federal funds. This stand-alone legislation fills in the gaps found in Title VII of the Civil Rights Act of 1964 and other legal documents.

Violence Against Women Act (VAWA): Landmark federal legislation enacted in 1994 (and reauthorized several times) to address gender-based violence, such as intimate partner abuse, sexual victimization, and stalking offenses.

DISCUSSION QUESTIONS

1. How can institutions balance the responsibilities to prevent sexual assault but also protect the autonomy and dignity of victims?
2. Compare the many forms (e.g., requiring all employees to disclose, involving law enforcement) of mandatory reporting procedures. Which approach do you advocate and why?
3. Which form of reporting procedure appears most effective in responding to the needs of victims while ensuring campus safety?

Notes

1 Various terms exist to describe compelling third parties to report knowledge of sex assault and abuse. The process has been described as "mandated reporting" (American Association of University Professors [AAUP], 2012, 2016; Mancini et al., 2017; Pappas, 2018), "compelled disclosure" (Holland, Cortina, & Freyd, 2018), and "third-party reporting" (Krivoshey, Adkins, Hayes, Nemeth, & Klein, 2013). In the absence of a single and precise definition, I use these terms interchangeably. When relevant, I specify whether the process involves law enforcement or simply university officials.

2 While the role of the RE substantively, at least, seems to align with a "mandated reporter" it is important to note that the former is terminology used in federal legislation, whereas the latter terms (e.g., "mandated" or compelled reporters) appear to be used more frequently in institutional-level policies and state legislation.

3 Holland and colleagues (2018) observed, "university compelled disclosure policies may or may not involve law enforcement" (p. 257). The analysis did not evaluate which policies encompass police involvement versus only university administration, nor was it able to assess how investigation of a third-party report was handled, as compared to one received directly by a victim/survivor (see also Richards, 2018, for a recent examination of Title IX investigations).

4 The law makes no distinction between third-party reports (e.g., "a mandated report") and allegations disclosed directly by victims/survivors.

5 This study examined disclosure of assault generally (i.e., not in the context of mandatory reporting).

6 For example, the AAUP cautions (2012, p. 371): "Faculty members should be aware that they could be called to testify in a criminal proceeding about a conversation with a student regarding sexual assault and may want to consider professional liability insurance as a safeguard."

References

American Association of University Professors (AAUP). (2012). *Campus sexual assault: Suggested policies and procedures*. Washington, DC: Author.

American Association of University Professors (AAUP). (2016). *The history, uses, and abuses of Title IX*. Washington, DC: Author.

Brown, L. G., & Gallagher, K. (2013). Mandatory reporting of abuse: A historical perspective on the evolution of states' current mandatory reporting laws with a review of the laws in the Commonwealth of Pennsylvania. *Villanova Law Review, 59*(6), 37–80.

Brown, S. (2018, August 16). Many professors have to report sexual misconduct: How should they tell their students that? *Chronicle of Higher Education*. Retrieved from https://www.chronicle.com/article/Many-Professors-Have-to-Report/244294

Brubaker, S. J., & Mancini, C. (2017). The impact of increased state regulation of campus sexual assault practices: Perspectives of campus personnel. *Journal of School Violence, 16*(3), 286–301.

Cantalupo, N. C. (2014). Institution-specific victimization surveys: Addressing legal and practical disincentives to gender-based violence reporting on college campuses. *Trauma, Violence, & Abuse, 15*(3), 227–241.

Cantor, D., Fisher, B., Chibnall, S., Townsend, R., Lee, H., Bruce, C., & Thomas, G. (2017). *Report on the American Association of Universities (AAU) campus climate survey on sexual assault and sexual misconduct*. Rockville, MD: *American Association of Universities*.

Dowler, L., Cuomo, D., & Laliberte, N. (2014). Challenging "the Penn State way": A feminist response to institutional violence in higher education. *Gender, Place & Culture, 21*(3), 387–394.

Engle, J. C. (2015). Mandatory reporting of campus sexual assault and domestic violence: Moving to a victim-centric protocol that comports with federal law. *Temple Political & Civil Rights Law Review, 24*(401), 401–421.

Fisher, B. S., Daigle, L. E., Cullen, F. T., & Turner, M. G. (2003). Reporting sexual victimization to the police and others: Results from a national-level study of college women. *Criminal Justice and Behavior, 30*(1), 6–38.

Heldman, C., Ackerman, A., R., & Breckenridge-Jackson, I. (2018). *The new campus anti-rape movement*. Lanham, MD: Lexington.

Holland, K. J., & Cortina, L. M. (2017). The evolving landscape of Title IX: Predicting mandatory reporters' responses to sexual assault disclosures. *Law and Human Behavior, 41*(5), 1–11.

Holland, K. J., Cortina, L. M., & Freyd, J. J. (2018). Compelled disclosure of college sexual assault. *American Psychologist, 73*(3), 256–268.

Hyman, A., Schillinger, D., & Lo, B. (1995). Laws mandating reporting of domestic violence: Do they promote patient well-being? *Journal of the American Medical Association, 273*(22), 1781–1787.

Karjane, H. M., Fisher, B. S., & Cullen, F. T. (2002). *Campus sexual assault: How America's institutions of higher education respond*. Washington, DC: U.S. Department of Justice.

Krivoshey, M. S., Adkins, R., Hayes, R., Nemeth, J. M., & Klein, E. G. (2013). Sexual assault reporting procedures at Ohio colleges. *Journal of American College Health, 61*(3), 142–147.

Lhamon, C. (2014, April 29). Questions and answers on Title IX and sexual violence. Washington, DC: U.S. Department of Justice. Retrieved from http://www2.ed.gov/about/offices/list/ocr/docs/qa-201404-title-ix.pdf

Mancini, C., Pickett, J. T., Call, C., McDougle, R. D., Brubaker, S. J., & Brownstein, H. H. (2017). Sexual assault in the ivory tower: Public opinion on university accountability and mandatory reporting. *Sexual Abuse, 31*(3), 344–365. doi:10.1177/1079063217706707

Mancini, C., Pickett, J. T., Call, C., & Roche, S. P. (2016). Mandatory reporting (MR) in higher education: College students' perceptions of laws designed to reduce campus sexual assault. *Criminal Justice Review, 41*(2), 219–235.

Marshall, R. (2014). Will it really save you? Analyzing the Campus Sexual Violence Elimination Act. *Legislation and Policy Brief, 6*(2), 271–293.

McMahon, S., Wood, L., Cusano, J., & Macri, L. M. (2018). Campus sexual assault: Future directions for research. *Sexual Abuse, 31*(3), 270–295. doi:1079063217750864

Moylan, C. A. (2017). "I fear I'm a checkbox": College and university victim advocates' perspectives of campus rape reforms. *Violence Against Women, 23*(9), 1122–1139.

Moylan, C. A., Hatfield, C., & Randall, J. (2018). Campus sexual assault climate surveys: A brief exploration of publicly available reports. *Journal of American College Health, 66*(6), 445–449.

Newins, A. R., & White, S. W. (2018). Title IX sexual violence reporting requirements: Knowledge and opinions of responsible employees and students. *Journal of Aggression, Conflict and Peace Research, 10*(1), 74–82.

Pappas, B. A. (2018). How can we increase reporting of sexual misconduct on campus? *University of Minnesota.* Retrieved from https://genderpolicyreport.umn.edu/how-can-we-increase-reporting-of-sexual-misconduct-on-campus/

Purdue University. (2018). *Title IX compliance guide for mandatory reporters.* Retrieved from https://www.purdue.edu/titleix/complianceGuide%20/index.php

Rennison, C. M., & Addington, L. A. (2018). Comparing violent victimization experiences of male and female college-attending emerging adults. *Violence Against Women, 24*(8), 952–972.

Rennison, C. M., Dragiewicz, M., & DeKeseredy, W. S. (2013). Context matters: Violence against women and reporting to police in rural, suburban and urban areas. *American Journal of Criminal Justice, 38*(1), 141–159.

Renzetti, C. M., Edleson, J. L., & Bergen, R. K. (Eds.). (2010). *Sourcebook on violence against women* (2nd ed.). Thousand Oaks, CA: SAGE.

Richards, T. N. (2018). No evidence of "weaponized Title IX" here: An empirical assessment of sexual misconduct reporting, case processing, and outcomes. *Law and Human Behavior, 43*(2), 180–192. doi:10.1037/lhb0000316

Richards, T. N., Branch, K. A., Fleury-Steiner, R. E., & Kafonek, K. (2017). A feminist analysis of campus sexual assault policies: Results from a national sample. *Family Relations, 66*(1), 104–115.

Richards, T. N., Branch, K. A., & Hayes, R. M. (2013). An exploratory examination of student to professor disclosures of crime victimization. *Violence Against Women, 19*(11), 1408–1422.

Richards, T. N., & Kafonek, K. (2016). Reviewing state legislative agendas regarding sexual assault in higher education: Proliferation of best practices and points of caution. *Feminist Criminology, 11*(1), 91–129.

Sachs, C. J., Peek, C., Baraff, L. J., & Hasselblad, V. (1998). Failure of the mandatory domestic violence reporting law to increase medical facility referral to police. *Annals of Emergency Medicine, 31*(4), 488–494.

Savino, C. (2015). "Nobody's saying we're opposed to complying": Barriers to university compliance with VAWA and Title IX. *Cornell Law Library.* Retrieved from http://scholarship.law.cornell.edu/cllsrp/9

Sinozich, S. & Langton, L. (2014). *Rape and sexual assault victimization among college-age females, 1995-2013.* Washington, DC: Bureau of Justice Statistics.

Swan, S. L. (2015). Between Title IX and the criminal law: Bringing tort law to the campus sexual assault debate. *University of Kansas Law Review, 64*, 963–986.

University of Oregon. (2017). *Student sexual and gender-based harassment and violence complaint and response (policy tracking worksheet).* Eugene, OR: Author.

U.S. Department of Education. (2011, April 4). *Dear colleague letter.* Retrieved from https://www2.ed.gov/print/about/offices/list/ocr/letters/colleague-201104.html

U.S. Department of Education. (2016). *The handbook for campus safety and security reporting.* Retrieved from https://ifap.ed.gov/eannouncements/attachments/HandbookforCampusSafetyandSecurityReporting.pdf

Weiner, M. H. (2017). A principled and legal approach to Title IX reporting. *Tennessee Law Review, 25*(1), 71–185.

Weiss, K. G., & Lasky, N. V. (2017). Mandatory reporting of sexual misconduct at college: A critical perspective. *Journal of School Violence, 16*(3), 259–270.

Author's Note

The author acknowledges the support of many generous individuals in completing this project. First and foremost, she thanks the editors of this important volume, Drs. Claire M. Renzetti and Diane R. Follingstad, for undertaking this critical topic and their helpful comments and suggestions on an earlier draft of the chapter. She also extends her gratitude to several scholars in the field who provided their expertise in the revision of this chapter: Drs. Callie M. Rennison, Tara N. Richards, Kathryn Holland, Sarah Jane Brubaker, Brian A. Pappas, Jennifer Freyd, and Amy Cook.

III Process Issues

CHAPTER FOUR

Confidentiality Throughout the Investigation, Hearing, and Disciplinary Process for Campus Adjudication of Sexual Misconduct

Melissa M. Carleton

Whenever multiple people live through the same experience, they will come away with different perspectives of the same story—often very different perspectives, but not less true. When they tell that story to others, hearing it may impact the listeners in such a way that they enfold the story into their own existence, from their own perspective.

The listener may retell it to others, not necessarily because they wish to gossip, but because the story changed them in some way, or they need help processing it, or it expresses some truth that resonates with them that they need to share. They may tell that story because they are asked to as part of the sexual misconduct investigation process. They may tell that story because it expresses injustice to them. The reasons for retelling are endless, and many are entirely appropriate. Ultimately, every time someone tells their own story, they give up some control of that story, and every time someone else tells that story, the original storyteller loses more control.

But who owns that story? Is it only owned by the ones who lived it? And when does it infringe on the rights of others when the story is retold? This balancing of the rights of the storytellers is at the core of the issue of confidentiality when sexual misconduct is investigated and adjudicated, and the laws dictate the framework for where that balance rests. This chapter will explore the laws that restrict or allow this sharing of information as they relate to cases involving reported sexual misconduct on a college campus.

Note that throughout the chapter, criminal terms such as "victim" or "perpetrator" are used to reflect the language of the law being discussed in the particular circumstance; institutions would be more accurate to refer to parties as complainant and respondent, or whatever policy terms the institution uses to address the parties.

A Hypothetical: Chris and Sam

Chris and Sam engage in sexual activity. Chris believes the encounter is completely consensual. Sam does not and, after seeing a counselor for a few weeks, files a complaint with the campus Title IX coordinator. An investigation ensues, and the evidence ultimately substantiates that nonconsensual sexual contact occurred, in violation of the university's policy. As to whether nonconsensual sexual intercourse occurred, no policy violation is found. Chris is permitted to stay on campus with various behavioral restrictions, including staying away from Sam and undergoing counseling. Chris is also placed on probation until graduation, which in this case means automatic suspension in the case of additional misconduct.

The decision is upsetting to both parties. Sam is irate that Chris has not been dismissed permanently and warns friends, graphically, about Chris's dangerous behavior. Sam's best friend, Riley, spends 2 months in counseling after hearing the details because they trigger Riley's own memories about a previous sexual assault that occurred in high school. Sam's other best friend, Dylan, is particularly incensed and puts up posters around campus with Chris's face and the caption, "Chris raped my friend and the school did nothing!" The posters advise *not* to call the Title IX coordinator in cases of sexual assault because "the Title IX office is the first step to the official cover-up."

The Title IX coordinator, who spent a significant amount of time ensuring that the investigation was thorough and impartial, is personally aggravated by the posters but is also troubled that it may prevent others from reporting and having concerns addressed. Chris, on the other hand, feels humiliated by the posters, harassed by those on campus who move away in the dining hall, and furious at being called a "rapist" despite having been found not to have engaged in nonconsensual sexual intercourse. Chris writes a letter to the editor to decry the terrible treatment and Sam's supposed lies during the investigation, which "goes viral" on the internet. Ultimately, neither Chris nor Sam can search for their own names on the internet without being immediately connected with the case.

Chris and Sam file lawsuits against each other and the college. The complaints are scathing, and both sides feel that the investigation "split the baby" to limit liability for the school. The Title IX coordinator is vilified in every direction, causing the university's president to place the coordinator on administrative leave—partly so the institution can look into the concerns, and partly because the coordinator is now experiencing mental health issues due to stress and anxiety.

In this case, it is easy to see how the story has gotten much bigger than the parties. It has begun affecting others, across campus and beyond its borders. Where are the lines, and where, one might ask, have they been crossed?

Restraints on Telling Your Own Story

For Chris and Sam, there are few legal restrictions to prevent them from telling their own story, and those that do exist are rooted in state laws and case decisions. The primary restriction on one's own self-report is a claim of **defamation**, which can be brought in a civil lawsuit as a claim for money damages. Defamation is an intentionally false statement that causes harm to someone else's reputation. There are two general types of defamation: Slander is spoken defamation, and libel is written defamation.

Certain types of statements are considered "defamation per se," which means that plaintiffs need not prove the statements caused harm to their reputation in order to make a claim for defamation. These categories differ by state but generally include statements that accuse the plaintiff of criminal activity and statements that accuse the plaintiff of being unchaste or of engaging in other sexual misconduct. Chris, then, may choose to pursue Sam and Dylan for their statements accusing Chris of sexual assault.

And what can Sam and Dylan do to counter such a charge of defamation? Truth is a defense to a defamation claim, but to invoke this defense, they will need to put evidence before the court that the underlying allegations are true. In other words, to mount a successful defense, Sam will have to retell the story of the sexual encounter, and the court will have to decide whether the sexual encounter was nonconsensual—essentially, re-deciding what the university has already done through its own investigation.

Invasion of privacy is another commonly invoked claim in lawsuits where individuals believe their story was made public against their will. It is often defined as publicity that places a person in a false light in the public eye or discloses embarrassing private facts about a plaintiff. Publicity typically requires that the story be spread very broadly, often through traditional media or social media. This is a broader claim than defamation, and it is not a valid claim in all states because some courts believe it overlaps too much with the First Amendment right to free speech. In our hypothetical case, if Chris used Sam's name in the viral post, Sam may claim that this was an invasion of privacy (and potentially defamation, depending on the content).

Telling falsehoods in a way that harms another is not just an issue for a civil lawsuit. Lying to law enforcement about criminal conduct can result in criminal charges. For example, if a person were to lie to law enforcement and allege that they were a victim of a crime they fabricated, that person could be charged with obstruction of justice, perjury, or another similar criminal offense; a person under investigation who lied to police could similarly be charged. Individuals found guilty of obstructing justice or perjuring themselves may be subjected to penalties such as a fine or jail time, depending on the circumstances and state law. Therefore, based on both the potential civil and criminal penalties that could apply when lying, complainants and respondents alike should be mindful to tell the truth as they share their stories with others.

Complainants, respondents, and witnesses may also be requested or required to limit the telling of their story during an active investigation, either a sexual misconduct investigation by an educational institution or a criminal investigation by law enforcement. The reason for this, at least in criminal cases, is that additional charges could apply for interfering with an investigation or obstructing justice. In all cases, the instruction to not talk about a case is typically based on concerns for the integrity of the investigation. If a complainant, respondent, or witness starts talking about the underlying facts of a case with other witnesses, it runs the risk of interfering with the investigation. Stories start to sound the same. Memories start to be filled in by statements from other people. This may create credibility concerns where all the witness accounts align too perfectly, leaving an investigator to wonder whether witnesses are colluding about their testimony. Talking about the investigation may also create concerns about retaliation, particularly in small campus communities where the witnesses and parties are in close proximity.

Educational institutions that wish to instruct witnesses and parties to limit the circumstances in which they speak about the case so as to preserve the integrity of the investigation should be mindful of the need of those individuals to share their stories to get support through what can be an emotionally difficult process. They may need to talk to friends, family, and confidential resources to get support. Institutions, therefore, should try to find a balance between protecting the investigation and allowing their students to access the assistance they need. Public institutions will also need to be mindful of constitutional free speech rights, which place restrictions on how they may limit speech.

Confidentiality Laws Applying to Institutions of Higher Education

What about the Title IX coordinator and other administrators in this case? What rights do they have to tell their own stories to explain and defend their actions and correct what they feel to be misstatements made by others? The answer is not many. Institutions of higher education and, by proxy, their employees, are not permitted to share confidential information about students at will, even to correct public misstatements of fact. There are certain key restrictions that limit administrators, faculty, and other staff members from the disclosure of student information.

Family Educational Rights and Privacy Act

The primary law that imposes confidentiality rights on campus is the Family Educational Rights and Privacy Act (FERPA) (20 U.S.C. §1232g; 34 C.F.R. Part 99). This federal law and its regulations prohibit educational institutions from the **disclosure** of **personally identifiable information** contained in **education records**, unless the educational institution has either the consent of the postsecondary student or one of several exceptions are met.

The most commonly used exception is that school officials can access student records if they have a legitimate educational interest in such records. This allows for the institution to do what it needs to do to function, while still protecting an individual's privacy. Other common exceptions include the release of **directory information** (as defined by the institution's policy), the disclosure of information in a health or safety emergency, and the disclosure of records to a school where the student seeks to enroll, intends to enroll, or has enrolled, so long as the disclosure is for purposes related to the student's enrollment or transfer.

Postsecondary students are often concerned with whether their parents will learn of their involvement in a sexual misconduct case where there is no ongoing health or safety emergency. FERPA allows, but does not require, institutions to disclose any and all personally identifiable information from education records to parents if the student is a dependent for tax purposes, so the practices of each institution may vary as to whether a disclosure is made under these circumstances. Even if institutions permit such disclosures in routine situations such as tuition statements and grades, they may want to consider more carefully whether notifying parents regarding less-routine topics such as their adult child's sexual activity (consensual or not), gender identity, and sexual orientation should reasonably fall within the bounds of that disclosure, even if permitted by law. In other words, just because an institution *can* disclose something, query whether it should.

FERPA also allows, but does not require, the disclosure of alcohol and drug-related discipline to the parent of a student of postsecondary education where the student has violated any federal, state, or local law, or any rule or policy of the institution, governing the use or possession of alcohol or a controlled substance. This disclosure can only be made if the institution determines that the student has committed a disciplinary violation with respect to that use or possession. Further, the student must be under the age of 21 at the time of the disclosure to the parent for the FERPA exception to allow such disclosure without permission of the student (34 C.F.R. § 99.31(a)(15)). While it is true that many sexual misconduct cases involve some alcohol or drug use, in practical terms, it is often the case that students in sexual misconduct cases are not subject to discipline for alcohol or drug use due to the institution's "amnesty" policy. Such policies often provide that a party will not be disciplined for alcohol or drug use as it may relate to a complaint regarding sexual misconduct so as not to discourage reporting of what is typically a more serious offense. Where such a policy exists, the alcohol or drug violation would not trigger a disciplinary finding, and the prerequisite to disclosure under this FERPA exception would not be met.

In addition to the drug and alcohol exception, FERPA allows postsecondary institutions to make certain disclosures relating to certain violent or sexual crimes. Under one regulation, the institution may disclose to a victim of certain offenses the final results of the disciplinary proceedings of the alleged perpetrator (34 C.F.R. § 99.31(a)(13)). The list of offenses includes arson, assault, burglary, homicide, kidnapping, robbery, and forcible sex offenses such as rape, as well as non-forcible sex offenses such as statutory rape or incest (34 C.F.R. § 99.39). The disclosure is limited to the name of the student, the violation committed, any essential findings supporting the institution's conclusion, and the sanctions imposed. These disclosures may be made to the victim regardless of whether the institution concluded a violation was committed.

Postsecondary institutions may also disclose the same information to anyone—victim, parent, or third party—if the individual is found to have violated an institutional policy by committing one of these offenses (34 C.F.R. § 99.31(a)(14); 34 C.F.R. §99.39). This exception, however, does not allow the institution to disclose the names of other students, such as victims or witnesses, without the prior written consent of those students. This provision, then, would not allow the institution to disclose Chris's name, as he was ultimately found not to have committed nonconsensual sexual intercourse.

These two exceptions allowing disclosures relating to certain violent or sexual crimes are permissive in nature, in that FERPA does not require an institution to make the disclosures. Some institutions, by policy or practice, do not make such disclosures. Public institutions subject to public records laws, however, may be required to make such disclosures if the information is requested under a state's freedom of information laws, as federal law does not restrict the disclosure. Therefore, this determination will be state specific.

Public records analysis can complicate the notion of confidentiality in sexual misconduct cases. For example, where a sexual misconduct investigation involves employees rather than students, institutions may be required to release those records under state law. If an investigation involves students, the records may still be requested, although FERPA will often require extensive redaction of all personally identifiable information prior to release.

When criminal conduct is alleged, it is not uncommon for local law enforcement to conduct an investigation concurrently with that of the educational institution. However, FERPA complicates the release of such educational investigatory records to police. Where there is no imminent health or safety emergency, the institution must either obtain the written consent of the students whose records are requested, or law enforcement must subpoena the information from the institution. The institution is then obligated to notify the students of the request and give them a deadline by which they may move the court to "quash" (invalidate) the subpoena. Such notice is not required in certain situations where the court order or subpoena requires secrecy, for example due to homeland security concerns (34 C.F.R. § 99.31(a)(9)).

It is important to note that while FERPA restricts the sharing of confidential student information, the U.S. Supreme Court has ruled that there is no private right of action under the law. That means that while violations may be addressed by the U.S. Department of Education, an individual whose confidentiality was violated may not sue to redress a FERPA violation in a court of law (*Gonzaga University v. Doe*, 2002).

In our hypothetical case, the disclosures by Chris and Sam do not implicate FERPA because they are not bound by FERPA's restrictions. FERPA, however, does limit what the Title IX coordinator and the university can say when trying to respond to what Chris and Sam have shared with the general public about the case. Depending on the facts of the case, it is possible that the university would be permitted to share that Chris was found responsible for nonconsensual sexual contact if it rises to the level of a forcible sex offense. Otherwise, it is likely that the university will be unable to address any misunderstandings that the public may have about the case without consent from Chris and Sam, or a careful analysis of applicable exceptions to that consent.

Health Insurance Portability and Accountability Act

The Health Insurance Portability and Accountability Act (HIPAA) prohibits covered entities from the disclosure of protected health information without authorization. Campus student health and counseling centers often qualify as covered entities for purposes of HIPAA compliance, which can lead to the question of whether certain records are protected under HIPAA or FERPA. In November 2008, the U.S. Department of Health and Human Services and the U.S. Department of Education issued Joint Guidance on the Application of FERPA and HIPAA to Student Health Records (U.S. Department of Education, n.d.), which helps institutions sort out which law applies to records under the circumstances of a particular situation.

For purposes of a campus sexual misconduct investigation, the records are protected from unauthorized disclosure in either event, although written consent may be required for on-campus and off-campus investigators to obtain the medical or counseling records if protected by HIPAA. Regardless of which law protects the records, once the records become part of the investigatory record, they may be subject to disclosure to the other party. Therefore, if Sam were to request the inclusion of Sam's own counseling records in the investigation for consideration as evidence, Chris would have the right to review the records to the extent that they were relevant.

Individuals who are concerned about the privacy of their personal information would be well advised to consult with the investigator, prior to providing such consent, to obtain a clear understanding of how relevant information will be shared and what information is subject to redaction. Educational institutions would be well advised to make these practices transparent, consistent, and aligned with the need to get the best evidence on the table for consideration during the investigation (see, for example, an August 2016 Dear Colleague Letter by the U.S. Department of Education, which restricted the sharing of counseling and medical records within the institution, in anticipation of litigation, without a court order or consent (U.S. Department of Education, 2016)).

Clery Act

The Clery Act is a federal law that only applies to institutions that receive funds under the Higher Education Act (20 U.S.C. § 1092(f)). Under current Clery regulations, an institution's sexual misconduct policy must include certain procedural protections, at least with respect to cases involving allegations of domestic violence, dating violence, sexual assault, and stalking (34 C.F.R. § 668.46). The regulations also require the sharing of certain information to provide emergency notifications and timely warnings to the campus community to help ensure awareness and safety of students, faculty, and staff.

Under Clery regulations, an institution's policy regarding domestic violence, dating violence, sexual assault, and stalking must provide for timely and equal access by the accuser, the accused, and appropriate officials to any information that will be used during informal and formal disciplinary meetings and hearings. Clery regulations specifically state that the sharing of such information to those parties does not constitute a violation of FERPA (34 C.F.R. § 668.46(l)). Clery regulations also require simultaneous notification in writing, to both the accuser and the accused, of the result of any institutional disciplinary proceeding that arises from one of these allegations, the institution's procedures for the accused and the victim to appeal the result of such proceeding (if available), any change to the result, and when such results become final. The result of a disciplinary proceeding that is shared must include any initial, interim, and final decisions by the institution, as well as the rationale for the result and the sanctions.

The institution is also required by Clery to release emergency notifications and timely warnings to campus. Emergency notifications typically involve a dangerous and widespread concern, such as a viral outbreak or the approach of a tornado, and therefore do not typically implicate confidentiality concerns. In contrast, timely warnings are alerts to campus that are intended to warn of a criminal incident so that people can protect themselves. Timely warnings, therefore, may be issued in relation to reports of sexual misconduct. While Clery regulations require the institution to withhold as confidential the names and other identifying information of victims, there is no such requirement with regard to the release of information regarding the alleged perpetrators. This information, however, may be shared under the health and safety emergency exception found in FERPA (34 C.F.R. §§ 99.31(b)(6) and 99.36).

Disclosure Within the Title IX Process Itself

Title IX regulations mandate that every educational institution adopt a grievance procedure by which complaints regarding sex discrimination may be reported and addressed. Inherent in that requirement is the need to communicate the information reported so that it may be addressed appropriately to eliminate the discrimination or harassment, prevent its recurrence, and remedy its effects. For example, upon receiving a report of sexual assault, the Title IX coordinator may find the need to communicate with residence life staff to obtain a room change for one or both parties as appropriate; communicate with the dean of students to facilitate academic accommodations, as requested; communicate with the Campus Safety Department to notify them of the issuance of a no-contact directive or no-trespass order; communicate with internal investigators to assign the case; confer with legal counsel regarding unusual circumstances or risks; and communicate with the health and counseling centers to help the parties access needed services. These communications are permissible under FERPA's exception allowing the disclosure of information to school officials with a legitimate need to know. Each of the individuals receiving the information, as school officials of the same institution, would be subject to FERPA's prohibitions against disclosure of confidential student information.

Within an investigation, however, it may also be necessary for investigators to share information with non-employees in order to facilitate the investigative process and gather the evidence needed to make an informed decision about whether the institution's policy has been violated. For example, the investigator in our hypothetical case will need to share information regarding Sam's allegations with Chris so that Chris can adequately respond to them. When the investigator hears Chris's side of the story, the investigator may re-interview Sam to share Chris's side of the story and ask for a response. The investigator will also need to offer at least some basic details to the witnesses to frame the relevant questions (e.g., the date of the incident, the location, the setting). The failure to share this information may result in less evidence for consideration and, ultimately, not as thorough an investigation or as well-reasoned a decision. On the other hand, at least some of the information may be protected by FERPA. What then?

The U.S. Department of Education's January 2001 "Revised Sexual Harassment Guidance: Harassment of Students by School Employees, Other Students, or Third Parties," has at least some response to this concern. According to that guidance,

> *In 1994, as part of the Improving America's Schools Act, Congress amended the General Education Provisions Act (GEPA)—of which FERPA is a part—to state that nothing in GEPA "shall be construed to affect the applicability of ... Title IX of the Education Amendments of 1972. ..." The Department interprets this provision to mean that FERPA continues to apply in the context of Title IX enforcement, but if there is a direct conflict between requirements of FERPA and requirements of Title IX, such that enforcement of FERPA would interfere with the primary purpose of Title IX to eliminate sex-based discrimination in schools, the requirements of Title IX override any conflicting FERPA provisions.* (p. vii)

Based on this guidance, it appears that the sharing of information during the process, not just with school officials but with other individuals, will not violate FERPA, as long as the sharing of the information is done in the furtherance of the institution's obligations to investigate, adjudicate, and otherwise resolve Title IX complaints.

This would appear to protect the institution when information and evidence need to be shared between the parties, either through an investigative process or hearing model, so as to elicit additional witnesses, questions, evidence, and other information potentially helpful to the factfinders. However, the sharing of this information can also give rise to concerns that the parties themselves, in turn, may share the information outside of the process, as they may not be individually bound by the restrictions of FERPA anyway. While no sharing of information can ever be without risk, institutions have relied on a number of ways to protect such information from redisclosure, including technological solutions that do not allow the material to be printed, downloaded, or screenshotted; requiring parties to sign nondisclosure agreements before being permitted to review the information in any format other than in person under administrative supervision; and including disciplinary action in their code of conduct for those individuals who redisclose the records without permission of the other students involved.

Disclosure After the Process Concludes

The U.S. Department of Education's statements regarding the intersection of FERPA and Title IX appear to protect the sharing of information as necessary to facilitate the process. But what is the rule after the process is over and all internal appeals have been exhausted? Should the parties still have access to the records and, if so, what restrictions should be imposed? Recall that the records relate to at least two parties and often cannot reasonably be redacted without revealing critical information about other parties and witnesses in the case. If a party were to wish access to the records later, perhaps to consider a lawsuit or the filing of a federal complaint, or perhaps to assist in mental health treatment related to the underlying incident, what disclosure is fair at that point? Should the reason for accessing the records matter in determining whether the records are disclosed? The law is unclear in this circumstance, and institutions have differing practices, often evolving from the institution's own experiences in post-resolution disclosure.

Tension Points Relating to Confidentiality

In every case involving allegations of sexual misconduct, it is highly likely that at least one of the parties will come away disappointed, confused, or angry at the result. In our hypothetical case, this is true for both parties. Each had their own perspective on the situation, and ultimately with regard to each of the two charges, one perspective was determined to be more persuasive than the other, for whatever reason, based on the other evidence available. It may feel to both parties that their own story has somehow been invalidated. Investigators should work to make the process fair and transparent and to help the parties feel heard so as to minimize their dissatisfaction with the result. Despite best efforts of the investigators, adjudicators, and Title IX coordinator, however, one or both parties may feel that an injustice has occurred. The reactions to such an outcome can take many forms, all of which may implicate confidentiality concerns.

Warnings of Danger

When a respondent is found not responsible for a policy violation, the complainant and their friends may feel that the respondent's continued presence on campus constitutes a danger to others. As was the case with Sam and Dylan, the complainant and/or their friends may choose to share their story with others in the hope of warning away other potential victims. The same may be the case on the other side, where the respondent and their friends may want to warn others away from a complainant whom they feel wrongly accused them of serious misconduct, in this case as Chris did via a public post.

These behaviors can quickly feel antagonistic, threatening, and harassing to the other party. Depending on the nature of the comments, they may rise to the level of prohibited retaliation. The U.S. Supreme Court has held that Title IX prohibits retaliation against a person who claims sex discrimination, and that one experiencing such retaliation may sue (*Jackson v. Birmingham Board of Education*, 2005). Retaliation against an employee is typically defined as taking an adverse employment action against an individual, such as firing, disciplining, or demoting them, because they engaged in a protected activity, such as reporting sexual harassment. The definition of retaliation is not well defined outside of the employment setting, so institutional policies typically set forth definitions of retaliation that will be enforced among students.

These behaviors may also create a hostile environment through sexual harassment, although the bounds of this argument are still being established through case law. The U.S. Supreme Court, in *Davis v. Monroe County Board of Education* (1999) held that this sort of "hostile environment" occurs when unwelcome conduct of a sexual nature is "so severe, pervasive, and objectively offensive, and that so undermines and detracts from the victims' educational experience, that the victims are effectively denied equal access to an institution's resources and opportunities." It is common for educational institutions to use broader language adopted by the U.S. Department of Education in previous guidance that considers a hostile environment to exist where the behavior is "severe, persistent, *or* pervasive,"[1] so individual policies should be consulted to determine the sexual harassment standards that will be enforced at a particular institution.

How might this be applied by a court? In one recent high-profile case, a female student reported that she had been sexually assaulted by a male student. An investigation was completed, and the male respondent was found "not responsible" for a policy violation. The complainant continued to maintain that the respondent had raped her, and as part of her highly publicized senior thesis project, she carried a mattress around campus as a physical demonstration of the burden that she carried because of what he had done to her. On one occasion, other students brought mattresses to the respondent's class, and he was identified as a "rapist" on fliers distributed throughout campus by other students.

The respondent sued the university, alleging that the university was deliberately indifferent to sexual harassment against him. The court dismissed the case, finding that the comments were not sufficiently gendered or sexual in nature under the facts as presented to rise to the level of sexual harassment, nor had the respondent experienced a sufficient deprivation of access to educational opportunities such that the conduct would rise to the level of sexual harassment (*Nungesser v. Columbia University*, 2017). The decision would appear to provide support for one who reports a rape to call their rapist a rapist regardless of the university's disciplinary outcome (at least under a Title IX analysis), but a reader might also conclude that a slightly different set of facts may lead the court to take a more sympathetic approach to the respondent, thus emphasizing that this area of law is still developing.

At public institutions, of course, free speech rights under the First Amendment may limit the institution's ability to redress the comments and protect a student from related harm. Private institutions may provide similar free speech rights by contract as well. What options, then, are available for the students involved? This is often where defamation suits begin, requiring the re-litigation of whatever claims were adjudicated by the institution in the first place.

Media Attention and the Public's "Right to Know"

The important role of media in exposing injustices in this society cannot be denied, and where injustice lies, the media and the public alike may have strong beliefs in the right to access information, even confidential information, to bring bad deeds to light. In cases involving sexual misconduct on campus, these beliefs are no less strongly held. Yet, as we have seen, FERPA prohibits the release of personally identifiable information from student records without either consent of the student(s) or the existence of another exception—none of which involves release to the media. This can increase tension in an already tense situation.

Sometimes, it is the students themselves who go to the media to express concern about the handling of the case, the outcome, or both. When this happens, the students may feel vindicated, or they may lose control of their story in a way that was initially unexpected or unintended. For example, in one case, two students reported being sexual assaulted by a professor and were dissatisfied with the outcome (*University of Kentucky v. The Kernel Press*, 2017). The students anonymously sought the help of their campus paper to expose the professor, but when the paper requested the investigative file, the public institution refused to comply with much of the public records request. The institution filed suit to defend its position on the grounds that FERPA prohibited disclosure.

As the legal battle continued through multiple appeals, the students, in effect, switched sides, filing an amicus brief in support of the institution's refusal to disclose the documents with their identities. As explained by the court in one decision,

> *The complaining witnesses contend that what began as a "well-intended journalistic search for information" has devolved into a public dispute that ignores the interests of the victims. They argue the [student newspaper] has now published more than twenty articles about the story, despite the complaining witnesses' requests to stop, thereby forcing them to relive the trauma they have suffered. The confidentiality offered to the complaining witnesses during [the institution's] investigation was integral to the decision to come forward and report in the first place. The complaining witnesses feel that relinquishing the documents to the [newspaper], even with redactions, would allow the public to quickly deduce their identities.* (University of Kentucky v. The Kernel Press, 2017)

Of course, sometimes students approach the media without any expectations of anonymity, sharing their story for their own reasons. This can contribute to theories of retaliation or creation of a hostile environment toward other students, as discussed. Where the student alleges misconduct on the part of an administrator, different concerns may arise. For example, if an administrator has been accused in the media of being a bad actor in a case involving sexual misconduct, FERPA can severely limit their ability to respond to such accusations, even where the public statements about their involvement or their actions are objectively false. This is not without irony, as the law limits the public's right for the institution to put forth the truth, be it for its own protection or the protection of others. It is often only in the context of a lawsuit that administrators may tell their own stories without restrictions on the right to defend themselves from the accusations (34 C.F.R. § 99.31(a)(9)(iii)).

Perhaps the most well-known case of this nature involves an article published by *Rolling Stone* magazine on November 19, 2014 entitled, "A Rape on Campus: A Brutal Assault and Struggle for Justice at UVA." The article told the story of a student, identified as "Jackie," who alleged she had been sexually assaulted at a fraternity party on September 28, 2012. According to the article, which has since been retracted by the magazine, when Jackie met with the University of Virginia's Title IX coordinator, the coordinator discouraged her from pursuing the matter and made derogatory statements about the institution, such as describing it as "the rape school."

The article was later discredited by a number of sources, and on March 23, 2015, the Charlottesville Police Department issued a statement that there was "no substantive basis of fact to conclude" that the incident described in the article had occurred (*Eramo v. Rolling Stone, LLC*, 2016). The Title IX coordinator subsequently filed a defamation lawsuit against the magazine and the author of the article, obtaining a jury verdict in her favor for a total of $3 million; she later reached a confidential settlement with the magazine. The fraternity named in the article likewise sued, obtaining a settlement against the magazine for a reported $1.65 million.

What happens when a story accuses a student instead of an administrator? Students are under no FERPA obligations and thus may respond to news sources when asked. But they may or may not have the means or support to effectively counter the allegations in the press. Where one student goes to the media with an attorney, or perhaps a national organization backing them, another student may not have a truly equal opportunity to respond without similar resources at their disposal. The loudest or most well-spoken or best-represented student, then, may ultimately be seen as the one in the right, leading to potentially unfortunate consequences for others involved. Given that sexual misconduct allegations are already a battleground in our current culture wars, a skewed story in the press may affect the ability of others to share their own stories, to defend themselves, or to avoid being vilified by the public.

In the end, institutions and, in fact, the parties themselves, may have little ability to control a public story about a sexual misconduct case. If possible, the institution may consider reaching out to the parties remaining at the institution (regardless of whether they were the ones to engage the media) to determine whether any additional protections or supports may be needed to help them continue to access the institution's educational programs and activities despite the publicity.

Criminal Charges, Lawsuits, and Confidentiality

When a party has been wronged, the ultimate redress may lie with the courts. Criminal charges are typically not brought directly by a victim, but instead are at the discretion of the prosecutor, with the requirement of an indictment by a grand jury in some states. The victim must be subjected to cross-examination by the defense due to the right to confront one's accuser in a criminal trial as provided by the Sixth Amendment (*Pointer v. Texas*, 1965). This may somewhat limit the ability of accusers to protect their confidentiality completely, although courts may offer some protection through their own rules, and ethical journalists typically do not name an accuser in the media without consent. There are no such confidentiality protections for the criminal defendant during the case, but one who is found not guilty can sometimes request that the case be sealed to protect their reputation. This is heavily dependent on state law.

In civil cases, parties often will attempt to file their complaint using a pseudonym, such as John or Jane Doe. This anonymization of their identities can help to protect their internet presence to at least some extent and prevent future educational institutions, employers, and social connections from discovering their involvement with the case. While the Federal Rules of Civil Procedure do not explicitly permit pseudonymous parties, the practice has been allowed on occasion, most notably perhaps in *Roe v. Wade* (1973).

Exact standards for proceeding in such a manner differ between courts, but generally, pseudonyms are permitted when the particular circumstances of the case justify it, such as when there is a strong interest in privacy or avoiding physical harm, or when the lawsuit is of public importance but requiring the party to name themselves would prevent the suit from being brought. This often results in a balancing of public versus private interests.

For example, in *Doe v. University of South Carolina* (2018), the court allowed both the plaintiff (the accused) and the alleged victim to proceed under pseudonyms because their privacy interests "outweigh the public's interest in access to their identities." The court further found that the public was not prejudiced by the use of the pseudonyms, in that doing so would promote public access to the court records themselves. In *Doe H. v. Haskell Indian Nations University* (2017), however, the court denied a victim-plaintiff's request to proceed by pseudonym, noting that the plaintiff had already testified in open court in three trials; the facts, circumstances, and identities of the individuals involved were known to the community; and the plaintiff was not a minor at the time of the underlying allegations.

In lawsuits involving multiple students and the educational institution, it is common practice for the parties to request that the court issue a protective order to prevent the public release of certain confidential information related to the case. These protective orders often include protections for documents held by the educational institution and protected by FERPA from disclosure, medical or mental health records, and other records that would typically be protected by law. The issuance of such orders permits the public to review the pleadings in the case but shields the most sensitive information, allowing the parties the ability to participate in discovery without the ongoing concern of unauthorized disclosure.

Conclusion

Individuals may have differing perspectives on a single incident, but it is the combination and the weighing of those perspectives that allow investigators and adjudicators to make the best decisions as to whether a policy violation has occurred. The sharing of these perspectives is subject to some legal limitations—more so in the case of employees of an educational institution due to FERPA—but it is not absolutely barred in all circumstances. Parties and their advocates should be aware of the legal contours of confidentiality and find the best way to pursue their needs, preferably in a way that does not violate another's rights.

KEY TERMS

Directory information: FERPA defines this term to include information such as a student's name, address, telephone number, date and place of birth, enrollment dates, participation in school activities, weight and height of members of athletic teams. Institutions have some ability to customize what they consider to be directory information, so check their policies for more specific information.

Disclosure: FERPA defines disclosure as permitting access to or the release, transfer, or other communication of personally identifiable information contained in education records by any means, including oral, written, or electronic means, to any party except the party identified as the party that provided or created the record (34 C.F.R. § 99.3).

Education records: FERPA defines education records as those records that are directly related to a student and maintained by an educational agency or a party acting for that agency. The regulations state that personal notes are not education records where they are kept in the sole possession of the maker, are used only as a personal memory aid, and are not accessible or revealed to any other person except a temporary substitute for the maker of the record. Law enforcement records, employee records, treatment records (e.g., psychotherapy notes), and alumni records are excluded from the definition of education records (34 C.F.R. § 99.3).

Personally identifiable information: Defined by FERPA to include the student's name; names of the student's parents and other family members; address of the student or the student's family; Social Security numbers; student identification numbers; biometric records (e.g., fingerprints or retina scans); student's date of birth, place of birth, and mother's maiden name; other information that, alone or in combination, is linked or linkable to a specific student that would allow a reasonable person in the school community who does not have personal knowledge of the relevant circumstances to identify the student with reasonable certainty; and information requested by a person who the educational institution reasonably believes knows the identity of the student to whom the education record relates (34 C.F.R. § 99.3).

DISCUSSION QUESTIONS

1. If you could rewrite privacy laws, would there be any situation in which you would allow an institution to disclose information about a case to the press beyond whatever might be required under public records law? If so, what would be the impact, if any, of your new rule on the parties, the witnesses, and the administrators? Does it promote the elimination of harassment and discrimination on campus as well as getting to the truth?
2. Consider the actions of Dylan in our hypothetical case. What might the impact be on Chris, Sam, and other members of the campus community? At what point, if any, should the institution step in to address Dylan's conduct and consider potential discipline based on the legal restrictions outlined in this chapter? Does it make a difference if the institution is public versus private?
3. Does the public nature of the case change what the institution should be doing in the aftermath of this case to ensure that both Sam and Chris—both still students at the institution—can continue accessing the institution's programs and activities?

Notes

1 At the time of writing, proposed regulations would conform this language to that used by the courts and remove this distinction. Readers are urged to consult the U.S. Department of Education's latest Title IX regulations and guidance.

References

Davis v. Monroe County Board of Education, 256 U.S. 629 (1999)
Doe v. University of South Carolina, 2018 WL 1215045 (D.S.C. 2018)
Doe H. v. Haskell Indian Nations University, 266 F. Supp. 3d. 1277, (D. Kan. 2017)
Eramo v. Rolling Stone, LLC, 314 F.R.D. 205 (W.D. Va., January 26, 2016)
Gonzaga University v. Doe, 536 U.S. 273 (2002)
Jackson v. Birmingham Board of Education, 544 U.S. 167 (2005)
Nungesser v. Columbia University, 244 F. Supp. 3d 345, (S.D. New York 2017)
Pointer v. Texas, 380 U.S. 400 (1965)
Roe v. Wade, 410 U.S. 113 (1973)
University of Kentucky v. The Kernel Press, Case No. 16-CI-3229, (Fayette County Court, 8th Div., 2017)

U.S. Department of Education. (2001). *Revised sexual harassment guidance: Harassment of students by school employees, other students, and third parties.* Washington, DC: Author.

U.S. Department of Education. (2016, August 24). Dear colleague letter to school officials at institutions of higher education. Retrieved from https://studentprivacy.ed.gov/sites/default/files/resource_document/file/DCL_Medical%20Records_Final%20Signed_dated_9-2.pdf

U.S. Department of Education and U.S. Department of Health and Human Services. (November 2008). *Joint Guidance on the Application of the* Family Educational Rights and Privacy Act (FERPA) *and the* Health Insurance Portability and Accountability Act of 1996 (HIPAA) *To Student Health Records.* Washington, DC: Author.

CHAPTER FIVE

Civil Rights Investigations and Comprehensive Prevention of Sexual Misconduct

Nancy Chi Cantalupo

Contrary to what is depicted on television cop shows, there are several different methods by which police can investigate and determine the accuracy of allegations of sexual misconduct. The range of options is even wider for schools, including institutions of higher education (IHEs), because schools' handling of such allegations is governed by *non*-criminal laws, including the federal civil rights statute, Title IX of the Education Amendments Act of 1972 (Title IX); the federal education statute, Jeanne Clery Disclosure of Campus Security Policy and Campus Crime Statistics Act (Clery Act), which was amended by the Violence Against Women Act of 2013 (VAWA); and various state laws regarding civil rights and/or education. Although the state laws are beyond the scope of this chapter, the federal laws allow schools to use a wide range of investigative methods,[1] as long as those methods are consistent with the **comprehensive prevention** goals of both Title IX and the Clery Act. IHEs, therefore, are not limited to the kinds of investigative procedures typically used by police and prosecutors in the criminal justice system.[2] Instead, they are free to choose the kind of investigation method that is most likely to fulfill their specific legal obligations, as well as the methods that will be best for their campus communities as a whole.

This chapter sets forth the reasons why **civil rights investigations** are the most likely to fulfill IHEs' legal obligations under Title IX and the Clery Act to establish a comprehensive system to prevent gender-based violence, including "sexual misconduct," sexual harassment, domestic violence, dating violence, and stalking.[3] In doing so, it explains what civil rights investigations are and how civil rights investigations comprehensively prevent sexual misconduct. It also draws from a detailed set of practice recommendations that I drafted for the American Bar Association Commission on Domestic and Sexual Violence

(ABA CDSV), for use by college and university professionals who are conducting internal IHE investigations, many of whom are not attorneys. Because a detailed discussion of the full standards document is beyond the scope of the chapter, this chapter will focus instead on the underlying principles that animated the practice recommendations. Accordingly, the remainder of the chapter discusses, first, why IHE investigations of gender-based violence should take a comprehensive prevention approach, including the basis for this approach in federal law. The chapter then discusses the different models for investigations of campus gender-based violence commonly available to IHEs and explains why IHEs should select one of the **civil rights investigation models** to conduct investigations in these cases.

Comprehensive Prevention

The comprehensive prevention approach discussed in this chapter originates with the public health model of prevention first articulated by the Centers for Disease Control and Prevention (CDC) (2004) and explained in greater detail later. Comprehensive gender-based violence prevention is required most explicitly by U.S. Department of Education regulations under the Clery Act, but the regulations under Title IX also take a comprehensive prevention approach.

First, the Clery Act requires that IHEs provide "programs to prevent dating violence, domestic violence, sexual assault, and stalking" and defines such programs as "comprehensive, integrated and intentional programs, initiatives, strategies, and campaigns intended to end dating violence, domestic violence, sexual assault, and stalking" (Legal Information Institute, 2014). Because I was a negotiator in the negotiated rulemaking that adopted this definition (U.S. Department of Education, 2018) and chaired the subcommittee that drafted several iterations of this language, I can confirm that the drafters of this definition, now a part of the Clery Act regulations and therefore codified in federal law, intended "comprehensive" to refer to the CDC public health model.

Although Title IX's regulations, particularly as interpreted by various guidance documents issued by the ED's Office for Civil Rights (OCR), do not refer directly to the CDC public health comprehensive prevention approach as the Clery Act regulations do, OCR's and courts' interpretations of Title IX for the last 20-plus years are consistent with a comprehensive prevention approach to gender-based violence. Both court and OCR enforcement of Title IX recognize that the statute requires schools of all kinds, including IHEs, to prevent sexual harassment, a legally recognized form of sex discrimination, which includes most gender-based violence affecting the IHE's community. With regard to OCR's enforcement, a guidance document followed since the Clinton administration and confirmed as recently as September 2017 by the current Secretary of Education, the 2001 "Revised Sexual Harassment Guidance" (Revised Guidance) states the following: "Schools are responsible for taking prompt and effective action to stop the harassment and prevent its recurrence. A school also may be responsible for remedying the effects of the harassment on the student who was harassed" (Office for Civil Rights, 2001). Similarly, the standard that courts follow under Title IX has been articulated by the U.S. Supreme Court in *Davis v. Monroe County Board of Education* (1999) as prohibiting schools from acting with "deliberate indifference" to known instances of sexual harassment, defining "deliberate indifference" as actions or failures to act that cause students, at a minimum, "to undergo" harassment or "make them liable or vulnerable" to it (*Davis v. Monroe County Board of Education*, 1999).

Comprehensive prevention incorporates three forms of prevention: primary, secondary and tertiary. Primary prevention seeks to prevent gender-based violence before it starts. Secondary prevention includes methods that respond to gender-based violence immediately or very soon after the violence occurs, often focusing on interventions to address the trauma of gender-based violence and the harms that gender-based violence victims[4] experience, affecting their health, their relationships with others, and their ability to work and/or go to school. Tertiary prevention addresses the long-term consequences of gender-based violence, not only on the immediate victims but also secondary victims, those responsible for committing gender-based violence, and the community as a whole (Centers for Disease Control, 2004).

The systems IHEs put in place to investigate and resolve complaints of gender-based violence between students are key components to effective secondary and tertiary prevention. IHEs may be called on to investigate a complaint of gender based violence either immediately after the violence occurs or at some later point, and the form and results of their investigations have important short- and long-term consequences for many IHE members and the school itself. In addition, the effectiveness of an IHE's investigation of gender-based violence complaints influences the effectiveness of primary prevention programs, since students are less likely to take primary prevention educational messages seriously when the IHE's investigations do not indicate that the IHE itself takes gender-based violence seriously. For instance, an increasingly popular primary prevention program is bystander intervention, which trains students to recognize situations in which a fellow student may be in danger and teaches them methods of safely intervening in those situations. However, because the IHE is the most important bystander, if the IHE seems unwilling to investigate cases, or does so using methods that revictimize the survivor, students will question why they should be responsible for intervening as bystanders when the IHE is not.

Civil Rights Investigation Models: The Investigative Model or the "IDP Hybrid"

For the reasons already stated, the methods used by IHEs to investigate gender-based violence complaints should be structured and implemented so as to advance comprehensive prevention goals. Based on information that I gathered from the IHE professionals I consulted in my research for the ABA CDSV "Recommendations for Practice" document, IHEs have four basic options for such investigations. These options include the "Investigative Model," the "Hearing Model," the "Investigation & Hearing Hybrid" (IH Hybrid), and the "Investigation & Deliberative Panel Hybrid" (IDP Hybrid). Of the four models, the Investigative Model and the Hearing Model are the older options, whereas the hybrids are more recent innovations. For the reasons discussed next, both the Investigative Model and the IDP Hybrid qualify as civil rights investigation models.

In general, the Investigative Model uses investigators who have demonstrated professional and culturally competent expertise, knowledge, and skills in areas including but not limited to the dynamics of gender-based violence, trauma-informed interviewing and investigation techniques (including cultural and linguistic skills), and methods for building trust with those involved in the investigation and in the integrity of the investigatory process itself. The role of these professional investigators is to gather evidence and interview the parties (i.e., the complainant and respondent) and any witnesses in separate, individual meetings, then write an investigative report where they review the evidence and make factual findings. In contrast, the Hearing Model is an **adversarial model** that generally depends on the parties involved in the allegations to present evidence and witnesses in support of their own factual account, usually while both parties are present, to a neutral panel of university community members who are not professional investigators. These panelists do not do their own investigation, but instead passively hear testimony and consider evidence presented by all parties and witnesses, then make factual findings based on that testimony and evidence. The Investigative Model has long been used in the employment context to address workplace sexual harassment under Title VII of the Civil Rights Act of 1964 and similar statutes (Whittenbury, 2013). This history constitutes a main reason why it is referred to as a civil rights investigation, and the Investigative Model continues to be popular and widely used. In contrast, while the Hearing Model has likewise been historically used (but in school disciplinary proceedings, not workplaces), it is increasingly less favored.

The hybrid models have both developed more recently as IHEs have struggled to find methods of investigating complaints of gender-based violence that better fit the educational context. The IH Hybrid model, which is *not* a civil rights investigation model, combines the Investigative Model with a hearing panel so that the investigators' report goes to the hearing panel and the panel reviews it along with hearing testimony from parties and witnesses, then makes factual findings based on the report and the testimony. In contrast, the IDP Hybrid, which *is* a civil rights investigation model, depends on the professional investigators to make factual findings as in the Investigative Model, then adds a "Deliberative Panel" review of the investigation report. The Deliberative Panel is made up of IHE community members, excluding students due to the invasion of privacy and risks of disclosure involved in having fellow students hear or see deeply personal information or evidence about their classmates, especially evidence collected through a "rape kit" such as the photos of broken blood vessels on the survivor's backside that were viewed by the hearing panel in a Harvard University student survivor's hearing discussed later. The IDP Hybrid gives the members of the Deliberative Panel copies of the investigation report and requires the investigators to appear before the panel to answer questions before the panel makes a final decision about whether an IHE policy violation has occurred. The parties may also appear before the panel, at their option, to make statements, although the goal of the parties' statements is not to present new or additional evidence beyond the evidence in the investigators' report, but to give the parties an opportunity to speak directly to the IHE decisionmakers, without any kind of filter. Conceivably, the parties' statements might lead the Deliberative Panel to add to the questions that they ask the investigators, but those questions would still be directed at the investigators and be focused on such purposes as clarifying why a party's statement and the investigatory report present different accounts of the facts or determining why the investigators' report does not include evidence to which the party's statement points.

These models have important similarities and differences, with the most important difference dealing with each model's effectiveness as a method of comprehensive prevention. Most importantly with regard to similarities between models, nothing in the basic structure of any of these models would cause an IHE to violate the federal laws that apply to IHEs' obligations regarding gender-based violence and complainants' or respondents' rights, including under Title IX, the Clery Act, and U.S. constitutional law regarding accused students' due process rights. A model complies with these federal laws as long as it (1) provides a mechanism for investigation (e.g., does not tell student victims that they must report to police in order to get any investigation); (2) uses rules that guarantee "due process" or "fair process" procedural rights *equally* to complainants and respondents (including with regard to notice of the investigation and the right to be heard by those investigating); (3) investigates and resolves a complaint of gender-based violence promptly and without undue delay; and (4) otherwise does not conflict with the *spirit* of the Clery Act, VAWA, and Title IX.

In particular, all four models comply with schools' "due process" obligations for student conduct proceedings under U.S. constitutional law and, as long as they give equal "process," or procedural rights, to victims, will also comply with Title IX and the Clery Act, as amended by VAWA 2013. It has long been acknowledged that the legal requirements for due process in campus disciplinary procedures generally are quite minimal, as they only give accused students at state institutions (who are at risk of being suspended or expelled) rights to "some kind of notice and … some kind of hearing" (*Goss v. Lopez*, 1975). Accused students at private schools receive a much vaguer right to fundamental fairness based on the institution's contractual obligations to the student. However, in the context of campus gender-based violence, the Clery Act, VAWA 2013, and Title IX have combined to provide students accused of gender-based violence with rights that they do not receive for other kinds of misconduct. These additions to accused students' rights have come as a result of the expansion of rights for student victims and complainants guaranteed by the VAWA 2013 amendments to the Clery Act, expansions which then extend to accused students because, in Title IX proceedings, in particular, OCR expects schools to provide equal procedural rights to both students.

An example of such an expansion relates to students' ability to bring attorneys to student conduct proceedings. Neither the constitutional due process rights of accused students at state schools nor the rights to fundamental fairness for private school students require schools to allow an accused student to bring an attorney into student conduct proceedings. However, VAWA 2013's language that complainants are allowed an "advisor of their choice" in such proceedings was interpreted by the U.S. Department of Education in its regulations implementing VAWA 2013's changes to the Clery Act to allow attorneys as advisors. When combined with Title IX's "procedural equality" (Cantalupo, 2016, p. 286), both respondents and complainants now may have an attorney with them during the proceeding (Cantalupo, 2016). Importantly, as with issues of due process generally, nothing in the statute or regulations regarding "an advisor of their choice" applies differently to the different investigatory models. The Clery regulations interpret that provision to guarantee a student the right to bring an advisor to all meetings and interactions related to the investigation (Federal Register, 2014, p. 62774), not only to a traditional "hearing," as such a hearing is defined in the Hearing Model. Therefore, student complainants and respondents may now bring advisors, including advisors who are attorneys, to all parts of an investigation, regardless of the model chosen (see also chapter 6).

Similarly, none of these models inhibits IHEs any more or less than the others in terms of fulfilling the obligations they have under Title IX, Clery, and VAWA that do not deal with investigations. Indeed, in order to comprehensively prevent gender-based violence, IHEs must have various policies, procedures, and programs that guide it in addressing gender-based violence, even if the survivor never initiates an investigation. For instance, IHEs must provide clear paths by which students can disclose (confidentially) or report (non-confidentially) gender-based violence, as well as provide educational accommodations to students who have been subjected to gender-based violence, regardless of whether an investigation ever occurs and which investigation model the IHE uses to investigate the allegations (Cantalupo, 2015).

Although it is important to acknowledge the significant commonalities between these models, their differences in effectiveness at achieving the comprehensive prevention goals articulated earlier clearly elevate certain models above others. The characteristics of certain models are more likely to be effective because their designs show an understanding of the scope and dynamics of campus gender-based violence that others lack. In addition, most IHEs face significant resource restrictions while simultaneously feeling a particular commitment to provide sufficient support to all students, victims or accused, involved in gender-based violence cases. Together, these considerations push in favor of IHEs adopting the civil rights investigation models (i.e., the Investigative Model, the IDP Hybrid, or some variation of these two models), because these models most efficiently and effectively engage in comprehensive prevention, particularly in light of IHEs' limited resources.

Civil Rights Investigations as Tertiary Prevention

The Investigative Model and the IDP Hybrid fit better into the comprehensive prevention approach because they qualify as both tertiary and secondary prevention strategies. For instance, with regard to tertiary prevention, the IDP Hybrid and Investigative Model are more effective due to their greater conduciveness for post-proceeding treatment of those who are found responsible for committing gender-based violence, as well as their greater sustainability as long-term responses to violence.

First, the Investigative Model and IDP Hybrid are more likely to encourage accused individuals who are found responsible for committing gender-based violence to respond to nonpunitive sanctions such as those based on principles of restorative justice or those requiring treatment to learn how to stop committing gender-based violence. Several scholars and IHE professionals favor integrating restorative justice-based sanctioning methods in gender-based violence cases (Coker, 2017; see also chapter 11).

Recall that the structures of the Hearing Model and the IH Hybrid are adversarial in nature because they require the parties to present evidence that supports one party's account of events, undermines the other party's evidence, or both. In many cases, adversarial proceedings will compel the parties to attack each other's credibility and evidence, polarizing the parties or increasing preexisting polarization and their hostile feelings toward one another. At the sanctioning stage, such a situation is unlikely to support restorative justice methods, which require the parties to agree on a certain sanction or sanctions. In addition, the parties are more likely to have a "zero-sum" attitude about sanctions, where they are going to be satisfied only with a sanctioning decision at one end of the spectrum, either expulsion or a borderline non-sanction such as writing a research paper on sexual assault. These adversarial models are thus less likely to create openness to restorative justice or treatment sanctioning options with which IHEs may wish to experiment.

In addition, sanctions perceived by some as overly punitive, especially expulsion, are often not supported by either student victims or IHE professionals, because of several unintended consequences that could ultimately further harm the student victim or other students who could be victimized. First, those who are expelled (including through firing, if the accused is a faculty member) can and do go to new schools, and those schools may not be notified of disciplinary actions taken by the previous school, making it easy for those expelled persons to commit gender-based violence again, if they tend toward repeat perpetration. Second, accused individuals who are expelled or fired but do not go to another school may stay in the neighborhood of the school from which they have been expelled, but the school may not be able to compel nonviolent behavior from them because the school no longer has jurisdiction over or the ability to control such former students or employees. Even methods such as barring the accused individual from campus or seeking a court-issued protective order may be insufficient. An IHE cannot bar the accused person from property that the IHE does not own but that may be adjacent or close to campus and therefore regularly frequented by the complainant. Similarly, protective orders may not be available under applicable laws, especially if the gender-based violence at issue does not involve intimate partners.

The IDP Hybrid and Investigative Model are more sustainable because they are more efficient as a resource matter and more likely to be affordable in the long-term for IHEs. Conducting gender-based violence investigations competently and well requires a lot of training in the dynamics and scope of gender-based violence, in both general and trauma-informed investigation techniques, in the IHE's policies and procedures, and in the legal requirements of Title IX, Clery, VAWA, the constitutional law related to accused students' rights, and applicable state laws. It is likely to be more efficient and effective to focus such in-depth training on a limited number of specialized employees who can develop expertise in the training areas over time.

Unfortunately, adversarial hearing panels are structured in exactly the opposite fashion. The hearing panels used by the Hearing Model and IH Hybrid are commonly drawn from existing IHE faculty, staff, and (increasingly rarely, for the reasons already noted) students, who serve on these panels on top of their full-time jobs. Because such service is an extra responsibility, hearing panel members generally rotate on and off such panels, often on an annual basis, requiring new people to be trained each year. Thus, the employees participating in these hearings have no specialty in such investigations or in other skills beyond pure investigation skills, such as appropriate cultural or linguistic skills. Instead, they are either generalists or specialists in another area. Nor do they have time to develop expertise, as they serve on hearing panels temporarily.

Moreover, because adversarial hearing panel members generally have no expertise in gender-based violence, training them in such basic competencies requires significant resources. However, at the end of their rotation, they are often replaced by other untrained faculty and staff, and IHEs may get little to no return on their investment in training, especially if there are no gender-based violence complaints that initiate a hearing in that year. If there are gender-based violence complaints, they are unlikely to be frequent enough during these temporary panel members' time on a panel for them to develop expertise. On the other hand, if there are multiple complaints of gender-based violence in a year, although assigning an employee to multiple gender-based violence hearing panels potentially allows that employee to develop expertise in such cases, doing so is quite unfair to that employee when each case is an extra responsibility on top of the employee's regular job.

This burden is exacerbated by the nature of gender-based violence complaint hearings, which are unusually exhausting and carry significant risk of secondary trauma. To the extent that panel members may be asked to be on panels because they are assumed to have or actually have certain cultural and/or linguistic skills needed (due, for instance, to being members of a racial and/or ethnic minority), the burden is likely to fall even more disproportionately on certain panel members, often based on gender, ethnicity, or sexual orientation.

Therefore, using an investigation method that relies even in part on an adversarial hearing is at least highly inefficient and stressful for the hearing panelists, especially hearing panelists already disproportionately burdened due to being expected to represent marginalized communities, and at most could incur for the IHE a significant and repeated training cost for little if any discernable return. Moreover, although the use of existing IHE employees to staff the panels seems low cost at first, properly training those employees increases expenses significantly and carries greater risks of expensive liability if the training is inadequate or the panel's lack of experience causes members to commit errors. In addition, because of the sustainability concerns already articulated, these savings, if they exist at all, are only short-term. Long-term, IHEs are more likely to spend significantly more money on constantly training new hearing panel members as they rotate on and off the panels, without a likely return on that significant investment. In contrast, because the **civil rights investigation models** rely on professional investigators who will investigate many cases over time, the investigators can act as repositories for skills, institutional knowledge, and experience that can not only sustain, but also improve the IHE's expertise in preventing gender-based violence. Investigators can be hired for, or trained in, cultural and linguistic skills and in methods to minimize bias on the basis of race, gender, and sexual orientation by, for instance hiring investigators who are trained in understanding and counteracting the dynamics of race discrimination and implicit bias, a much preferable result than disproportionately burdening and tokenizing hearing panel members of color. Hiring professional investigators may certainly have high up-front costs from the salaries and/or retainers that highly trained people are paid, but in the long term, those investigators will be less expensive because they are a long-term investment from which the IHE will benefit well into the future.

Aside from the expenses and inefficiencies regarding training and personnel issues, the models involving adversarial hearings are inefficient in other ways. Hearings for gender-based violence complaints are often multi-day affairs, requiring the panel members, parties, advisors and any other staff involved to clear days on their calendars, a particularly complicated logistical matter because panel members may have to fulfill normal job responsibilities that have little if any overlap with their duties as hearing panel members. This formidable logistical endeavor cannot avoid expending significant resources that ultimately contribute little to nothing to the investigation itself, as well as making it more difficult for an IHE to investigate promptly, one of the central requirements under both Title IX and Clery/VAWA.

In contrast to the inefficiencies of the models involving hearings, the Investigative Model and IDP Hybrid use the IHE's resources more cost-effectively and sustainably, even though the IDP Hybrid requires existing IHE members to sit on the Deliberative Panel in addition to their regular jobs. The Deliberative Panel responsibility is much less extensive and does not require as much training for panel members as the adversarial models do. Regardless of whether professional investigators are hired to work in-house as employees or are hired on a case-by-case basis, the IHE can bring in investigators with the applicable expertise, contract with an outside professional for specific cases, and/or train a limited number of existing employees who will be responsible for multiple investigations (including potentially those not involving gender-based violence) and who will be able to develop expertise in such investigations and improve their quality over time. Although, as already noted, this will certainly be expensive at first, in the long term it will be cheaper and more effective. Finally, because investigators interview the parties and witnesses individually, even with an investigatory team made up of multiple investigators, as best practice suggests, scheduling can be expected to be significantly easier, and the investigation can be completed more quickly, compared to finding one time period when all parties, witnesses, and panel members are able to attend a hearing.

The civil rights investigation models are also more conducive to creating a consortium of IHEs that would share the expense of hiring professional investigators (Smith & Gomez, 2016). Such a consortium not only allows IHEs to share expenses, it also enhances the independence of the investigators (who would report to the consortium rather than the individual IHE) and provides a mechanism for separate IHEs that are geographically close to address gender-based violence complaints brought by a student at one campus against a student at another campus. These advantages of an investigation consortium are facilitated when the evidence on which the decision is being made is collected by the consortium's investigators only, as would be the case in the IDP Hybrid and the Investigative Model. In contrast, the IH Hybrid model, which includes investigators but still requires an adversarial hearing, typically allows the parties and witnesses to present additional evidence, which may or may not be in the investigators' report, regardless of its probative value, all in the context of an adversarial hearing where members of the specific IHE's community, not the consortium, make decisions. When the specific IHE's hearing panel makes a decision on evidence that the specific IHE's panel alone has heard, much of the purpose of entering into such a consortium in the first place is defeated.

It is important to note that the models requiring adversarial hearings have resource implications for the parties as well as IHEs. Some students and/or their families have the resources to hire lawyers to advise students and others do not. This is true of both complainants and respondents, so that inequality can exist not only between complainants and respondents but also between respondents and between complainants, where some respondents or complainants can afford an attorney and others cannot. Concerns about investigations where a respondent has an attorney but the complainant does not, or vice versa, have long been discussed, including during the negotiated rulemaking amending the Clery Act regulations, when negotiators debated whether the statutory language authorizing students to bring "an advisor of their choice" to conduct proceedings allowed the advisor to be an attorney (Vendituoli, 2014).

The structures of the adversarial Hearing Model and IH Hybrid exacerbate such income disparities and inequalities between students. Both of these adversarial models would create strong incentives for schools, complainants, and respondents to hire lawyers, because these models most closely model themselves after court proceedings and systems that lawyers are trained to navigate but most non-lawyers are not. In these systems, the ultimate decisionmakers, especially regarding procedural matters, are judges who were usually lawyers before becoming judges. Because the Hearing Model and the IH Hybrid rely more on procedures familiar to lawyers but unfamiliar to non-lawyers, both complainants and respondents will feel more pressure to hire attorneys, perhaps regardless of whether they can afford them. IHEs, in turn, will feel pressure to hire lawyers to run their hearings so that the school is not placed in the difficult position of acting in the role of a judge and managing the behavior of attorneys who have more legal or judicial training, experience, or skills than the IHE staff ultimately making the decision. This is a serious problem because some IHEs, including many minority-serving and commuter/community colleges, cannot afford in-house lawyers. Although IHEs have good reasons to hire lawyers as investigators in the Investigative Model and the IDP Hybrid, non-lawyers have been shown to be effective investigators where these models are used in other settings, such as many workplaces. Moreover, even while acknowledging the insights and arguments of several scholars with regard to the benefits to survivors (Behre, 2016; Weiner, 2017) of retaining a lawyer either for pay or *pro bono*, the non-court-like procedures of the Investigative Model and the IDP Hybrid will make it more likely that parties can protect their interests even if they do not prefer or cannot afford to hire a lawyer. Thus, in the face of these disparities and in the interest of not exacerbating such inequalities, the civil rights investigation models present the best options for conducting investigations that are as equally protective as possible of students, regardless of income level. They do so because they seek to avoid exacerbating the disparities and inequalities that come with the realities of impoverished students and economic disparities between students.

Civil Rights Investigations as Secondary Prevention

The Investigative Model and IDP Hybrid also constitute a form of secondary prevention. To be effective as a secondary prevention strategy, IHE gender-based violence investigations must be trauma-informed, because secondary prevention aims to minimize the harm to the gender-based violence victim by intervening as quickly as possible after the harassment or violence has occurred and addressing the victim's needs. Trauma-informed investigations recognize, first, that some student victims initiate an investigation for trauma-related reasons, whether due to the increased fear and trauma they experience from potentially or actually encountering the individual(s) they have accused of gender-based violence on campus, or because they seek more abstract goods like empowerment and community acknowledgement of the wrong they experienced. Second, a trauma-informed investigation acknowledges the ways in which investigations can *re*-traumatize student victims. The IDP Hybrid model, in particular, and the Investigative Model to a lesser extent, allow complainants to access the positive aspects of the trauma-informed investigation while minimizing the re-traumatizing elements. The models that include adversarial hearings are significantly less trauma-informed because they are much more likely to re-traumatize victims.

The adversarial Hearing Model and IH Hybrid are more likely to re-traumatize a complainant in several ways. First, these models require a complainant to repeatedly recount—and in recounting, often to relive—much of the trauma of the original victimization. Whenever an adversarial hearing is involved in an investigation, a complainant will typically be required to recount the violence as many as six times (two to three of which could be avoided in a non-adversarial model), and several of those times will likely be to groups of people and potentially in the presence of the named harasser. More specifically, the complainant will have to recount the violence at least once to whomever the complainant first discloses the harassment (either to a first responder who may not be further involved in the investigation or to someone who acts in no official capacity for the IHE or law enforcement). When the complainant makes an official report, if it is not to the person to whom the complainant already disclosed, the complainant will have to recount the victimization at least one more time. The complainant will likely take advantage of the right to bring an "advisor of her/his choice" to the proceeding, as guaranteed by the Clery Act since 2013, necessitating at least one further recounting to whomever the complainant chooses as an advisor. The complainant will also need to disclose at least once to the person designated by the IHE to "prosecute" the case if the IHE conducts "criminalized" hearings (i.e., adversarial hearings that imitate court procedures in criminal, as opposed to civil, cases[5]), or to the investigators *and* the "prosecutor" if the IHE uses a criminalized hearing as a part of the IH Hybrid model. In this sense, the IH Hybrid potentially requires the most retelling and reliving of the violence. And the complainant will have to recount the victimization at least once to the hearing panel, a retelling that may be the most re-traumatizing of all because it usually involves telling a *group* of people that likely includes faculty members and/or other campus community members, and even fellow students (at IHEs that are unaware of or opposed to the trauma-informed practice of not putting students on such panels). The potential re-traumatizing effects of this final retelling may be worsened if the complainant must potentially recount the harassment or violence in the presence of the person(s) accused of committing these acts. These repeated retellings are *only* for the investigation; most complainants will need counseling and medical care, potentially requiring more recounting of the violence to health professionals.

Trauma-informed investigations minimize the number of times a gender-based violence victim must recount the violence. For instance, best practices for law enforcement often suggest methods by which police, prosecutors, and others such as Sexual Assault Nurse Examiners (SANEs) can work together to minimize the number of times sexual assault survivors must recount the violence they have experienced. Dr. Kim Lonsway and Sergeant (Retired) Joanne Archambault, who between them have about 5 decades of research on and practical experience with law enforcement investigations of sexual assault, advise law enforcement to develop methods for reducing the number of times victims are interviewed or have to recount their victimizations to law enforcement, including by having police and SANEs conduct preliminary interviews together, having police and prosecutors conduct comprehensive interviews together, and not passing a survivor between law enforcement for trivial and avoidable reasons like a shift change (Lonsway & Archambault, 2008).

In the campus gender-based violence context, the Investigative Model and IDP Hybrid likely need several fewer such recountings. Complainants will likely want to access their rights to an advisor and may initially tell a first responder or confidante who is not the advisor or an investigator, so those first two retellings are likely to happen regardless of the investigation model used. However, unlike the models involving adversarial hearings, the civil rights investigation models open up the possibility that complainants may have to recount the victimization only one more time, when they tell the investigators what happened in a first (and potentially only) interview, for which any follow-up interviews will tend to revisit only limited parts of the original account, as opposed to requiring a full recounting to an entirely new person or persons, as both of the models with adversarial hearings typically do.

The re-traumatizing effects resulting from the greater number of retellings required by the adversarial Hearing Model and IH Hybrid are exacerbated by the adversarial hearing requirement of divulging deeply private information to a larger number of people, including potentially people with whom the complainant has an ongoing relationship that will be inevitably affected by the disclosure of this private information. An example of the secondary victimization adversarial hearings can cause was movingly but painfully described by a student survivor at the launch of the "Not Alone" report by the White House Task Force to Protect Students from Sexual Assault. In her introduction of Vice President Joseph Biden, this student discussed how traumatic it was for her to "sit in a room full of Harvard professors as they look[ed] at a magnified photo of [her] backside covered in bruises and broken blood vessels" (The White House, 2014). These dynamics are likely to be even more traumatic if the school is small and the survivor is more likely to be forced to interact with campus community members who were on the hearing panel and thus privy to the invasive disclosures that the process requires.

In contrast to the two models with adversarial hearings, the Investigative Model and IDP Hybrid can limit the number of people who see such private disclosures to many fewer persons. Because the investigators meet with each party and witness separately and alone, with only the student party's advisor and the investigators present, survivors must endure only a fraction of the retraumatizing privacy invasions required by the adversarial hearing models. Although the IDP Hybrid model presents the chance that a survivor might make a statement to the hearing panel, that choice is under the control of the survivor, since the IDP Hybrid allows parties to make a statement but does not require them to do so (as the adversarial hearing models do).

Hearings can also fail to separate the complainant and respondent during the course of the proceedings, a failure that is problematic in light of both court and U.S. Department of Education recognition that separating the student victim from the accused student, especially if requested by the victim, is critical to avoiding a Title IX violation (Cantalupo, 2009). For instance, in Title IX litigation, many courts have found that the failure to separate student victims and accused students can be evidence of the school's "deliberate indifference" to sexual harassment (Cantalupo, 2009), an indirect acknowledgement of the re-traumatizing effects of failing to separate students (Cantalupo, 2012). Likewise, courts in cases brought by accused students' alleging due process violations have upheld the use of a screen to separate complainants and accused students in student conduct proceedings (Cantalupo, 2012). Both sets of cases confirm that because these are not criminal proceedings, there is no legal right to "confront" one's accuser. While screens, remote testimony, or other methods can be and have been used to separate complainants and respondents, these devices must be added to the usual adversarial hearing structure, which has traditionally included no such separating devices. Since the Investigative Model and IDP Hybrid separate complainant and respondent throughout the process (except, in the case of the IDP Hybrid, if survivors decide of their own free will to give a statement to the Deliberative Panel), special efforts to separate the parties are not necessary with these civil rights investigation models.

Although the Investigative Model and IDP Hybrid fairly equally avoid the re-victimizing aspects just discussed, the IDP Hybrid more effectively facilitates the positive aspects of trauma-informed investigations. First, the option for complainants to voluntarily choose to stand up and speak out about the gender-based violence to a panel of campus community members has an empowering effect. The IDP Hybrid allows parties the opportunity to make a statement to the Deliberative Panel, after the investigation report has been finalized, providing the parties with the option to present their perspectives after actually seeing the report and allowing them to be heard directly by IHE decisionmakers. Because the Deliberative Panel represents the campus community in a way that a single or pair of investigators cannot, when parties make a statement to the Deliberative Panel they can accurately feel that they are speaking more directly to the campus community.

Second, the Deliberative Panel provides safeguards against investigators who are not competent, are biased in some way, or are otherwise not in line with the policies and values of the institution.[6] As with the empowerment function of making a statement to the Deliberative Panel, the IDP Hybrid retains a positive characteristic associated with more traditional hearings, while eliminating the non-trauma-informed adversarial hearing characteristics.

Both civil rights investigation models are also more trauma-informed than the models involving adversarial hearings because each establishes a better balance between an investigation's promptness, due process protections, and certainty (in terms of the ultimate decision) than the adversarial hearing models do. Promptness and the certainty of the decision, in particular, are both important to complainants' healing from trauma, especially if the complainant's fear of or actual encounters with the accused student repeatedly trigger a traumatic response. Separation of the survivor and accused student that lasts until the survivor graduates or leaves may be necessary for survivors to reestablish educational trajectories as close to their original trajectories as possible, and the longer an investigation takes, the longer survivors must wait before starting the long road to rebuilding normalcy in their educations and lives. Indeed, as noted, separating the survivor and the accused student is widely acknowledged as a trauma-informed practice, even by courts that often do not articulate separation as "trauma-informed" (and are not medical professionals well educated in trauma or trauma-informed practice) but nevertheless recognize the harm that *failure* to separate survivors and accused students does to survivors. This recognition can be seen in the failure-to-separate-as-deliberate-indifference Title IX cases already mentioned (Cantalupo, 2009, 2012).

Unfortunately, the parties' due process concerns can work at cross purposes with an investigation's promptness, and both promptness and increased process can diminish certainty. Increased process takes more time, interfering with promptness, but insufficient process and rushed investigations can lead to decisions that are more likely to be overturned if there is a right to appeal or an additional proceeding (such as a lawsuit against the IHE by any student party). Increased process may also undermine accuracy,[7] by, for instance increasing the likelihood that witnesses will meet and talk about their evidence during the lengthier investigation. Decisions that are less accurate and more uncertain thus make the entire matter drag on before a final decision can be reached and are not prompt in a different way, interfering with the complainant's healing from trauma.

The Investigative Model and IDP Hybrid are more likely to be prompt without sacrificing due process for all parties or certainty in the resolution of the investigation. The two models strike that balance differently, with the Investigative Model emphasizing promptness while the IDP Hybrid favors enhanced due process. Nevertheless, the design and structure of both models make them more likely to be prompt than the adversarial hearing models due to their reliance on professional investigators employed solely to conduct investigations, either full-time or on a case-by-case basis. This focus means that the investigation is the investigators' priority, rather than being an additional duty besides their other duties unrelated to gender-based violence or investigations, as is usually the case with adversarial hearing panel members. In addition, professional investigators' experience and expertise in conducting investigations will likely cause them to work more efficiently and proactively, allowing them to complete investigations more quickly and promptly without sacrificing the quality of the investigation. Similarly, this professional expertise is likely to increase the investigation's high quality and result in accurate factual findings that will be less challengeable and therefore more certain. Moreover, professionals who are dedicated entirely to conducting such investigations are likely to be more neutral and more independent in their fact-finding than faculty, staff, and students who are intertwined with and influenced by the community in multiple ways that may interfere with the primarily technical character of the fact-finding process. This neutrality and independence thus also enhance the fairness of the process offered to the parties.

The investigators in the Investigative and IDP Hybrid models will conclude their investigation by synthesizing all of the evidence they have gathered, both from interviews and from other sources (e.g., security camera footage), and write a report summarizing the evidence, making credibility determinations, resolving conflicts in the evidence, and concluding whether the IHE's policy has been violated. The ABA Recommendations for Practice also advise that IHEs adopt a procedure by which the complainant(s) and respondent(s) each get a first draft of the report and have a time-limited opportunity to review, object to, or ask for clarification on matters in the report, as well as identify evidence missing from the report (all in writing), as long as the investigators learned about that evidence or the evidence became available after the investigator had completed the evidence-gathering stage. The investigators should then also have a time-limited opportunity to add, delete, or change the report based on the parties' feedback before finalizing and sending it to the Deliberative Panel, if the IDP Hybrid is being used. The parties' feedback and any response from the investigators should be included in the record that the Deliberative Panel considers. Under these procedures, the parties receive much of the process associated with hearings, but without either significant delay or the pressure of on-the-spot decisions and responses by the investigators and the parties.

Although the advantages just listed apply to both the Investigative Model and the IDP Hybrid, the Investigative Model emphasizes promptness over process. Because the Investigative Model does not involve any kind of hearing, the model has fewer steps and therefore investigations can be completed more quickly. For example, investigations will not be slowed down by the time required to find common times and arrange other logistics for the fairly sizeable groups of people involved in either hearings or a Deliberative Panel meeting to gather.

The fact that the IDP Hybrid model does involve such complex scheduling provides an example of how it balances promptness, process, and certainty differently than the Investigative Model, emphasizing process more than promptness. The IDP Hybrid increases the due process protections offered to all parties because parties are given an opportunity to speak directly to panel decisionmakers after seeing and responding to the investigators' report and because of the greater accountability that investigators have due to panel oversight. This increased process also potentially provides greater certainty in the decision reached by the panel, as the panel's oversight guards against either perceptions of or actual bias, shoddy evidence-gathering, or other reasons that may cause some to question the accuracy of the investigators' fact-finding, while still not involving so many steps (i.e., process) in the investigation that it cannot be completed promptly.

Consistent with its emphasis on process more than promptness, the IDP Hybrid faces many difficulties similar to the adversarial hearing models, but at lower levels. For instance, because the Deliberative Panel's questioning is limited to the investigators, is based on the investigation report, and does not involve presentations of evidence by the parties (which is likely to significantly and unpredictably lengthen the time needed for the hearing), a Deliberative Panel meeting is generally limited to one day at most. Many, if not most, adversarial hearings require many days. Deliberative Panel meetings are likely to be easier to schedule—and, therefore, are likely to be held more promptly—than adversarial hearings because adversarial hearings involve a larger number of people (whereas both panels will include investigators, parties, and perhaps their advisors, Deliberative Panel hearings would not include witnesses), who must be available for longer (sometimes much longer) periods of time. Besides being easier to schedule and thus likely to make the investigation as a whole more prompt, the shorter hearings of the IDP Hybrid are less stressful for all involved. The design of adversarial hearings is more stressful because such hearings require people already in a highly stressful conflict to replay that conflict in front of third parties who must make virtually immediate decisions with very little time to consider conflicting evidence that has just been presented to them. In contrast, in the IDP Hybrid, the investigators have more time to do the difficult fact-finding work of gathering, weighing, and synthesizing the evidence for their report, and the Deliberative Panel has more time to read and deliberate on the evidence presented in the report.

The value of such an approach is particularly obvious when compared to the other hybrid investigation model among the four models reviewed here, the Investigative & Hearing Model. As suggested by the name, in the IH Hybrid, an investigation similar to that done in the Investigative and the IDP Hybrid Models is done, but the investigators' report is considered in the adversarial hearing that follows it as only one part of the evidence that the hearing panel members consider. Unlike in the IDP Hybrid, where the investigators' report establishes, with generally only minor exceptions, the full universe of evidence that is considered, IH Hybrid hearing panels also consider evidence presented at the hearing by the parties and witnesses, even if those parties' and witnesses' evidence is already addressed in the investigators' report. To the extent that the evidence presented in the investigators' report conflicts with the evidence presented in the adversarial hearing by parties or witnesses, the hearing panel is back to making very quick decisions with little time for consideration (and the parties are back to having to replay their conflict before an audience). Even worse, the IH Hybrid hearing panel may come to a different decision from that of the investigators because the panel and the investigators considered different evidence in making their decisions. Should such a conflicting decision occur, it automatically makes the ultimate decision less certain and more challengeable. The IDP Hybrid avoids this problem because the Deliberative Panel is not hearing new evidence that is not already in the investigators' report.

Although all four of the investigatory models commonly used by IHEs to investigate and resolve gender-based violence complaints aim to be prompt, to provide due process, and to reach certain and supportable conclusions, the models using adversarial hearings sacrifice too much of the promptness needed by survivors to obtain reasonably quick resolutions to their complaints that will allow them to go back to their studies and try to reestablish normalcy in their lives as soon as possible. In contrast, the civil rights investigation models offer a more trauma-informed balance because they manage to provide due process without sacrificing promptness.

Conclusion

Although IHEs have wide discretion in how they investigate gender-based violence within their campus communities, the requirements in federal law that IHEs engage in comprehensive prevention of gender-based violence, as defined by the CDC and subcategorized into primary, secondary, and tertiary prevention methods, push in favor of using the Investigative Model and the IDP Hybrid. Related to these legal considerations, these models' greater sustainability and efficiency in light of IHEs' limited resources, as well as their more trauma-informed character, qualify these civil rights investigation models as methods of both tertiary and secondary prevention.

KEY TERMS

Adversarial hearings and **adversarial models:** These investigation models rely primarily or exclusively on members of the IHE community, who are usually not professionally-trained or -experienced investigators, to conduct a fact-finding process to determine whether and to what extent an accusation of gender-based violence is accurate. In these models, a hearing panel of IHE community members listens to presentations of evidence by others (usually the complainant and respondent or their representatives), who, depending on the rules of the proceeding and the parties' resources, *may* interview witnesses and gather other evidence to present to the hearing panel. These models are called "adversarial" because the complainant(s) and the respondent(s) present different and almost always conflicting accounts of what happened between them, and the hearing panel must decide which account is more credible. The types of adversarial hearing models discussed here include the "Hearing Model" and the "Investigation & Hearing (IH) Hybrid."

Civil rights investigations and **civil rights investigation models:** These investigation models rely primarily or exclusively on professional investigators to conduct a fact-finding process to determine whether and to what extent an accusation of gender-based violence is accurate, including by interviewing parties and witnesses and gathering other evidence that supports or contradicts the allegations. These models are designated as "civil rights" investigations because they have traditionally been used in investigations of conduct like gender-based violence, which violates civil rights laws like Title IX (dealing with equal educational opportunity) and Title VII (dealing with equal employment opportunity), and because they fulfill the comprehensive prevention goals of those civil rights laws more effectively than other models. The types of civil rights investigation models discussed in this chapter include the "Investigative Model" and the "Investigation & Deliberative Panel (IDP) Hybrid."

Comprehensive prevention: Refers to a kind of prevention, first articulated by the Centers for Disease Control and Prevention, that includes three forms of prevention: primary (prevention that seeks to prevent gender-based violence before it starts), secondary (prevention that responds to gender-based violence immediately or very soon after the violence occurs in order to reduce the trauma and harm of gender-based violence to the victim), and tertiary (prevention that addresses the long-term consequences of gender-based violence for direct and secondary victims, perpetrators, and the community as a whole).

DISCUSSION QUESTIONS

1. What factors should IHEs consider when selecting a model for investigating campus gender-based violence?
2. Why does the author criticize adversarial hearing models and decide that civil rights investigation models are better for investigating complaints of campus gender-based violence? Do you agree or disagree with the author's position in this regard?
3. How can an investigation model promote or obstruct an IHE in achieving its goals to comprehensively prevent campus gender-based violence, including primary, secondary, and/or tertiary forms of gender-based violence prevention? Which model do you think best accomplishes the goal of comprehensive prevention? Why?

Notes

1 Note that, as of this writing, the U.S. Department of Education (ED) has issued a Notice of Proposed Rulemaking that attempts to change the regulations under which it enforces Title IX in a way that will depart drastically from how the U.S. Department of Education has enforced Title IX since the first regulations were passed in 1975. Based on the public comments regarding Title IX and sexual harassment in a previous call for public comments, in which 99% of the commenters expressed support for past Title IX enforcement and urged the U.S. Department of Education not to change the regulations (Buffkin, Cantalupo, Cool, & Orlando, 2018), this attempt is likely to face significant enough challenges that whether the proposed rules will ultimately be passed into law and survive any subsequent legal challenge is uncertain. For these reasons, this chapter discusses Title

IX's requirements based on ED's traditional enforcement of Title IX, not the proposals of the current administration.

2 As already indicated, it is important to recognize that even law enforcement is not limited to a finite number of investigative methods. Although traditional police investigations of reported sexual violence tend to use a limited number of methods, police departments are increasingly adopting approaches that are broader in scope. For instance, the You Have Options Program that has been adopted by police departments in Oregon, Colorado, Washington and Virginia (Lill, 2016) offers victims three options for how to report a sexual assault to police: an "Information Only report, a Partial Investigation, and a Complete Investigation" (You Have Options Program, n.d.).

3 This chapter uses the term "gender-based violence" as an umbrella term that refers to violence directed at cisgender women or gender minorities, including cisgender men and boys who are targeted because they are perceived as insufficiently masculine, as well as transgender and gender non-conforming persons. It includes conduct often referred to using more specific terms from the federal statutes, including "sexual harassment," a term used in connection with conduct prohibited by anti-sex discrimination laws such as Title VII and Title IX, and including conduct that also fits the Clery/VAWA terms "sexual assault," "domestic violence," "dating violence," and "stalking." Of the terms listed here, only "sexual misconduct" is not a legal/statutory term, even though it has been used by the U.S. Department of Education during the Trump administration. It is unclear whether this usage was deliberate or the result of imprecision by the drafters.

4 Note the usage of terms like "victim": When discussing other authors' research, I try to use the same terms they use for the subjects of their research. In other cases, I generally use "victim" and "survivor" interchangeably to refer to those who have reported or disclosed in some way that they have experienced gender-based violence. In the context of claims, complaints, and lawsuits involving accusations against a specific person for harassment/violence, I use "accuser," "complainant," or "plaintiff" to refer to victims or survivors and "respondent" to refer to the person accused of harassment/violence. I also use "named," "accused," "alleged," or "reported," either as an adjective or a noun, to designate someone who has been accused of harassing or victimizing someone else. I do not use "defendant" at any point because this chapter does not discuss the criminal process, so there are no defendants in these cases. I have selected all of these terms self-consciously with a goal of capturing and respecting, admittedly imperfectly, the self-identification of the people to whom these terms refer. Therefore, I use "named," "accused" and "victims"/"survivors"/"accusers" regardless of whether a neutral factfinder has found an accused individual responsible for harassing or victimizing someone. I do so because, based on my 20-plus years of working on gender-based violence in education as a student activist, university administrator, attorney, researcher, and scholar, I have observed that those who report or disclose in some way that they have experienced sexual harassment self-identify as victims, survivors, accusers, complainants, and plaintiffs at different points in time and in different contexts, but these self-identities almost never have anything to do with the judgment of a neutral factfinder. Likewise, those who have been accused of harassing or victimizing someone else generally refer to themselves as "accused" or use similar terms even when they have been found responsible for such conduct by a neutral factfinder.

5 Such criminalized hearings are incompatible with Title IX's civil rights approach to preventing sexual harassment and gender-based violence and put IHEs that adopt such procedures at risk of inadvertently violating Title IX (Cantalupo, 2012, 2016).

6 Note that this additional layer of safeguards is not present in any of the other models. The Investigative Model has no built-in check on bad investigators (beyond the standard check of firing investigators who do a bad job), and the Hearing Model has neither investigators nor any check on potential bias or incompetence of the hearing panel members. The IH Hybrid does not have the hearing panel review the investigator's work; the panel only considers the investigator's work/report as one piece of evidence. The hearing panel can

discount or reject the investigator's report if they think it has problems, but that is not the only reason why they might reject the report (e.g., they might reject the report because the report was *not* biased but the hearing panel *is*), and there is nothing in the IH Hybrid that gives the IHE a specific process by which to evaluate the investigator.

7 "Accurate" and "accuracy" as used here refer to the technicalities of accessing, collecting, preserving, and assessing evidence that is most relevant and probative to the matter in controversy, not to standards of review (e.g. the "preponderance of the evidence" or "clear and convincing evidence" standards). Although certain standards of review are often assumed to be more accurate than others, each standard of review actually chooses the type of *in*accuracy it will risk, in light of other values (Cantalupo, 2019, p. 332).

References

Behre, K. A. (2016). Ensuring choice and voice for campus sexual assault victims: A call for victims' attorneys. *Drake Law Review, 65*, 293–363.

Buffkin, T., Cantalupo, N. C., Cool, M., & Orlando, A. (2018). Widely welcomed and supported by the public: A report on the Title IX-related comments in the U.S. Department of Education's Executive Order 13777 Comment Call. *California Law Review Online, 9*, 71–103. Retrieved from https://papers.ssrn.com/sol3/papers.cfm?abstract_id=3255205

Cantalupo, N. C. (2009). Campus violence: Understanding the extraordinary through the ordinary. *Journal of College and University Law, 35*, 613–690.

Cantalupo, N. C. (2012). "Decriminalizing" campus institutional responses to peer sexual violence. *Journal of College and University Law, 38*, 483–527.

Cantalupo, N. C. (2015). Five things student affairs professionals should know about campus gender-based violence. *NASPA Research and Policy Institute*. Retrieved from https://www.naspa.org/images/uploads/main/5Things_Gender_Based_Violence.pdf

Cantalupo, N. C. (2016). For the Title IX civil rights movement: Congratulations and cautions. *Yale Law Journal Forum, 125*, 281–303.

Cantalupo, N. C. (2019). Dog whistles and beachheads: The Trump administration, sexual violence, and student discipline in education. *Wake Forest Law Review, 54*, 303–362.

Centers for Disease Control and Prevention. (2004). *Sexual violence prevention: Beginning the dialogue*. Atlanta, GA: Author. Retrieved from https://www.cdc.gov/violenceprevention/pdf/svprevention-a.pdf

Coker, D. (2017). Crime, logic, campus sexual assault, and restorative justice. *Texas Tech Law Review, 49*, 147–210.

Davis v. Monroe County Board of Education, 526 U.S. 629 (1999)

Goss v. Lopez, 419 U.S. 565 (1975)

Legal Information Institute. (2014). 34 CFR § 668.46 - Institutional security policies and crime statistics. Retrieved from https://www.law.cornell.edu/cfr/text/34/668.46

Lill, A. (2016). Oregon detective pioneers new sexual assault reporting program. *NPR*. Retrieved from https://www.npr.org/2016/09/22/491932615/oregon-detective-pioneers-new-sexual-assault-reporting-program

Lonsway, K. A., & Archambault, S. J. (2008). Incomplete, inconsistent, and untrue statements made by victims: Understanding the causes and overcoming the challenges. *End Violence Against Women International*. Retrieved from http://www.evawintl.org/Library/DocumentLibraryHandler.ashx?id=630

Office for Civil Rights. (2001). *Revised sexual harassment guidance: Harassment of students by school employees, other students, or third parties*. Retrieved from https://www2.ed.gov/about/offices/list/ocr/docs/shguide.html

Smith, G. M., & Gomez, L. M. (2016). The regional center for investigation and adjudication: A proposed solution to the challenges of Title IX investigations in higher education. *Dispute Resolution Magazine,* 27–33. Retrieved from https://www.americanbar.org/content/dam/aba/publications/dispute_resolution_magazine/spring2016/7_RCIA.authcheckdam.pdf

The White House. (2014, April 20). Vice President Biden speaks on preventing campus sexual assault [Video file]. Retrieved from https://www.youtube.com/watch?v=m6-Fz_VO_Ss

U.S. Department of Education. (2018). *Negotiated rulemaking 2013-2014 Violence Against Women Act (VAWA).* Retrieved from https://www2.ed.gov/policy/highered/reg/hearulemaking/2012/vawa.html

Vendituoli, M. (2014, June 20). Colleges face new requirements in proposed rules on campus sexual assault. *Chronicle of Higher Education.* Retrieved from https://www.chronicle.com/article/Colleges-Face-New-Requirements/147275

Violence Against Women Act, 34 CFR 668 (2014). Retrieved from https://www.gpo.gov/fdsys/pkg/FR-2014-10-20/pdf/2014-24284.pdf

Weiner, M. H. (2017). Legal counsel for survivors of campus sexual violence. *Yale Journal of Law and Feminism, 29,* 123–206.

Whittenbury, B. K. (2013). *Investigating the workplace harassment claim.* Chicago, IL: American Bar Association.

You Have Options Program. (n.d.). Sexual assault reporting. Retrieved from https://www.reportingoptions.org/

IV Disciplinary Hearings for Sexual Misconduct

CHAPTER SIX

The Role of Attorneys in Campus Adjudications Involving Sexual Misconduct

Kelly Alison Behre

Attorneys are now a common fixture in many campus disciplinary proceedings. What was once a relatively informal legal system is becoming increasingly technical, adversarial, and litigious. This chapter will introduce students' legal rights to counsel in campus disciplinary proceedings and discuss some of the different roles attorneys play in campus disciplinary cases involving sexual misconduct violations.[1]

There are several confusing issues underpinning the debate about the role of attorneys in campus adjudications involving sexual misconduct. First, people often automatically associate sexual assault with the criminal justice system. They may picture a courthouse scene from shows like *Law and Order: SVU*, where a prosecutor presents a case before a judge or jury and a criminal defense attorney represents a criminal defendant by questioning and cross-examining witnesses, presenting evidence, and offering opening and closing arguments. Criminal defendants facing potential jail time have a constitutional right to counsel, because the government is seeking to deprive them of their right to liberty through incarceration. Campus adjudications are different: They are administrative proceedings that create a different set of rights, because expulsion from a university, rather than incarceration, is the most severe sanction available. Second, the short explanation of the role of attorneys in campus adjudications—both in cases involving sexual misconduct and in cases involving other forms of campus misconduct—is that "it depends." It depends on the location of the university, the type of university, and the internal policies created by the university. Moreover, students' right to counsel and the role of counsel in campus misconduct cases are not static.

They shift with new federal and state legislation, modifications to federal administrative guidance, recent decisions by federal and state judges, and revisions to individual school policies.

Legal Rights in Campus Disciplinary Proceedings

Universities enjoy a lot of flexibility in the behavior they prohibit through their student conduct codes and the process they use to determine responsibility for student conduct code violations. Different universities prohibit different kinds of behavior, including criminal behavior (e.g., theft, assault, sexual assault, vandalism, illicit drug use, underage drinking), academic behavior (e.g., cheating, plagiarism), and honor-based or community violations (e.g., lying to administrators, disrupting class, curfew violations, premarital sex, legal alcohol consumption). Students' rights in campus adjudications differ depending on the type of school they attend. Students attending public universities are entitled to **notice and opportunity to be heard** (to tell their side of the story) before their school expels them (*Dixon v. Alabama State Board of Education*, 1961). Some federal courts have further held that students facing long suspensions or expulsion from public universities have the right to counsel, but not necessarily **active participation by counsel** in a disciplinary hearing (*Gorman v. University of Rhode Island*, 1988). Students attending private universities have fewer rights under federal law, but courts have held that private universities disciplining students must act in good faith and follow their own written procedures (which sometimes include a right to an attorney at varying levels of participation).

A few states currently have their own laws granting students attending their public universities the **right to retained counsel**. For example, the West Virginia Supreme Court of Appeals established a right for student respondents to have retained counsel at West Virginia public university disciplinary hearings (*North v. West Virginia Board of Regents*, 1977). In North Carolina, students responding to non-academic violations at public universities have the right to have an attorney actively participate in all campus disciplinary procedures at their own expense (NC.G.S. §116-40.11, 2013). In Arkansas, both students disciplined by a public university with a suspension longer than 10 days and the students who filed the complaints resulting in that discipline have the right to hire (at their own expense) an attorney to fully participate in appeals processes (Ark. §6-60-109, 2015). In North Dakota, both students responding to violations that could result in a suspension or expulsion and student complainants reporting those violations have the right to be represented by an attorney (N.D.C.C. § 15-10-56, 2015).

Although all students may hire and consult an attorney about campus disciplinary issues (assuming they can afford to do so), students do not have a constitutional right to active representation by an attorney during a campus investigation or adjudication hearing. In most states, universities may bar students from bringing their attorney with them to interviews or hearings for most types of student misconduct. In almost all states, schools may limit students' attorneys to serving in an **advisor** role, which usually means allowing an attorney to sit next to the student client and quietly provide advice during campus proceedings while prohibiting an attorney from speaking or conducting direct and cross-examinations during hearings. The law provides minimum requirements for schools to protect student rights; however, individual universities have discretion to expand those rights by allowing attorneys to fully participate in each stage of a campus adjudication or even providing attorneys to students free of charge.

Rights Specific to Campus Sexual Misconduct Cases

Both complainants and respondents in campus sexual misconduct cases currently have a federal right to counsel that does not apply to students in any other type of campus discipline case. Title IX of the Education Amendments Act of 1972 prohibits universities from engaging in sex discrimination. The U.S. Department of Education issued guidance clarifying that under Title IX universities are obligated to respond to reports of sexual harassment, including sexual violence, by taking immediate and appropriate steps to determine what occurred, take steps reasonably calculated to end the harassment, and remedy the effects of harassment on the victim (Office for Civil Rights, 1997). The Campus Sexual Assault Victims' Bill of Rights of 1992 instructed universities to provide the same opportunities to students reporting campus sexual assault as they do to respondents by allowing complainants to have others present during any institutional disciplinary proceeding. The category of students included in this equitable right was expanded to include victims of domestic violence, dating violence, and stalking through the Campus Sexual Violence Elimination (SaVE) Act, which amended the Jeanne Clery Act through the Violence Against Women Reauthorization Act of 2013. The regulations interpreting the Clery Act instruct schools not to limit the choice of advisor for either party (34 CFR §668.46(k)(2)(iv)).

Title IX and the Clery Act apply to all universities receiving federal financial aid, including private universities. Therefore, even if students would not otherwise have the right to counsel in their campus disciplinary process involving non-sexual misconduct violations, both complainants and respondents have the right to bring attorneys with them to all meetings and hearings involving sexual misconduct violations. Federal law does not currently require schools to allow attorneys to actively participate in investigation interviews and hearings, but instead requires schools to allow attorneys to accompany and advise their student clients during campus sexual misconduct and dating violence adjudication proceedings.

Role of Respondents' and Complainants' Attorneys in Campus Investigations and Adjudications

The challenge in discussing the role of attorneys in campus disciplinary adjudications is the wide array of processes used by different schools in their student discipline cases and the varying roles attorneys play in those processes. Although respondents remain much more likely than complainants to engage independent legal representation, the roles of attorneys representing respondents and complainants in campus disciplinary proceedings involving sexual misconduct are similar. In universities using a civil hearing model that allows attorneys to participate in a traditional representation role, attorneys will often provide opening and closing arguments and conduct direct and cross-examinations. In universities using a hearing model that limits attorneys to the role of advisor, attorneys may assist student clients with drafting questions for witnesses and preparing evidence. In universities using an investigation model, attorneys might help student clients suggest helpful witnesses for the investigators to interview and assist student clients in reviewing investigation reports.[2] In schools that utilize an appellate process, attorneys might assist with written appeals or provide representation in appellate hearings. The following is a non-comprehensive list of the roles attorneys for respondents and complainants may play in campus sexual misconduct adjudications along with a few illustrative examples.

Pre-Report Consultation

Attorneys for victims of campus sexual misconduct may provide students with information about their various reporting options by describing the process, helping them assess legal needs, discussing available confidential and non-confidential resources, and safety planning, particularly in cases involving intimate partner violence.

Example

A student seeks an attorney's advice about a sexual assault. He discloses that an acquaintance raped him after a party a few months ago. He tells the attorney that his assailant is now enrolled in two of the same classes as him and that he has stopped attending those classes because he experiences so much anxiety about the possibility of seeing the assailant there. He worries that if his grades drop, he will lose his scholarship. He also describes to the attorney his fear that if he reports the sexual assault to the school or reaches out for supportive services, his assailant will follow through with threats to contact his parents and pastor to tell them he is gay. His attorney brainstorms with him about his legal options, including the potential ramifications of each reporting option, and safety plans with him about non-legal options and community resources.

Legal Screening

Attorneys for both respondents and complainants may provide legal screenings for their student clients. Complainants' attorneys may screen clients to identify legal needs related to the sexual assault, including civil protection orders, housing issues, employment issues, education and loan issues, family law issues, criminal issues, privacy issues, and campus interim measures, such as changes to campus housing, class schedules, and no contact directives. Respondents' attorneys may provide legal advice about how related criminal and civil restraining order cases could impact campus disciplinary processes and vice versa.

Example

A student discloses to an attorney that her ex-boyfriend sexually assaulted her several times during the past year and engaged in other controlling behaviors and stalking. She reported the assaults to her college, which issued a mutual no-contact directive and opened an investigation. Last week, the student and her roommate returned to their off-campus apartment late at night to find her ex-boyfriend sitting in their living room. The student's roommate called the police, and they are currently investigating. She and her roommate want to break their lease to move somewhere where they feel safe. The student also reports that she has seen her ex-boyfriend standing in the parking lot outside the restaurant where she works off campus. She stopped going to work and fears she will lose her job. She is also losing sleep and tells the attorney she has missed several class assignments. Her attorney discusses her options under the ongoing campus and criminal investigations, including available campus interim measures and retaliation, and brainstorms about any potential civil options under applicable restraining order laws.

Example

An attorney represents a student who tells the attorney that his ex-girlfriend falsely accused him of sexual assault. He explains that the school issued a mutual no-contact directive before the investigation was even completed and that he was asked to withdraw from one of his classes in which she is also enrolled. He has an interview scheduled with the university investigator next week. He also tells the attorney that after his school issued a no-contact directive, he tried to contact his ex-girlfriend's roommate to pick up some personal items at their apartment. When she never responded, he let himself into their apartment when he thought they were at a concert. He tells the attorney that he left as soon as they got home, but a police officer left him a phone message this week to discuss the incident. He also tells the attorney that one of his ex-girlfriend's co-workers screamed at him in the parking lot near her work when he was walking to his car from another store, accusing him of stalking his ex-girlfriend. His attorney advises him of his rights under the campus and criminal investigations and tries to determine the current status of those investigations.

Investigation

Regardless of the type of adjudication model used by the university, attorneys for both complainants and respondents can assist their student clients during the investigation phase. They may help students identify potential witnesses who might have information about the alleged misconduct; related issues, such as incapacity or alibis; or prior disclosures or confessions. They can also assist in finding evidence that might have some value to the investigator or adjudicator, such as texts, social media posts, photographs, videos, or medical records. In some cases, attorneys may advocate for the inclusion or exclusion of certain types of evidence in an investigative report or hearing.

Example

A student tells an attorney that a classmate accused him of sexual assault. He believes the complainant's texts to her friends will reveal contradictions in her report to the school that she was too incapacitated to consent to sex. The school investigator provides the attorney with a copy of a few texts the complainant sent shortly before and after the alleged assault, but the attorney wants to review more of the complainant's texts to adequately defend the client. The investigator also sent the attorney a redacted copy of a report from a sexual assault forensic examination completed 2 days after the alleged assault. The respondent believes that some of the information redacted from the report could help his case. The attorney contacts the school and requests the complete record of the complainant's texts from the past month and an unredacted copy of the forensic examination report.

Example

A student tells her attorney that she disclosed that another student raped her to her dormitory resident advisor last week, who then reported to the school's Title IX coordinator. Upon request, this student met with the Title IX investigator and provided copies of text messages she sent and received from the respondent the day after the assault, along with text messages to her sister about the assault 3 days later. Upon request, she also provided a redacted copy of her medical records from the sexual assault forensic exam. The Title IX coordinator contacted the student today to request that she bring her cell phone to the campus police so that they can download every text and image she sent or received in the past month in order to determine which information to share with the respondent's attorney before the hearing. She is angry that her school would consider sharing her personal texts or photos with the student who raped her. She tells her attorney that the Title IX coordinator also requested an unredacted copy of her medical records so that she could decide whether to share the entire record with the respondent's attorney before the hearing. The student explains that she is particularly upset by the invasion of her privacy and worries that the respondent's attorney might try to use her history of anxiety and current medications she had to disclose to the hospital against her in the hearing. The attorney discusses the student's options with her regarding the school's requests.

Reviewing Investigation Reports

Attorneys representing students at universities that utilize a single investigator model or a hybrid investigator hearing model may assist their student clients in reviewing investigation reports. They may help student clients identify factual errors, missing evidence, faulty assumptions, or unsupported findings of facts or conclusions.

Example

A complainant's attorney reviews a lengthy investigation report with her client. The attorney realizes that the investigator never interviewed two of the witnesses the complainant suggested could corroborate her disclosures about the respondent's sexual misconduct. The attorney also realizes that the timeline contained in the summary section is incorrect. The attorney helps the client file a written response pointing out the inaccuracies.

Example

A student brings his attorney a copy of an investigation report with proposed findings of facts indicating that he violated the campus conduct code by committing acts of sexual misconduct by sharing a video without the consent of the woman engaging in sexual acts with him in the video. After reviewing the report, the attorney notices that the investigator never asked the client's roommate about whether it was common for the client to leave his unlocked cell phone all over campus, even though the client claimed that he often lost his phone and that someone else must have sent the video from his phone. The attorney further notes that the investigation report is missing any indication that any of the witnesses actually viewed the video. The attorney helps the respondent create a list of follow-up questions for the witnesses.

Hearings

Universities that use a hearing model or hybrid investigator hearing model for violations of their student conduct code involving sexual misconduct employ a variety of hearing procedures and rules about attorney participation. Regardless of the type of hearing, respondents' and complainants' attorneys can help their student clients prepare. At universities that limit attorneys' roles to that of advisors, attorneys may help clients prepare an opening and closing statement, draft written questions for the witnesses, prepare evidence, and prepare an impact statement. Attorneys serving in an advisor role can consult with their student clients throughout the hearing by advising them about whether to answer questions or provide rebuttal testimony, helping them develop new questions for witnesses and present evidence, walking them through formal or informal objections, and aiding them in the development of arguments or responses to arguments. At universities where attorneys can actively participate, they can conduct direct and cross-examinations and make opening and closing arguments.

Example

An attorney represents a respondent at a school using a hybrid investigation hearing model. After reviewing the investigation report, the attorney drafts questions for the hearing officer to ask the complainant, respondent's witness, and the investigator during the upcoming hearing and helps the client draft an opening statement and an impact statement. During the hearing, the attorney sits with his client and passes him notes before he answers questions to ensure that he does not contradict any of his earlier statements.

Example

An attorney represents a complainant at a school with a hearing model. The attorney helps the client create a witness and evidence list. The attorney provides an opening statement to the hearing panel and conducts direct and cross-examination of the witnesses. The attorney argues irrelevance when the respondent's attorney tries to question the client about the client's sexual history with other students. The attorney provides a closing statement arguing that a preponderance of the evidence shows the respondent sexually assaulted the client.

Internal Appeals

Many universities offer some kind of appellate process to both complainants and respondents. The process varies from schools allowing an automatic or *de novo* appeal (allowing a do-over of the previous investigation or hearing) to schools limiting appeals to specific grounds, such as the discovery of relevant evidence not previously available, an unreasonable decision based on the investigation or hearing record, or disproportionate sanctions. Attorneys for respondents and complainants may play an essential role in assisting their student clients in identifying grounds for an appeal, drafting a written appeal, and responding to an appeal submitted by the other party.

Example

An attorney represented a complainant in a campus sexual misconduct case at a school using a single investigator model. The investigator concluded that the respondent did not violate the student conduct code. The attorney reviews the report and believes it misstates the college's definition of sexual assault and incorrectly identifies the complainant's consent to kiss the respondent at a party as affirmative consent to engage in sexual intercourse in the respondent's car a few hours later. The attorney submits an appeal requesting a school hearing by arguing that the investigator's findings were unreasonable based on the written record.

Example

An attorney represented a respondent at a student misconduct hearing in which the attorney fully participated by conducting questioning of the respondent and his witnesses, cross-examining the complainant and her witnesses, and providing a closing argument. The hearing panel found the respondent responsible for violating the student conduct code by engaging in nonconsensual sexual touching of the complainant and sanctioned the respondent with a one-semester suspension. The respondent has never been in trouble before, and he is concerned that his graduate school fellowship offer might be withdrawn if he does not obtain his degree on time. The attorney submits a written appeal arguing that the sanction is disproportionate to the finding.

Post-Appeal Representation

Although not part of the campus disciplinary process, attorneys often assist student clients with post-appeal civil litigation or complaints. Attorneys for complainants may help clients file lawsuits against schools or submit complaints to the U.S.

Department of Education's Office for Civil Rights. Attorneys for respondents may help clients file lawsuits against schools, including requests for emergency stays of sanctions. Both parties may also file lawsuits against one another.

Example

An attorney represented a respondent through an initial investigation and hearing in an advisor role. The hearing panel found the respondent responsible for violating the school conduct code for sexual misconduct and sanctions him with a 2-year suspension. Upon reviewing the decision, the attorney discovers that the panel relied on notes from several witness interviews conducted by one of the panel members that were never made available to the respondent. The attorney submits an internal appeal, but the administrator tasked with considering appeals denies review. The attorney files a writ of administrative mandate with the state court arguing that the school failed to provide the respondent with a fair hearing because it did not follow its own disciplinary procedures requiring the panel to inform the parties about all relevant witness information and it included the investigator on the hearing panel.

Example

After a football player raped her outside of a school party, a student disclosed the assault to her friends, contacted the police, and submitted to an evidentiary exam at a local hospital. Her parents requested counseling services and academic accommodations to help her with the resulting trauma, but the school failed to provide her with any support. The parents reported the rape to the football coach, but he stopped returning their calls. The student felt fearful that she might run into the football player on campus. Her grades dropped, causing her to lose her academic scholarship and eventually withdraw from school. The student later learned that at least one other student previously reported the football player for rape but that the school's administrator in charge of school discipline claimed that there was nothing the school could do. The student hires an attorney who files a federal lawsuit against the university for sex discrimination under Title IX for its deliberate indifference to reports of the football player's sexual assaults and failure to provide the reporting student with adequate resources.

Debates About the Role of Attorneys Representing Complainants and Respondents in Campus Sexual Misconduct Adjudications

The increased national attention to campus sexual assault—first created by student survivors demanding increased federal enforcement of Title IX and then by accused and disciplined student advocates demanding increased due process rights for respondents—created a renewed debate about the role of counsel in campus disciplinary proceedings (Behre, 2019). The debate about the appropriate role of attorneys in campus adjudications involving sexual misconduct is informed by how one identifies the goals and values of campus administrative proceedings and the protections that respondents and complainants need to ensure fairness.

Universities generally view campus misconduct processes as an educational, rather than an adversarial or punitive, process intended to teach students how to take responsibility for their actions and learn from them. They value their ability to draft student conduct codes and procedures to enforce those codes that reflect the values of their individual educational communities. Some universities worry that increased participation by attorneys in the adjudication process will limit the educational and developmental goals of the process, because respondent attorneys may advise their clients against speaking directly to the hearing officer or panel and taking responsibility for their actions. Schools also express concern that increased participation by attorneys may impede their ability to reach an accurate outcome in campus investigations and adjudications, because attorneys acting on their ethical obligation of zealous advocacy and loyalty to clients may use technical loopholes or aggressive posturing to convince a school to dismiss a complaint against a student who violated a school code (American Council on Education, 2019; Association of Title IX Administrators, 2018; King & White, n.d.).

Schools express concern that increased participation by respondents' attorneys could cause an unequal campus response to student code violations based on the students' ability to afford private counsel. They also contend that increased participation by attorneys in campus disciplinary proceedings will create a new financial burden on schools forced to hire additional staff and attorneys to regulate an adversarial legal system (American Council on Education, 2019). Although individual universities may concede that they have not always responded appropriately to campus sexual assault reports or conducted their disciplinary process in a fair manner, most want to maintain autonomy and flexibility in determining the best system for their educational community with limited interference from courts and politicians.

Proponents for increased due process rights for respondents argue that students facing campus sexual misconduct violations need more robust legal protection, including attorney representation in live hearings that resemble criminal and civil legal models (Bartholet et al., 2014; Bartholet, Gertner, Halley, & Gersen 2017; Rudovsky et al., 2015; Shibley, 2016). They point to cases where universities violated respondent students' basic procedural rights in support of their argument that respondents need increased legal representation to protect them from inept or biased school administrators, particularly during a time when universities face more scrutiny from the federal government or the public for responses to campus sexual assault (Safko, 2016). Those in favor of requiring all universities to allow students' attorneys to fully participate in hearings argue that this requirement could reduce appeals and civil lawsuits and improve fairness for all parties.

Disciplined and accused student advocates suggest that even though campus sexual misconduct adjudications do not result in incarceration, university expulsions and suspensions can seriously impact a student's future. They point to affirmative consent definitions of sexual misconduct found in many student conduct codes coupled with use of the preponderance of the evidence burden of proof evidentiary standard to suggest that students responding to campus sexual misconduct especially need legal representation because they have fewer legal protections than they would in a criminal case. Some reference the racism of our criminal legal system and the school-to-prison pipeline to express concern that campus sexual assault adjudications may also disproportionately harm respondents of color (Gersen & Suk, 2016; Halley, 2015; Trachtenberg, 2017). Others suggest that the criminal law system is better suited to respond to campus sexual assaults.

Survivors and victim advocates suggest that a civil rights framework, rather than the criminal justice system, is the appropriate lens with which to view campus sexual assault. Title IX scholars remind us that schools have a legal obligation to prevent sexual violence on campus. High rates of campus sexual assault combined with low reporting rates perpetuate the cycle of sexual violence on campuses, because assailants know they will not be held accountable and victims fear they will not be believed or that their reports will be met with hostility (Cantalupo, 2012). In order to break this cycle, schools must design a system that encourages more victims to report and provides them with appropriate resources to maintain their access to education (Behre, 2016; Cantalupo, 2012). Schools that instead adopt adversarial hearing models that resemble criminal hearings risk increasing the trauma for victims of sexual violence (Campbell, 2008), because the role of attorneys hired to represent respondents in campus adjudications is to convince the hearing officer or panel that their client is not responsible for the violation, a goal often accomplished by attacking the credibility or character of the complainant. Victim advocates suggest that when schools adopt "criminal" investigation and adjudication models that exacerbate victim trauma, they likely decrease victim reporting rates and the school's ability to respond to sexual violence and protect students on its campus.

Title IX scholars generally agree that schools must create procedures that are fair to both complainants and respondents (Brodsky, 2017; Buzuvis, 2017), but they raise the question as to why due process advocates are so focused on sexual assault cases rather than general procedural rights for students facing other forms of serious campus discipline (Anderson, 2016; Behre, 2019; Brake, 2017). Title IX advocates suggest that the call for extraordinary protections for the relatively small proportion of campus respondents facing sexual misconduct violations resembles the history of criminal law's explicit credibility discounting of women who reported sexual assault and signals skepticism of sexual assault complainants (Anderson, 2004, 2016; Brake, 2017; Tuerkheimer, 2017). They share a concern about the impact of racism on school discipline but point out that female students of color and LGBT students are more likely to experience sexual assault, less likely to report, and less likely to be believed by schools (Johnson, 2017). They also express concern that when attorneys participate in campus adjudicatory hearings, student respondents are more likely than student complainants to have legal representation, creating an inequitable system for victims (Behre, 2016; Weiner, 2017). The debate about how to best investigate and adjudicate campus sexual assault persists in federal agencies and state legislatures and on individual campuses.

Other Roles for Attorneys in Campus Investigations and Adjudications

Universities are increasingly using attorneys in roles other than representation of student complainants and respondents. Universities hire attorneys as investigators or contract with attorneys or law firms to act in an investigatory role. Attorneys may serve in a prosecutorial-type role in campus hearings by representing the university's interests. Universities frequently hire attorneys or judges to act as hearing officers for initial hearings or appellate hearings. Attorneys may fill roles as Title IX coordinators, compliance officers, or legal advisors to assist universities with procedural questions during campus disciplinary investigations and hearings. Universities also hire attorneys to conduct audits of their sexual misconduct disciplinary procedures or to represent them in litigation filed by students. Universities are increasingly utilizing attorneys in more roles in order to ensure compliance with the patchwork of laws and policies governing campus adjudications and to better inoculate themselves or defend against lawsuits by both respondents and complainants.

KEY TERMS

Active participation by counsel: "Active participation" generally refers to an attorney's ability to engage in traditional representation activities during a hearing, such as direct and cross-examination of witnesses, submission of evidence, and legal argument.

Advisor: An attorney acting in an advisory role may be prohibited from speaking during a campus hearing or interview.

Notice and opportunity to be heard: A form of procedural due process that references a respondent's right to receive notification about the allegations made against them and the student's opportunity to tell their side of the story. Specific requirements vary under the law.

Right to retained counsel: A legal right to hire and obtain legal advice from a lawyer a party hires at their own cost.

DISCUSSION QUESTIONS

1. What role, if any, do attorneys play in your school's student conduct process? Does that role change in cases involving sexual misconduct?
2. If you could create your school's procedures for investigating and adjudicating student conduct cases involving sexual misconduct, would you include attorneys? If so, in what roles? What, if any, limitations would you place on their participation?

Notes

1 The rights of faculty and staff accused of sexual misconduct against students generally fall under employment law and are therefore not discussed in this chapter.

2 On November 29, 2018, the U.S. Department of Education proposed a new regulation to Title IX that would require universities to provide student respondents in campus sexual misconduct violations with a live hearing and the right to cross-examination conducted by retained counsel. The notice and comment period ended on February 15, 2019. If the new rule is adopted, then all schools would move to a live hearing model (U.S. Dept. of Education, 2018).

References

American Council on Education. (2019, January 30). Comments in response to the Department of Education's November 29, 2018, notice of proposed rulemaking amending regulations implementing Title IX of the Education Amendments of 1972, Docket ID ED-2018-OCR-0064. Retrieved from https://www.acenet.edu/news-room/Documents/Comments-to-Education-Department-on-Proposed-Rule-Amending-Title-IX-Regulations.pdf

Anderson, M. J. (2004). The legacy of the prompt complaint requirement, corroboration requirement, and cautionary instructions on campus sexual assault. *Boston University Law Review, 84*(4), 945–1022.

Anderson, M. J. (2016). Campus sexual assault adjudication and resistance to reform. *Yale Law Journal, 125,* 1940–2005.

Ark. Code § 6-60-109 (2015)

Association of Title IX Administrators. (2018, October 5). ATIXA position statement on cross-examining the urge to transform college conduct proceedings into courtrooms. Retrieved from https://cdn.atixa.org/website-media/o_atixa/wp-content/uploads/2015/03/18120439/ATIXA-Position-Statement_Cross-Examination-final.pdf

Bartholet, E., Brewer, S., Dershowitz, A., Desan, C., Donahue, C., Elhauge, E., … & Wilkins, D. (2014, October 15). Opinion: Rethink Harvard's sexual harassment policy. *Boston Globe.* Retrieved from https://www.bostonglobe.com/opinion/2014/10/14/rethink-harvard-sexual-harassment-policy/HFDDiZN7nU2UwuUuWMnqbM/story.html

Bartholet, E., Gertner, N., Halley, J., & Gersen, J. S. (2017, August 21). Fairness to all students under Title IX. Retrieved from http://nrs.harvard.edu/urn-3:HUL.InstRepos:33789434

Behre, K. A. (2016). Ensuring choice and voice for campus sexual assault victims: A call for victims' attorneys. *Drake Law Review, 65*(2), 293–362.

Behre, K. A. (2019). Deconstructing the disciplined student narrative and its impact on campus sexual assault policy. *Arizona Law Review.* Retrieved from https://papers.ssrn.com/sol3/cf_dev/AbsByAuth.cfm?per_id=1734818

Brake, D. L. (2017). Fighting the rape culture wars through the preponderance of the evidence standard. *Montana Law Review, 78,* 109–153.

Brodsky, A. (2017). A rising tide: Learning about fair disciplinary process from Title IX. *Journal of Legal Education, 77*(4), 822–849.

Buzuvis, E. E. (2017). Title IX and procedural fairness: Why disciplined student litigation does not undermine the role of Title IX in campus sexual assault. *Montana Law Review, 78,* 71–108.

Campbell, R. (2008). The psychological impact of rape victims' experiences with the legal, medical, and mental health systems. *American Psychologist, 26*(3), 701–717.

Campus Sexual Assault Victims' Bill of Rights of 1992, 20 U.S.C. § 1092(f) (1992)

Campus Sexual Violence Elimination (SaVE) Act of 2013, 20 U.S.C. § 1092(f) (2013)

Cantalupo, N. C. (2012). "Decriminalizing" campus institutional responses to peer sexual violence. *Journal of College and University Law, 38,* 483–527.

Cantalupo, N. C. (2016). For the Title IX civil rights movement: Congratulations and cautions. *Yale Law Journal Forum, 125,* 281–304.

Dixon v. Alabama State Board of Education, 294 F.2d 150 (5th Cir. 1961)

Gersen, J., & Suk, J. (2016). The sex bureaucracy. *California Law Review, 104,* 881–948.

Gorman v. Univ. of Rhode Island, 837 F.2d 7 (1st Cir. 1988)

Halley, J. (2015). Trading the megaphone for the gavel in Title IX enforcement. *Harvard Law Review Forum, 128,* 103–117.

Jeanne Clery Disclosure of Campus Security Policy and Campus Crime Statistics Act, 20 U.S.C. § 1092(f) (1990)

Johnson, A. M. (2017). Title IX narrative, intersectionality, and male-biased conceptions of racism. *Georgetown Journal of Law & Modern Critical Race Perspectives, 9,* 57–75.

King, T. & White, B. (n.d.). An attorney's role in the conduct process. *Association for Student Conduct Administration.* Retrieved from https://www.theasca.org/files/Best%20Practices/Attorney%20role%20in%20conduct%20process%20%202.pdf

North v. West Va. Board of Regents, 160 W. Va. 710, 233 S.E.2d 411 (1977)

N.C. Gen. Stat. § 116-40.11 (2013)

N.D. Code § 15-10-56, (2015)

Rudovsky, D. Bibas, S., Balganesh, S., Berman, M., Burbank, S. B., Fisch, et al. (2015, February 18). *Open letter from members of the Penn Law School faculty: Sexual assault complaints: Protecting complainants and the accused students at universities.* Retrieved from http://online.wsj.com/public/resources/documents/2015_0218_upenn.pdf

Safko, E. D. (2016). Are campus sexual assault tribunals fair?: The need for judicial review and additional due process protections in light of new case law. *Fordham Law Review, 84*(5), 2289–2333.

Shibley, R. L. (2016) *Twisting Title IX.* New York, NY: Encounter Books.

Title IX of the Educational Amendments Act of 1972, 20 U.S.C. §1681 (1972)

Trachtenberg, B. (2017). How university Title IX enforcement and other discipline processes (probably) discriminate against minority students. *Nevada Law Review, 18,* 107–166.

Tuerkheimer, D. (2017). Incredible women: Sexual violence and the credibility discount. *University of Pennsylvania Law Review, 166*(1), 1–58.

U.S. Department of Education, Office for Civil Rights. (1997). *Sexual harassment guidance 1997.* Retrieved from https://www2.ed.gov/about/offices/list/ocr/docs/sexhar01.html

U.S. Department of Education, Office for Civil Rights. (2011, April 4). *Dear Colleague Letter.* Retrieved from http://www2.ed.gov/about/offices/list/ocr/letters/colleague-201104.pdf

U.S. Department of Education, Office for Civil Rights. (2018, November 29). *Nondiscrimination on the basis of sex in education programs or activities receiving federal financial assistance,* 34 Fed. Reg. § 106.45(b)(3)(vi)-(vii). Retrieved from https://www.govinfo.gov/content/pkg/FR-2018-11-29/pdf/2018-25314.pdf

Violence Against Women Reauthorization Act. (2013). Pub. L. No. 113–4, codified at 20 U.S.C. § 1092(f)

Weiner, M. H. (2017). Legal counsel for survivors of campus sexual violence, *Yale Journal of Law & Feminism, 29,* 123–206.

CHAPTER SEVEN

Standards of Proof for Campus Sexual Misconduct Cases

Deborah L. Brake

The stunning spectacle of the recent Supreme Court nomination hearings, in which Christine Blasey Ford appeared before the Senate Judiciary Committee on live television to air her allegations against Brett Kavanaugh, who, in turn, angrily denied the allegations and told a very different story, is the perfect foil for the ongoing controversy over the appropriate **standard of proof** for resolving contested accounts of an alleged sexual assault in a campus disciplinary process. Indeed, the Kavanaugh hearings unleashed a perfect storm in the ongoing culture wars over how to approach wildly conflicting accounts of an alleged sexual assault. Who is more believable? Who has more at stake? In the pitched battle that ensued, Judge Kavanaugh's supporters invoked a presumption of innocence, contending that in the face of conflicting accounts, corroborating evidence is needed to overcome the presumption in his favor. In contrast, those on the other side rejected a criminal law reference point, framing the matter as more akin to a job interview than a criminal trial. The debate was eerily reminiscent of the competing sides in the clash over what Title IX requires of an educational institution in adjudicating allegations against a student accused of sexual misconduct. Should a university demand a heightened level of certainty before finding a student responsible for sexual misconduct, such as a clear and convincing evidence standard would require? Or is it enough for the proof to convince the factfinder that it is more likely than not that sexual misconduct occurred, as is consistent with the **preponderance of the evidence standard** typically used in civil cases?

Introduction to Standards of Proof and the Controversy Over Which Standard to Apply in Campus Sexual Assault Proceedings

Any standard of proof will reflect baseline judgments about the likelihood of truth and the costs of an erroneous outcome. When the risk of error is roughly equivalent for both sides and when the stakes of getting it wrong are comparable, the standard of proof should not privilege one side over the other in determining the likelihood of the truth or calibrating the costs of an erroneous outcome. The preponderance standard aligns with this calibration of the likelihood of truth and the stakes for the persons involved because it makes the resolution of contested allegations turn on whether it is more likely than not that the alleged wrongdoing occurred.

It is only when these premises are rejected that the preponderance standard is viewed as insufficiently protective of persons accused of wrongdoing. In the criminal realm, for example, the costs of an erroneous outcome for the accused—a prison sentence—justify a much higher level of certainty, requiring the factfinder to be convinced **beyond a reasonable doubt** that the accused committed the crime in order to impose criminal penalties. Civil cases, by contrast, threaten no such loss of liberty. The stakes in civil cases can be quite high, including hefty financial losses, costs to reputation, and court-ordered injunctions to take, or refrain from taking, certain actions. Yet, in nearly all civil cases, including civil actions for sexual assault, courts apply the preponderance of the evidence standard. A higher **clear and convincing evidence standard** is used by courts in only a tiny sliver of civil cases in which the stakes for one side have been deemed unusually high, approximating the loss of liberty in the criminal realm. These cases include involuntary civil commitment for psychiatric reasons, termination of parental rights, involuntary deportation, and the withdrawal of life support for an unconscious, terminal patient (to prove that it conforms to the patient's expressed wishes) (Kidder, 2019). In all other civil cases, including civil cases alleging rape and sexual assault, the preponderance standard applies, in recognition of the important stakes for both parties. How campus disciplinary processes for adjudicating sexual misconduct fit into this schema is the subject of heated debate.

In the firestorm over Title IX's regulation of campus sexual assault, no issue has generated more controversy than the standard of proof colleges and universities should use to resolve student conduct violations involving sexual misconduct. During the Obama Administration, the Office for Civil Rights (OCR) of the U.S. Department of Education drew fierce criticism for endorsing the preponderance of the evidence standard in the agency's guidance documents (OCR, 2011, 2014), prompting charges that the preponderance standard failed to sufficiently protect the rights of the (mostly male) accused students and tilted the scales too far in favor of the (mostly female) students alleging sexual misconduct. Appropriating feminist claims to "take rape seriously," critics of the preponderance standard have argued that precisely because sexual assault is a serious crime, it should not be found to have occurred without a higher-than-ordinary level of evidentiary certainty (Brodsky, 2017). Those taking this view have argued that colleges and universities should evaluate allegations of sexual assault using a clear and convincing evidence standard. Their perspective situates sexual assault as first and foremost a crime of violence committed by one person against another. These critics have not gone so far as to advocate using the criminal law's beyond a reasonable doubt standard in university student conduct cases involving alleged sexual misconduct. But they have argued that campus disciplinary processes should require clear and convincing evidence before finding a student responsible for sexual assault.

A very different understanding of sexual assault has animated the social movement to respond to sexual violence on campus, a movement that sparked the momentum behind the Obama Administration's efforts to strengthen Title IX enforcement as it relates to sexual assault. Frustrated and angered by the mishandling of sexual assault on college campuses, survivors of sexual violence formed new advocacy groups, such as Know Your IX, End Rape on Campus, and SurvJustice, and told their stories—using their own names and voices—of sexual violation, trauma, and betrayal by the institutions they attended (Brake, 2017). Joining with women's groups and student activists, survivors pressed for recognition that sexual assault is a civil rights violation against women and gender minorities and a denial of gender equality in education. Seen through this lens, sexual assault, which has long been recognized in the law as a severe form of sexual harassment, denies its victims, who are mostly women and LGBT persons, agency over their bodies and their sexuality and visits physical, emotional, and educational harms on the persons subjected to it. Understanding sexual assault as a civil rights violation and a form of sex discrimination would support using the same standard of proof that is used in civil rights cases, the preponderance of the evidence standard.

The conflict over the proof standard, then, tracks deep divisions over whether sexual assault should be addressed through campus policies designed to protect students' rights to nondiscrimination and provide a campus safe from gender-based violence or whether the criminal justice system is the better analogue for handling such matters in campus justice systems. To be clear, leaving sexual assault entirely to the criminal justice system is out of the question under current federal law. Title IX, as construed by courts and OCR, requires schools to respond to all complaints of sexual harassment, including sexual assault by other students, with a prompt and equitable grievance procedure. In addition, the Campus SaVE amendments to the Violence Against Women Act require educational institutions to have and publicize procedures for handling such matters, including a standard of evidence for resolving disputed allegations. Nevertheless, the choice of reference points, foregrounding sexual assault as either a serious crime or as a civil rights matter, drives the controversy over the proof standard.

The failure of the criminal justice system to provide meaningful recourse to sexual assault victims should caution against using criminal law evidentiary standards as the benchmark for student conduct proceedings. Indeed, the inadequacy of the criminal justice system has been a driving force behind the movement for justice for survivors on campus. The criminal justice system has proven notoriously unresponsive to sexual assault victims, resulting in low rates of prosecution, even lower rates of conviction, and additional trauma for victims, all of which contribute to extraordinarily low rates of reporting to police. Even if the criminal justice system were reformed to better respond to rape and sexual assault, it is not designed to address the needs of survivors. Many survivors of sexual assault in the college setting do not want their assailants sent to prison, but seek some form of campus justice, and are often in need of services and accommodations in order to stay in classes and succeed in school. The criminal justice system reflects a different set of values than Title IX or campus justice systems, with criminal justice emphasizing punishment and deterrence, and campus processes foregrounding educational access, student welfare, and community norms.

As troubled as the criminal justice system has proven to be for sexual assault survivors in general, it is particularly fraught for women from non-privileged backgrounds or marginalized communities to turn to law enforcement. Women of color, in particular, may have strongly negative impressions of police and law enforcement based on their experiences or those of family members and friends. Women who have immigrated or who have close family members who are undocumented also may have reasons to fear interactions with police and law enforcement. And women who are first-generation college students may have a heightened need for resources and support to minimize the educational interruptions that the criminal justice system cannot address. For all women, the criminal justice system is hardly a model of justice for addressing the harmful effects of sexual assault to educational opportunity. Borrowing campus proof standards for their resemblance to criminal proof standards seems particularly ill-suited for the many women who reasonably fear the worst from the criminal justice system.

At its core, the controversy over where sexual assault fits as a matter of justice, and the proper procedures and proof burdens for handling it, reflects a struggle over the legitimacy of treating sexual assault as a civil rights violation and a matter of gender equality. This divide is at the heart of the debate over the proof standard. When the U.S. Department of Education's Office for Civil Rights issued its 2011 Dear Colleague Letter (DCL) on sexual violence, which included a directive to educational institutions to use the preponderance standard for resolving disputed sexual assault allegations, it vindicated the principle that students have a right, grounded in Title IX's guarantee of sex equality, to accountability and redress for sexual violence—and other forms of sexual harassment—in educational settings. Critics of the DCL's position have appealed to a different understanding, that sexual assault is not a matter of civil rights, but a crime committed by individuals who are entitled to a presumption of innocence that can be overcome only by exceptionally convincing evidence, such as a clear and convincing evidence standard would require. The difference in the framing explains why the debate over the proof standard is so heated in the controversy over how Title IX applies to sexual assault and why the debate is as much about symbolism as it is about practical considerations of equity and fairness. This chapter addresses some of the pragmatic and symbolic aspects of the controversy and argues that Title IX's requirement of an "equitable" grievance procedure counsels in favor of using the preponderance standard to resolve sexual assault allegations.

Title IX's Evolving Framework for Responding to Sexual Assault

Given the trajectory of how sexual assault came to be recognized as a form of sex discrimination under the law, it is no surprise that Title IX's statutory language does not specify any proof standard for educational institutions to use in resolving sexual assault allegations—nor any other type of sex discrimination claim. Like many civil rights and nondiscrimination statutes, Title IX, enacted in 1972, sets forth a very broadly worded ban on sex discrimination. To flesh out the contours of the statute's broad language, the federal agency charged with enforcing Title IX (a precursor to the U.S. Department of Education) issued regulations in 1975, including a provision requiring federal funding recipients to have in place "prompt and equitable" grievance procedures for internally addressing sex discrimination complaints (Title IX Regulations, 2019). It took another decade to solidify the judiciary's understanding that sexual harassment is encompassed by a broadly worded statute banning sex discrimination, a principle that the Supreme Court first endorsed in a case involving workplace sexual harassment under a different statute, Title VII of the Civil Rights Act of 1964, in a 1986 decision (*Meritor Savings Bank v. Vinson*, 1986). A few years later, the Court applied that principle to Title IX (*Franklin v. Gwinnett County Public Schools*, 1992). From there, the Court charted a clear path to treating sexual assault, including when perpetrated by other students, as a form of sexual harassment covered by Title IX (*Davis v. Monroe County Board of Education*, 1999; *Gebser v. Lago Vista Independent School District*, 1998). Indeed, the foundational sexual harassment cases decided by the Supreme Court have all involved conduct that included one or more sexual assaults (*Davis v. Monroe County Board of Education*, 1999; *Franklin v. Gwinnett County Public Schools*, 1992; *Gebser v. Lago Vista Independent School District*, 1998; *Meritor Savings Bank v. Vinson*, 1986). In the late 1990s, in a pair of cases focusing on high schools, but with reasoning that is equally applicable to higher education, the Court held that federally funded educational institutions may be liable for monetary damages in court if they are deliberately indifferent to known sexual harassment, whether perpetrated by a school employee or a fellow student (*Davis v. Monroe County Board of Education*, 1999; *Gebser v. Lago Vista Independent School District*, 1998). Those decisions invited the federal enforcing agency, the U.S. Department of Education, to impose additional obligations on educational institutions in responding to sexual harassment, above and beyond merely avoiding deliberate indifference, as a condition of compliance in OCR's administrative enforcement process, which is a separate enforcement path from private lawsuits in court. The department did exactly that in guidance documents first issued in 1997 and revised in 2001.

In the decade that followed, numerous incidents came to light, many of which were investigated by OCR, in which allegations of sexual assault against students, including many involving charges against high-profile athletes, were mishandled, covered up, or discouraged by university officials. Scandals involving institutional cover-ups of widespread sexual abuse at places like the University of Colorado, Boulder, and the U.S. Air Force Academy, for example, made attention-grabbing headlines (Tani, 2017). OCR's experiences with mishandled sexual assault allegations by colleges and universities under investigation in administrative enforcement actions shaped the guidance documents to come, as OCR responded with increasing specificity about the appropriate procedures and processes universities should use in such matters. OCR investigated a number of institutions that used a clear and convincing evidence standard, including Harvard and the University of Montana, in which the agency faulted the institutions for how they handled sexual assault cases.

An explicit endorsement of a particular proof standard first appeared in official OCR guidance documents in the agency's 2011 Dear Colleague Letter on sexual violence (OCR, 2011). In that document, OCR encouraged institutions to evaluate sexual misconduct allegations under a preponderance of the evidence standard. Although this was the first time the agency expressly stated this in an official guidance document, it was not the first time the agency was on record as requiring institutions to resolve sexual assault allegations using the preponderance standard. As far back as 1995, OCR had included the use of the preponderance standard in a resolution agreement with a college under investigation for mishandling sexual assault allegations (Jackson, 1995). OCR again required the preponderance standard as part of a resolution agreement with Georgetown University in 2003 (Kallem, 2003). Both the 2011 DCL and a 2014 question-and-answer document subsequently issued by OCR endorsed the preponderance standard as the only standard that is consistent with the Title IX regulation requirement of an "equitable" grievance procedure.

When the Trump Administration took the reins at the U.S. Department of Education, critics of the Obama Administration's actions on sexual assault found a receptive audience. In the summer of 2017, Secretary of Education Betsy DeVos held a "Title IX Summit" in which she met with advocates for students allegedly unfairly accused of sexual assault and with experts on all sides. That very morning, acting assistant secretary for civil rights, Candice Jackson, was quoted in the *New York Times* as saying that "90 percent" of campus sexual assault allegations "fall into the category of 'we were both drunk,' 'we broke up, and six months later I found myself under a Title IX investigation because she just decided that our last sleeping together was not quite right' " (Green & Stolberg, 2017). While Jackson offered no evidence to back up her 90% statistic, and subsequently apologized for what she called "flippant" remarks, the statement seemed to accurately reflect the department's baseline judgment that alleged victims of sexual assault are less credible and have less at stake than accused students. As argued later, those two presuppositions are reflected in calls for a heightened proof standard.

Soon after its Title IX Summit, the U.S. Department of Education announced its decision to rescind the 2011 and 2014 guidance documents in a statement highlighting the plight of wrongly accused students. In place of the documents, the department issued an interim guidance document titled "September 2017 Q&A on Campus Sexual Misconduct," in which it provided answers to several questions and announced its intention to engage in formal rulemaking on the Title IX responsibilities of educational institutions in responding to sexual harassment. In contrast to the 2011 and 2014 documents, the 2017 Q&A stated that schools may apply either the preponderance standard or the clear and convincing evidence standard in making findings and conclusions based on the evidence, with the caveat that the standard applied to sexual misconduct "should be consistent with the standard the school applies in other student misconduct cases" (OCR, 2017, p. 5 n. 19). As justification for this policy reversal, the department cited a single court decision that was critical of a university's use of the preponderance standard in a sexual misconduct case. In that case, the court found many flaws with the university's process, including insufficient notice to the accused of the charges against him and a lack of meaningful opportunity to respond to the evidence against him (*Doe v.*

Brandeis University, 2016). The court's criticism of the university for applying a lower standard of proof to sexual misconduct than to other forms of student misconduct must be read in light of the myriad process failures the court identified. On the other hand, a wealth of legal authorities not mentioned in the 2017 Q&A support the continuing validity of using the preponderance standard in campus disciplinary proceedings for all student conduct violations, including sexual misconduct (Kidder, 2019).

A second justification proffered by the U.S. Department of Education for its policy change—that use of the preponderance standard may give rise to Title IX sex discrimination claims by students accused of sexual misconduct—also fails to withstand scrutiny. In the 2017 Q&A, the department stated that applying a lower standard of proof to sexual misconduct cases than the standard that the school applies to other kinds of (nonsexual) misconduct may amount to sex discrimination against the students accused of sexual assault, in violation of Title IX (OCR, 2017, p. 5, n. 19). Under the department's stated view, a male student who is found responsible for sexual assault under a preponderance of the evidence standard could bring a Title IX claim for sex discrimination against the university if the university applied a higher proof standard to other forms of (nonsexual) misconduct. This argument stretches the legal understanding of sex discrimination well beyond existing precedents. Courts have viewed the use of campus procedures favoring victims of sexual misconduct as revealing—at most—a special solicitude toward victims of sexual assault, which is not the same thing as, and does not provide evidence of, gender bias or sex discrimination against male students (Buzuvis, 2017).

In November of 2018, the department issued a "Notice of Proposed Rulemaking" (NPRM) in which it detailed proposed Title IX regulations addressing myriad aspects of university responses to sexual harassment, including the standard of proof used for resolving contested allegations. The issuance of the NPRM began a 60-day notice and comment period, during which members of the public were invited to submit comments on the proposed regulations. The comment period closed at the end of January 2019, with approximately 100,000 comments having been submitted for department review (Smith, 2019). At the time of this writing, the department was still in the process of considering the comments and had not yet issued its final regulations.

The position that the NPRM takes on the standard of proof goes further than the 2017 Q&A in setting limits on the use of the preponderance standard for resolving alleged sexual harassment. The 2017 Q&A required consistency between sexual misconduct and other student conduct violations (OCR, 2017). The NPRM goes beyond mandating consistency in student conduct proceedings and also requires parity with the standard of proof used for complaints against employees, including complaints against faculty (OCR,

2018, §106.45(b)(4)). The parity requirement for complaints against faculty is not limited to complaints about faculty misconduct covered by Title IX and seemingly applies to any type of misconduct by faculty. Significantly, the NPRM's parity requirement operates as a constraint on institutional discretion only if the institution uses the preponderance standard for sexual harassment. If the institution instead applies the clear and convincing evidence standard to sexual harassment, then it is free to apply the preponderance standard to other serious misconduct. In other words, in order to use the preponderance standard for sexual harassment, a university must ensure that it uses the preponderance standard for all other serious student misconduct and for complaints against faculty and employees. However, an institution that uses the clear and convincing standard for sexual harassment is not constrained in its selection of proof standards for other types of misconduct.

As a result, under the proposed NPRM, a school could permissibly single out sexual harassment for proof by clear and convincing evidence, while resolving all other misconduct complaints, including complaints alleging other forms of discrimination under the lower preponderance of the evidence proof standard. This singular parity constraint functions as a one-way ratchet that grants unlimited discretion to schools that use the clear and convincing evidence standard for sexual harassment but imposes strict parity requirements on schools that use the preponderance standard for sexual harassment allegations. In this way, the proposed regulations would permit schools to disfavor sexual harassment victims by imposing on them, but no others, a singularly stringent proof standard in campus disciplinary processes. This resolution of the controversy over the proof standard goes far beyond merely walking back the 2011 directive to schools to use the preponderance standard; it would permit a school to apply a tougher proof standard to sexual harassment cases than it applies to any other serious misconduct on campus.

It remains to be seen whether the department's review of public comments will have any impact on its final regulation of the proof standard. If the proposed regulations, in substance, go into effect, lawsuits challenging their validity and their constitutionality under the equal protection clause for relying on sex stereotypes about sexual assault victims will likely follow. Three organizations representing the interests of sexual assault survivors filed just such a lawsuit challenging the U.S. Department of Education's decision to rescind the 2011 and 2014 OCR guidance documents and replace them with the 2017 Q&A. A district court decision in March of 2019 dismissed the lawsuit, but on the narrow ground that the organizations lack standing to assert the legal claims of sexual assault survivors themselves who might be injured by the change in U.S. Department of Education policy (*SurvJustice v. DeVos*, 2019). The court's decision leaves open a path for students themselves to challenge any new regulations, using similar arguments that the changes will have a chilling effect on investigations, deter complainants from reporting sexual assault, and reflect gender stereotypes that treat sexual assault victims more skeptically than victims of other misconduct. Regardless of potential legal challenges, any new regulations may be undone by a subsequent administration. Given the controversy over the NPRM, their fate may ultimately be decided by the next presidential election (Smith, 2019). At present, all that is clear is that the NPRM's proposed regulation of the standard of proof will not be the final word on the matter.

Institutional Practice with Proof Standards

For all of the controversy sparked by the 2011 Dear Colleague Letter's directive to use a preponderance of the evidence standard, the preponderance standard had already long been the dominant standard used in campus disciplinary proceedings, including in matters involving sexual misconduct (Kidder, 2019). An influential model code of student conduct published in 1990 endorsed the preponderance standard for all student disciplinary matters, including sexual misconduct, explaining that only the preponderance standard strikes an equitable balance in accommodating the interests of the educational community, the accused student, and the complaining student (Stoner & Cerminara, 1990). In explaining their position, the model code authors pointed out that campus disciplinary processes lack many of the evidence-gathering powers to which litigants have access in the justice system, such as the power to subpoena witnesses and compel the production of documentary evidence. Requiring proof of sexual misconduct by clear and convincing evidence would create an insurmountable hurdle in many campus sexual misconduct cases where the only evidence is the conflicting testimonial evidence of the students themselves.

Even before the 2011 DCL, the vast majority of institutions that specified the standard of proof used in sexual misconduct cases were using the preponderance standard (Kidder, 2019). For those institutions that already used the preponderance standard to resolve sexual misconduct complaints, complying with that aspect of the DCL did not require any change. For schools that were using a clear and convincing evidence standard, however, complying with the DCL required a change in institutional policies on sexual assault, which some institutions resisted. Particularly for those institutions, the U.S. Department of Education's new flexibility permitting use of a clear and convincing evidence standard may make a difference. It is too soon to say how many colleges and universities will switch from a preponderance to a clear and convincing standard if the final regulations permit it. Early reactions from the higher education community to the Trump Administration's proposed changes, however, indicated that at least some institutions were disinclined to raise their proof standard as a result of the new administration's position. The leading association of student conduct professionals, the Association for Student Conduct Administration, issued a white paper advocating the continued use of the preponderance standard in student conduct proceedings involving sexual misconduct allegations, indicating that efforts to raise the standard are likely to encounter professional resistance (Loschiavo & Waller, n.d.).

One difficulty in assessing the impact of raising the proof standard on institutional practice is that it is not clear how much substantive difference separates the two standards. Students accused of sexual misconduct have been found not responsible under a preponderance standard, even where there is a reasonable basis in evidence for concluding that sexual assault likely occurred. For example, star football player Jameis Winston was found not responsible in the university's student conduct proceeding under a preponderance standard, even though a civil case against the university charging it with deliberate indifference to sexual assault was allowed to proceed (Novkov, 2015). Critics' charges that the preponderance standard sets an unfairly low bar for proving these cases is unsubstantiated. Data from campus cases adjudicated after the 2011 DCL show that a majority of accused students have been found not responsible even under the preponderance standard (Richards, 2019). That does not mean that the accusations were fabricated, but rather that the evidence did not meet the threshold of proof needed to show that misconduct more likely than not occurred. Even under a preponderance standard, proving sexual assault, without eyewitnesses, is a difficult endeavor. Moreover, even when a student is found responsible for sexual assault, it does not necessarily mean that the student will face a severe penalty. One study found only a 30% expulsion rate for students found responsible for sexual misconduct even after the 2011 DCL (Kingkade, 2014). That said, there is no way to know how many student conduct cases in which the student was found responsible under a preponderance standard would have come out differently under a clear and convincing standard, nor how many students adjudicated not responsible under a clear and convincing standard would face punishment if a preponderance standard had been applied.

One difficulty in assessing the effects of raising the proof standard is the fuzziness of exactly what kind of evidence suffices as clear and convincing enough to prove a sexual assault. The clear and convincing standard falls somewhere between a preponderance and the higher "beyond a reasonable doubt" standard in criminal law. But exactly where it falls on that spectrum is impossible to pinpoint, and different decision makers will likely vary in how much extra assurance of probability they require in order to find the standard met. One possible definition of clear and convincing evidence—"that proof which results in reasonable certainty of the truth"—is difficult, even for a lawyer, to differentiate from the criminal standard requiring proof beyond a reasonable doubt (Black & Garner, 2004).

As important as defining the standard is the determination of what evidence qualifies as clear and convincing when it comes to proving that sexual assault occurred. Very few types of civil cases are decided under the clear and convincing standard, and those that are—such as civil commitment and termination of parental rights—would be more likely to have some kind of documentary or objective proof beyond the testimony of interested persons. Proponents of using a clear and convincing evidence standard to adjudicate campus sexual assault have said precious little about what type of evidence it would take to qualify as clear and convincing. If both the complainant and the accused student tell conflicting stories, is additional evidence required in order to find that sexual assault occurred, and if so, what? Historically, "corroborating evidence" was required to convict a criminal defendant for rape, a requirement that reflected an ingrained distrust of women claiming rape. Such requirements were the subject of concerted feminist efforts at reforming rape law and have long been formally discarded in criminal law. Requiring clear and convincing evidence might effectively revive a corroboration requirement in campus processes given the lack of clarity in what clear and convincing evidence means in a case where testimonial evidence conflicts (Anderson, 2004).

Another complicating factor with a clear and convincing standard is that many sexual assaults in college involve alcohol or drugs—although it is worth noting that some research suggests that it is not alcohol consumption per se, but the setting in which alcohol is consumed that matters, with certain types of party cultures more important in predicting sexual assault than alcohol itself (Boyle & Walker, 2016). What does clear and convincing evidence require when one or both students were intoxicated? Might the complainant's use of drugs or alcohol, in itself, bar their testimony from being viewed as clear and convincing? The uncertainty in what the standard demands opens the door to *de facto* requirements of corroboration, despite the formal abandonment of this requirement in even the criminal law (Anderson, 2004).

Critics of the 2011 DCL's endorsement of the preponderance standard have expressed particular concern about the fairness of this requirement at institutions that use a clear and convincing standard for other forms of student misconduct. They argue that schools that use the clear and convincing standard for other student conduct matters should not be required to use a lower proof standard for sexual assault. This is a fair point in terms of consistency, but there are valid reasons why OCR, in 2011, directed all schools to use the preponderance standard for sexual harassment, even those that used a clear and convincing standard for other matters. Sexual assault, unlike many other student conduct violations, is not a victimless offense. The high stakes for the complaining student as well as for the accused student support a proof standard that holds both sides' accounts in equilibrium, as only the preponderance standard does. Another reason for treating sexual assault differently, even when other offenses must be proved by clear and convincing evidence, is that additional evidence above and beyond testimonial proof is unlikely to exist in sexual assault cases. Requiring clear and convincing proof of sexual assault is likely to be an insurmountable hurdle. Other student conduct violations, such as plagiarism, cheating, or property destruction, may be more likely to involve documentary evidence or other tangible proof so that a clear and convincing requirement may be more workable in such cases. Moreover, setting the scales of proof to favor the accused student has a special resonance when sexual misconduct charges are at issue, more so than other student conduct matters, since it taps into deeply ingrained skepticism of sexual assault victims' stories and aligns with **rape myths** that undermine survivors' credibility.

Finally, any reconsideration of the standard of proof for campus sexual assault must take into account institutional practices with respect to other types of discrimination charges. Educational institutions are required to have policies and procedures for addressing multiple forms of discrimination, including discrimination based on race, religion, and disability. Whatever proof standard is applied to sexual misconduct, a form of sexual harassment, which is itself a form of sex discrimination, should not be higher than that applied to allegations of other types of discrimination involving students at that institution. Schools considering raising their proof standard for sexual misconduct to require clear and convincing evidence must consider how such a change would impact the effectiveness of campus processes for addressing other kinds of discrimination and harassment. Requiring a higher threshold of proof for sexual harassment than for other types of prohibited harassment would create intractable dilemmas for students who stand at the intersection of protected categories, including women of color, and would inject problematic hierarchies of credibility and skepticism among discrimination complainants. On the other hand, extending the clear and convincing proof standard to other discrimination allegations, including racial harassment between students, would introduce difficult proof hurdles in those cases, too.

The Effect of a Higher Proof Standard on Institutional Incentives and Student Reporting

At the heart of the case for raising the proof standard above a preponderance of the evidence is the argument that colleges and universities, feeling the fire of the federal government's enforcement powers and the wrath of survivor activist groups, have overcorrected and are now railroading male students who have been wrongly accused of sexual misconduct. This narrative fails to account for the lingering institutional pressures that tilt in the opposite direction—pressures that incentivize higher education institutions to find accused students not responsible for sexual misconduct. It also fails to reckon with the effects of raising the proof standard on the already low rates of student reporting of sexual assault.

Institutional denial of sexual assault is practically baked into the campus ethos that lauds campus culture as collegial and idyllic. The "it doesn't happen here" phenomenon is rampant. In a 2015 *Inside Higher Education* survey of college and university presidents, 74% of respondents either agreed with or were noncommittal about the conclusion that sexual assault is a widespread problem on college campuses, but 78% disagreed with the statement that it was prevalent on their own campuses (Jaschik & Lederman, 2015). There is no benefit to an institution's reputation in concluding, after an airing of competing claims, that one (or more) of its students sexually assaulted another.

A university's reluctance to find an accused student responsible for sexual misconduct is especially pronounced when the accused student is highly valued by the institution as, for example, with athletes in highly valued sports programs, members of certain fraternities, and relatives of alumni or donors. In such situations, institutional reluctance to find accused students responsible for sexual misconduct can be difficult to overcome regardless of the proof standard applied. The Jameis Winston case is an example: The Florida State University found its MVP football player not responsible for sexual assault even under the preponderance standard. Far from being railroaded by a too-low proof standard, high-profile athletes accused of sexual misconduct have continued to evade responsibility in student conduct proceedings (Ladika, 2017).

Another consideration for how institutional practices discourage findings of responsibility for sexual misconduct is the role lawyers play in student conduct proceedings. One commentator has noted that allowing access to counsel in campus adjudications structurally favors accused students (Brubaker, 2018). Campus procedures typically allow students involved in such proceedings to select only one person as their advocate. Accused students typically select an attorney, while complaining students are more likely to choose a support person, such as a mental health provider or a non-lawyer victim advocate

(Brubaker, 2018). The support person may be very helpful in assisting a sexual assault survivor to endure the emotional toll of the adjudicatory process, but less influential than an attorney when it comes to navigating the process and obtaining the best outcome for the student in a campus disciplinary process (Weiner, 2017; see also chapter 6).

The Title IX liability standards that apply to schools in lawsuits brought by sexually assaulted students further contribute to the institutional incentives against finding accused students responsible for sexual misconduct. In order to hold an educational institution liable for damages under Title IX based on its response to alleged sexual assault, the accuser must prove that the school responded to the assault with deliberate indifference—a legal standard that requires more than mere negligence. As long as the institution investigated the allegations and followed reasonable procedures to resolve conflicting accounts, it is extremely unlikely that a court would find that it acted with deliberate indifference merely because it found the accused student not responsible for sexual misconduct. In cases in which universities have lost Title IX lawsuits brought by sexual assault victims, it is because of the process, not the outcome, as in a recent case where the court faulted Brown University for a "bungled" investigation "carried out so inartfully as to render it clearly unreasonable" (*Doe v. Brown University*, 2018). These institutional incentives are not outweighed by whatever pressures are brought to bear by the internal Title IX offices many universities have staffed in recent years. Even when staffed with good-faith, well-trained personnel, these offices are structured to prioritize bulletproofing for the university over providing redress for survivors (Brubaker, 2018). Following campus protocols, even when lengthy processes extend past the graduation of the involved students, and minimizing the risk of legal liability are the overarching objectives of university Title IX offices (Novkov, 2016; Tani, 2017)

The proposed regulations in the NPRM, if adopted, would further skew institutional incentives away from finding students responsible for sexual misconduct. In addition to changing the standard of proof, the NPRM proposes to raise the legal threshold for noncompliance in OCR's administrative enforcement process to match the institutional liability standard courts apply in lawsuits for damages. Until now, OCR (2001) has applied a negligence standard in its administrative enforcement of Title IX, asking whether a recipient of federal funds responded reasonably to correct and prevent sexual harassment of which it knew or should have known, and whether it used a fair and equitable process for handling allegations of sexual harassment. Because OCR's enforcement process offers a path to compliance in which institutions can avoid any monetary penalty by agreeing to come into compliance with Title IX, OCR—until the NPRM—has taken the position that the deliberate indifference standard, which the Supreme Court adopted for private lawsuits for damages, did not apply to OCR's administrative enforcement process. The NPRM proposes to change this, with the result of making it much less likely that OCR would find an institution noncompliant with Title IX based on its handling of sexual assault allegations.

As it stands, colleges and universities are more likely to risk liability for damages in a lawsuit brought by a student who was disciplined for sexual assault than to be found liable to sexual assault victims. Increasingly, male students who have been suspended or expelled for sexual misconduct have sued their colleges and universities, and in a growing number of such cases, courts have allowed the claims to proceed (Buzuvis, 2017). Although the case law still leaves plenty of room for universities to comply with due process and impose sanctions for sexual misconduct that it found through a fair and impartial process (Brodsky, 2017), a litigation risk-averse university may conclude that it is better off finding the accused student not responsible, thereby minimizing its risk of legal exposure.

Raising the proof standard to require clear and convincing evidence would not only compound the institutional incentives that already favor accused students, it would likely further deter sexually assaulted students from reporting sexual misconduct. Sexual misconduct is already widely recognized as an underreported problem. The rate of college students' reporting of sexual assault to law enforcement is low—in many studies reported to be in single digits (Krebs, Lindquist, Berzofsky, Shook-Sa, & Peterson 2016; Krebs, Lindquist, Warner, Fisher, & Martin, 2007). Women of color, women from less privileged class backgrounds, and women who are lesbian, bisexual, or transgender are particularly unlikely to report sexual misconduct (Brubaker, Keegan, Guadalupe-Diaz, & Beasley, 2017). Despite having additional channels for reporting, students in colleges and universities are even less likely than non-students in the same age group to report sexual assault (Sinozich & Langton, 2014). Although the AAU campus sexual assault survey found very low reporting rates overall, it also found a significant degree of variation by institution, suggesting that institutional factors, such as the perception of a fair process and responsiveness to reports, may influence reporting rates (Cantor et al., 2017).

Raising the proof standard so as to make it more difficult to prove sexual misconduct occurred can only further discourage reporting. Already, the fear of being disbelieved and unable to prove what happened is a major consideration in a student's decision about whether to report. Fear of peer retaliation would also likely be exacerbated by a higher proof standard. If the student conduct process finds an accused student not responsible, an outcome likely to be perceived as vindicating the accused student, the complaining student may be cast in a negative light with their peer group and depicted as a false accuser, rendering them vulnerable to jeers and shunning from other students.[1]

Tilting Baseline Judgments About Credibility and Harm

The debate over the appropriate proof standard for resolving sexual assault allegations is as contentious as it is because it taps into controversies that go to the heart of the culture wars over gender, sex, and sexuality: the relative credibility of the accuser and the accused, and the stakes for both sides. Calls for a heightened proof standard in the campus setting for sexual assault trade on an ingrained skepticism of sexual assault allegations and greater empathy for the consequences facing the accused student (Brake, 2017).

Baseline judgments about the believability of, and harm to, sexual assault victims tap into culturally resonant rape myths that undermine the credibility of, and empathy for, women alleging sexual assault. Rape myths are culturally shared beliefs and assumptions about rape that are not factually supported but serve to preserve the status quo and make rape difficult to challenge. Two particular rape myths underlie the intensity of the controversy over the standard of proof: (a) Women claiming sexual assault are not credible; and (b) even if true, women's accounts of the harm resulting from sexual assault are overblown. Both sets of beliefs are particularly salient for sexual assaults that do not fit the prototype of "real rape" (i.e., those not involving a stranger, a weapon, or lasting physical injuries—criteria that apply to the vast majority of sexual assaults in the college setting) (Sinozich & Langton, 2014).

The belief that women are unreliable and not credible when it comes to speaking out about sexual misconduct is as culturally ingrained as it is factually unsupported. Although we are now in the midst of a cultural upheaval in which women are speaking out, in new ways and with strength in numbers, about their experiences of rape and sexual assault—and finding unprecedented success in getting their stories heard—deep undercurrents of skepticism toward women remain (Epstein & Goodman, 2019). The last presidential election served as a painful reminder to many of how easy it is to undermine the credibility of women who accuse a powerful man of sexual misconduct. Despite having been caught on tape bragging about doing the very things that a dozen women came forward to accuse Donald Trump of doing, Trump successfully drew on tropes of lying, conniving women to call into question their accounts (including the pernicious suggestion that a particular woman wasn't attractive enough for him to have sexually assaulted). The #MeToo movement has since had considerable success in building public support for believing women's accounts, but recent polling data suggest that a strong backlash is brewing (Smith, 2018).[2] It remains a precarious thing for a woman, particularly when hers is the lone voice speaking out, to accuse a powerful man of sexual misconduct.

The recent Senate Judiciary Committee hearings on the nomination of Brett Kavanaugh to the Supreme Court offered the equivalent of a national seminar on the narrow path women must walk to credibly accuse a powerful man of sexual assault. Dr. Christine Blasey Ford testified about her experience of having been sexually assaulted by Brett Kavanaugh, with encouragement from one of his friends, when Ford and Kavanaugh were in high school. Dr. Ford powerfully shared how the event impacted her life, with a demeanor that was composed and even polite, despite appearing visibly shaken and afraid. Her records of telling people as early as 2012 rebutted aspersions that she acted as the dupe of politically motivated Democrats opposed to Judge Kavanaugh's nomination. Judge Kavanaugh angrily denied the allegations in his own testimony, and a lawyer retained by the Senate Judiciary Committee questioned Dr. Ford to probe her motives, memory, and reliability as a witness. Dr. Ford emerged from the hearings with her credibility questioned but largely intact, as acknowledged even by Senator Orin Hatch, a staunch supporter of Judge Kavanaugh's nomination, who called her an "attractive," and later an "appealing," witness. In the end, the nomination succeeded by the slimmest of margins, with statements of key senators voting to approve the nomination citing a "presumption of innocence" and a lack of "corroborating evidence" (Fram & Mascaro, 2018).

Notwithstanding this outcome, polls showed that most people believed Dr. Ford, a reaction that compares starkly to the public reception of Professor Anita Hill when she testified in the Senate hearings on the Clarence Thomas nomination more than two and a half decades earlier (Montanaro, 2018). As a married White woman, Dr. Ford's perceived credibility benefited from the privileges of race and marital status. Two and a half decades later, on the heels of the #MeToo movement, the extent of public support for Dr. Ford reflects the limits of cultural change when it comes to women's credibility. Dr. Ford managed to come across as warm, likeable, and believable only by staying within culturally approved boundaries of femininity and the emotional range expected of a credible victim. In other words, she was the perfect victim who could credibly accuse a powerful man of sexual assault: a White, married woman with children, from an upper middle-class background, highly educated, who presented her story in a way that exposed her vulnerability and emotion without veering into the territory of anger, shrillness, or hysteria. Yet, none of this was enough to overcome an angry man's outraged denials and sway the swing votes in the Senate. In the end, the generally positive public perception of Dr. Ford may ultimately say more about the precariousness of women's credibility in claiming sexual assault than about the extent of cultural change in the post-#MeToo era.

Despite the resilience of cultural skepticism of women alleging sexual assault, such skepticism is not borne out by facts. Numerous studies document widely held beliefs that the rate of false reporting is much higher than it actually is. One study found that police officers estimated the false reporting rate for sexual assault to be as high as 30–50% (Weiser, 2017). However, a recent comprehensive review of all studies to date on false rape reports found that the literature firmly supports a false reporting rate for rape at between 2–10%, which is no higher than for non-sexual crimes (Weiser, 2017). Even that may be artificially high, since some studies conflate "false" reports with unconfirmed reports, meaning they were labelled unfounded by law enforcement officers due to insufficient evidence (Weiser, 2017). A report may be unfounded for many reasons, including that an investigation was not carried out or that the victim later recanted their story, even though victims of sexual violence often recant under duress from the accused. Adherence to rape myths may also inflate the underlying statistics on false and unfounded charges. Circumstances commonly involved in campus sexual assaults, such as consumption of drugs or alcohol, prior acquaintance with the accused, and delay in reporting the assault, may cause investigators to inaccurately classify reports as unfounded, false, or baseless (Weiser, 2017). Notably, and perhaps counter-intuitively, the literature on false reporting has found false reports to be more common in reports of "stranger" rape, where no suspect is identified, than in reports accusing an assailant who is known to the complainant (Weiser, 2017).

Despite the lack of empirical support for high rates of falsely reporting sexual assault, widespread fear of false reports nevertheless persists because it dovetails with tropes of untrustworthy women and women who say no but mean yes. Such stereotypes are bolstered by traditional sexual mores that expect respectable women not to be sexually promiscuous, fueling suspicion that women who have casual sex make up lies after a consensual encounter to cover for their promiscuity. These beliefs fuel distrust of women's accounts of sexual assault and of women's sexual agency. Unlike civil and criminal trials, where revised evidence rules at least attempt (often unsuccessfully) to protect against using a victim's sexual history to undermine her credibility, few, if any, such protections exist in campus adjudicatory processes to guard against this. One recent survey of higher education sexual misconduct policies found that only a very small minority of university policies bar consideration of the complainant's sexual history or dress in the campus adjudication process (Richards et al., 2017).[3]

Credibility, always a concern for women accusing powerful men of sexual misconduct, is particularly a concern for women who lack the social and economic privileges of someone like Dr. Ford. Race, for example, influences how a victim's credibility is assessed, with racial and gender stereotypes combining in pernicious ways. Being both a racial minority and economically disadvantaged places women at higher risk of being discredited when bringing forth allegations of sexual assault, leaving them less likely to be vindicated than White and economically privileged women in campus adjudicatory proceedings (Weiser, 2017). Other relevant privileges bearing on credibility implicate gender identity and sexuality. LGBT students, who some research suggests experience sexual assault in college at higher rates than other student populations, are particularly vulnerable to having their credibility questioned, since they do not fit the prototype of male-female/heterosexual sexual assault (Cantor et al., 2015; Coulter et al., 2017; Mellins, 2017).

Another rape myth that is squarely engaged by calls for a heightened proof standard is that the harms to women from sexual assault are overblown or less impactful than the potential harms to men accused of sexual assault. Arguments for raising the burden of proof above a preponderance of the evidence in sexual misconduct cases prioritize the harms to students wrongly accused and minimize the effects on survivors of an erroneous finding of no responsibility. In this tilting of the balance of equities, students claiming sexual assault are cast as "snowflakes" in sexual encounters gone wrong, while accused men are regarded as victims of a hypersensitive sexual morality that threatens to destroy the rest of their lives. What begins as an understandable reluctance to impose lasting educational consequences on young men—particularly those with "bright futures"—becomes amplified in arguments for raising the proof standard into the predominant consideration. News media portrayals often feed into this narrative, revealing more concern for the impact sexual assault charges have on men than for how women are harmed by sexual assault and its aftermath when the institution sides with the accused (Weiser, 2017). This discourse recently played out in the Kavanaugh nomination hearings, as the lasting effects of the assault described by Dr. Ford were overshadowed by the anticipated harms to Judge Kavanaugh if he could not serve on the Supreme Court, teach adjunct courses, or coach basketball.

Although arguments for a heightened proof standard elevate the stakes of an erroneous decision for the accused above that of the accuser, it is important to understand that the driving concern about protecting a young man's future is not equally salient for all men. Privileged men—men who benefit from race and class privilege, as well as men who are institutionally valued as athletes, legacies, and members of certain well-connected fraternities—are the most likely to be able to leverage concerns about ruining a young man's bright future to their own advantage. Some critics of using the preponderance standard for campus sexual assault have cited legitimate concerns that men of color are especially vulnerable to unfair judgments of responsibility for sexual misconduct (Halley, 2015). While the risk of bias and unfairness toward men of color in sexual misconduct proceedings is indeed a pressing concern, there is no indication that raising the proof standard will protect men whose credibility might be undermined by race or class bias. In the criminal justice system, use of the highest proof standard, beyond a reasonable doubt, has not protected Black men from wrongful convictions or disparate outcomes. More likely, raising the proof standard will benefit the most privileged men—those for whom concerns about ruining bright futures and a presumption of credibility will be most salient. Raising the proof standard for campus sexual assault should not be viewed as an antidote to concerns about racial bias toward men of color, nor a substitute for institutional reforms directly addressing these concerns (Johnson, 2017).[4]

By prioritizing the risk of an erroneous outcome for accused students, shifting to a higher proof standard would telegraph the message that accusers have less to lose in these proceedings. Survivors of sexual assault have long struggled to convey the stakes in having their stories believed and the harms they suffer when they are silenced or ignored. Much of the #MeToo movement has been about the deep-seated need for recognition of the harms experienced by survivors of sexual assault. These harms are too often discounted by courts, law enforcement, and colleges and universities. Exemplifying this tendency, one federal court ruled that a rape of a college student by a fellow student was not "severe or pervasive" enough to deny the victim educational opportunity on campus (*Ross v. Mercer University*, 2007). As a legal precedent, the case is an outlier, cutting against the grain of the case law, which recognizes that a single rape is severe enough to constitute sex discrimination under Title IX. Yet, the court's decision reveals the staying power of rape myths that minimize the harm of sexual assaults that do not match the prototype of "real rape." The court's ruling that the rape was not severe enough to implicate Title IX is particularly stunning given that the plaintiff transferred to another college after her rapist went unpunished and required mental health services for suicidal ideation after the assault. Many survivors feel unable to remain in the same institution as their assailants when their claims are disbelieved. Those who do remain often experience declining grades, reduced extracurricular involvement, and worsened mental health (Bolger, 2016).

Heightened proof standards recalibrate the balance of equities between accuser and accused in a way that is particularly problematic for women who lack the privileges of race, socioeconomic status, and heteronormative sexuality and, consequently, find their experiences devalued. Racial and gender stereotypes can combine to minimize the harms of sexual assault experienced by women of color. Black women, in particular, have long been subjected to stereotypes that cast them as hypersexualized and invulnerable to sexual harms (Brubaker, 2018). Women subjected to such stereotypes are likely to fare poorly when their allegations of sexual assault are evaluated under a clear and convincing proof standard and their interests in a just outcome are compared to the stakes of a wrongful decision for an accused (likely male) student with a "bright future."

Finally, in calibrating the governing standard of proof, and thereby setting baseline expectations for the likelihood of truth and the relative weight of interests at stake, it is important to consider the effect on male victims. The debate over the standard of proof is often framed in zero-sum terms, as if protections for complainants benefit women at the expense of men. Such a zero-sum framing not only ignores the fact that both complaining and accused students have an interest in a fair process (Brodsky, 2017), it also erases and marginalizes the 9% of college-age sexual assault victims who are men (Weiser, 2017). Contrary to popular narratives, men are more likely to be sexually assaulted themselves than to be falsely accused of sexual assault (Weiser, 2017). As important, men who are sexually assaulted are even more unlikely than women to report it and more likely to fear not being believed if they do report (Weiser, 2017). Raising the proof standard from a preponderance to clear and convincing evidence would make it that much harder for men to invoke campus disciplinary procedures when they are victims of sexual assault.

Conclusion

Whatever regulations emerge from the Trump Administration's "Notice of Proposed Rulemaking" process will likely not be the final word on the standard of proof, which has been a flashpoint in the controversy over how educational institutions should respond to campus sexual assault. At present, the Trump Administration is poised to permit colleges and universities to adopt a clear and convincing evidence standard for all sexual harassment cases, including sexual assault, even if the institution uses a preponderance standard for other types of discrimination complaints and other student conduct violations. Colleges and universities should decline this invitation. Switching from a preponderance standard to the heightened clear and convincing evidence standard for sexual harassment cases would express skepticism about the credibility of sexual assault survivors, value the interests of accused students more highly than the interests of complainants, and deter sexual assault survivors from coming forward. If the final Title IX regulations issued by the U.S. Department of Education include the proposed changes to the proof standard in the NPRM, the next administration should make it a priority to revisit and revise the new Title IX regulations and restore the standard of proof to the preponderance of the evidence.

KEY TERMS

Beyond a reasonable doubt: The highest standard of proof used in the American legal system, limited to criminal cases and requiring reasonable certainty of guilt such that no other logical explanation exists.

Clear and convincing evidence standard: Requiring a higher probability than a preponderance of the evidence, but less than beyond a reasonable doubt.

Preponderance of the evidence standard: Requiring proof demonstrating that the fact in question is more likely true than not true; sometimes described as requiring at least a 51% probability of truth, such that if the evidence was in equipoise (a tie), the standard would not be met.

Rape myths: Attitudes and beliefs that are generally false but are widely and persistently held and that serve to preserve and defend the status quo of sexual violence.

Standard of proof: The amount of evidence or proof needed in order to resolve contested allegations of fact; the preponderance of the evidence standard, clear and convincing evidence standard, and beyond a reasonable doubt are all standards of proof, each requiring varying levels of probability.

DISCUSSION QUESTIONS

1. Given that most educational institutions have long used a preponderance of the evidence standard to resolve student conduct violations, including for sexual misconduct, why has the standard of evidence used in campus sexual assault cases become such a flashpoint of controversy?
2. What judgments about credibility and the costs of an erroneous outcome are reflected in a preponderance of the evidence standard? What judgments about credibility and the costs of an erroneous outcome are reflected in a clear and convincing evidence standard?
3. Is the selection between the two competing standards of evidence (the preponderance standard and the clear and convincing evidence standard) for campus sexual assault cases a zero-sum game between accusers and accused students? Or is this a false dichotomy?
4. What is the appropriate standard of proof for colleges and universities to use in campus sexual assault cases, and why?

Notes

1 There is still some uncertainty about how Title IX applies to peer retaliation against a student for reporting sexual assault. For a recent decision rejecting the defendant's argument that Title IX does not apply to peer retaliation, see *Niesen v. Iowa State University* (2017), holding that allegations that the plaintiff was "publicly humiliated and shamed by other students for claiming she had been sexually assaulted" could sustain a Title IX claim for peer retaliation if the school responded with deliberate indifference.

2 A National Public Radio poll conducted in 2018 found that 40% of respondents believed that the #MeToo movement had gone too far (Smith, 2018).

3 Only 18% of the policies reviewed in the study included provisions excluding consideration of the accuser's sexual history, and only 7% excluded consideration of the accuser's dress (Richards, Branch, Fleury-Steiner, & Kafonek, 2017).

4 Any assumption that a concern for racial injustice toward men of color is behind the Trump Administration's change in Title IX policy is belied by the U.S. Department of Education's recent actions rescinding the Obama Administration's Title VI guidance requiring educational institutions to address race-based disparate impact in school discipline (U.S. Department of Education, 2018).

References

Anderson, M. J. (2004). The legacy of the prompt complaint requirement, corroboration requirement, and cautionary instructions on campus sexual assault. *Boston University Law Review, 84*, 945–1022.

Black, H. C., & Garner, B.A. (2004). *Black's law dictionary* (8th ed.) St. Paul, MN: Thomson/West.

Bolger, D. (2016). Gender violence costs: Schools' financial obligations under Title IX. *Yale Law Journal, 125*(7), 2106–2181.

Boyle, K. M., & Walker, L. S. (2016). The neutralization and denial of sexual violence in college party subcultures. *Deviant Behavior, 37*(11), 1392–1410.

Brake, D. L. (2017). Fighting the rape culture wars through the preponderance of the evidence standard. *Montana Law Review, 78*(1), 109–154.

Brodsky, A. (2017). A rising tide: Learning about fair disciplinary process from Title IX. *Journal of Legal Education, 66*(4), 822–823.

Brubaker, S. J. (2018). Campus-based sexual assault victim advocacy and Title IX: Revisiting tensions between grassroots activism and the criminal justice system. *Feminist Criminology, 14*(3), 307–329.

Brubaker, S. J., Keegan, B., Guadalupe-Diaz, X., & Beasley, B. (2017). Measuring and reporting campus sexual assault: Privilege and exclusion in what we know and what we do. *Sociology Compass, 11*(12), e12543.

Buzuvis, E. E. (2017). Title IX and procedural fairness: Why disciplined-student litigation does not undermine the role of Title IX in campus sexual assault. *Montana Law Review, 78*(1), 71–108.

Cantor, D. Fisher, B., Chibnall, S., Bruce, C., Townsend, R., Thomas, G., & Lee, H. (2015, September 21). *Report on the AAU Campus Climate Survey on Sexual Assault and Sexual Misconduct.* University of Virginia. Retrieved from https://ias.virginia.edu/sites/ias.virginia.edu/files/University%20of%20Virginia_2015_climate_final_report.pdf

Cantor, D., Fisher, B., Chibnall, S., Bruce, C., Townsend, R., Thomas, G., & Lee, H. (2017, October 20). *Report on the AAU Campus Climate Survey on Sexual Assault and Sexual*

Misconduct. Westat. Retrieved from https://www.aau.edu/sites/default/files/AAU-Files/Key-Issues/Campus-Safety/AAU-Campus-Climate-Survey-FINAL-10-20-17.pdf

Coulter, R. W. S., Mair, C., Miller, E., Blosnich, J. R., Matthews, D. D., & McCauley, H. L. (2017). Prevalence of past-year sexual assault victimization among undergraduate students: Exploring differences by and intersections of gender identity, sexual identity, and race/ethnicity. *Prevention Science, 18*(6), 726–736. Retrieved from https://link.springer.com/article/10.1007/s11121-017-0762-8

Davis v. Monroe County Board of Education, 526 U.S. 629 (1999)

Doe v. Brandeis University, 177 F. Supp.3d 561, 607 (D. Mass. 2016)

Doe v. Brown University, 304 F. Supp.3d 252 (D. R.I. 2018)

Epstein, D., & Goodman, L.A. (2019). Discounting women: Doubting domestic violence survivors' credibility and dismissing their experiences. *University of Pennsylvania Law Review, 167*(2), 399–461.

Fram, A., & Mascaro, L. (2018, October 5). Brett Kavanaugh's confirmation to Supreme Court all but sure after Collins, Manchin announce their support. *Chicago Tribune*. Retrieved from https://www.chicagotribune.com/news/nationworld/ct-kavanaugh-vote-20181005-story.html

Franklin v. Gwinnett County Public Schools, 503 U.S. 60 (1992)

Gebser v. Lago Vista Independent School District, 524 U.S. 274 (1998)

Green, E. L., & Stolberg, S. G. (2017, July 12). Campus rape policies get a new look as the accused get DeVos's ear. *New York Times*, p. A1. Retrieved from https://www.nytimes.com/2017/07/12/us/politics/campus-rape-betsy-devos-title-iv-education-trump-candice-jackson.html

Halley, J. (2015). Trading the megaphone for the gavel in Title IX enforcement. *Harvard Law Review Forum, 128*, 103–117.

Jackson, G. D. (1995). *Letter from the regional civil rights director, Office for Civil Rights, United States Department of Education, to Jane Jervis, president, Evergreen State College.*

Jaschik, S., & Lederman, D. (n.d.). *The 2015 Inside Higher Ed survey of college and university presidents*. Retrieved from http://big.assets.huffingtonpost.com/2015IHE Presidents-Survey.pdf

Johnson, A. (2017). Title IX narratives, intersectionality, and male-biased conceptions of racism. *Georgetown Journal of Law and Modern Critical Race Perspectives, 9*(57), 57–75.

Kallem, H. (2003). Letter from Chief Attorney, D.C. Enforcement Office, Office for Civil Rights, United States Department of Education to Jane Genster, Vice President and General Counsel, Georgetown University.

Kidder, W. C. (2019). (En)forcing a foolish consistency?: A critique and comparative analysis of the Trump Administration's proposed standard of evidence regulation for campus Title IX proceedings. *Journal of College and University Law*, 45, forthcoming.

Krebs, C., Lindquist, C., Berzofsky, M., Shook-Sa, B., & Peterson, K. (2016). *Campus climate survey validation study: Final technical report*. Washington, DC: Bureau of Justice Statistics. Retrieved from https://www.bjs.gov/content/pub/pdf/ccsvsftr.pdf

Krebs, C. P., Lindquist, C. H., Warner, T. D., Fisher, B. S., & Martin, S. L. (2007). *The Campus Sexual Assault (CSA) Study*. United States Department of Justice. Retrieved from https://www.ncjrs.gov/pdffiles1/nij/grants/221153.pdf

Kingkade, T. (2014, September 29). Fewer than one-third of campus sexual assault cases result in expulsion. *Huffington Post*. Retrieved from https://www.huffpost.com/entry/campus-sexual-assault_n_5888742

Ladika, S. (2017, April 28). Sports and sexual assault. *CQ Researcher, 27*(16), 361–384.

Loschiavo, C., & Waller, J. L. (n.d.). *The preponderance of evidence standard: Use in higher education campus conduct processes*. Association for Student Conduct Administration. Retrieved from: https://www.theasca.org/files/The%20Preponderance%20of%20Evidence%20Standard.pdf

Mellins, C. A. (2017). Sexual assault incidents among college undergraduates: Prevalence and factors associated with risk. *PLoS ONE*, *12*(11), e0186471. Retrieved from: https://journals.plos.org/plosone/article?id=10.1371/journal.pone.0186471

Meritor Savings Bank v. Vinson, 477 U.S. 57 (1986)

Montanaro, D. (2018, October 3). Poll: More believe Ford than Kavanaugh, a cultural shift from 1991. *National Public Radio*. Retrieved from https://www.npr.org/2018/10/03/654054108/poll-more-believe-ford-than-kavanaugh-a-cultural-shift-from-1991

Niesen v. Iowa State University, 2017 U.S. Dist. LEXIS 221061 (S. D. Iowa Nov. 3, 2017)

Novkov, J. (2016). Equality, process, and campus sexual assault. *Maryland Law Review*, *75*(2), 590–620.

Office for Civil Rights. (2001, January). *Revised sexual harassment guidance: Harassment of students by school employees, other students, or third parties*. Retrieved from https://www2.ed.gov/about/offices/list/ocr/docs/shguide.pdf

Office for Civil Rights. (2011, April 4). *Dear Colleague Letter*. Retrieved from https://www2.ed.gov/about/offices/list/ocr/letters/colleague-201104.pdf

Office for Civil Rights. (2014, April 29). *Questions and answers on Title IX and sexual violence*. Retrieved from https://www2.ed.gov/about/offices/list/ocr/docs/qa-201404-title-ix.pdf

Office for Civil Rights. (2017, September). *Q&A on campus sexual misconduct*. Retrieved from https://www2.ed.gov/about/offices/list/ocr/docs/qa-title-ix-201709.pdf

Office for Civil Rights. (2018, November 29). Notice of proposed rulemaking: Nondiscrimination on the basis of sex in education programs or activities receiving federal financial assistance. *Federal Register*, *83*, 61462.

Richards, T. N. (2019). No evidence of "weaponized Title IX" here: An empirical assessment of sexual misconduct reporting, case processing, and outcomes. *Law and Human Behavior*, *43*(2), 180–192.

Richards, T. N., Branch, K. A., Fleury-Steiner, R. E., & Kafonek, K. (2017). A feminist analysis of campus sexual assault policies: Results from a national sample. *Family Relations*, *66*(1), 104.

Ross v. The Corporation of Mercer University, 506 F. Supp.2d 1325 (M.D. Ga. 2007)

Sinozich, S., & Langton, L. (2014). *Special report: Rape and sexual assault victimization among college-age females, 1995–2013*. Washington, DC: U.S. Department of Justice. Retrieved from https://www.bjs.gov/content/pub/pdf/rsavcaf9513.pdf

Smith, T. (2018, October 31). On #MeToo, Americans more divided by party than gender. *National Public Radio*. Retrieved from https://www.npr.org/2018/10/31/662178315/on-metoo-americans-more-divided-by-party-than-gender

Smith, T. (2019, January 30). Trump Administration gets an earful on new campus sexual assault rules. *National Public Radio*. Retrieved from https://www.npr.org/2019/01/30/689879689/education-department-gathers-feedback-on-new-campus-sexual-assault-rules

Stoner, E. N., II, & Cerminara, K. L. (1990). Harnessing the "spirit of insubordination": A model student disciplinary code. *Journal of College and University Law*, *17*(2), 89–122.

SurvJustice, Inc., v. DeVos, 2019 U.S. Dist. LEXIS 54616 (N.D. Ca. Mar. 29, 2019)

Tani, K. M. (2017). An administrative right to be free from sexual violence? Title IX enforcement in historical and institutional perspective. *Duke Law Journal*, *66*(8), 1847–1903.

Title IX Regulations, 34 C.F.R. § 106.8(b) (2019)

U.S. Department of Education. (2018, December 21). *Dear Colleague Letter*. Retrieved from https://www2.ed.gov/about/offices/list/ocr/letters/colleague-201812.pdf

Weiner, M. (2017). Legal counsel for survivors of campus sexual violence. *Yale Journal of Law and Feminism*, *29*(1), 123–206.

Weiser, D. A. (2017). Confronting myths about sexual assault: A feminist analysis of the false report literature. *Family Relations*, *66*(1), 46–60.

CHAPTER EIGHT

Incorporating What Is Known About Respondents and Their Perspectives Into Thoughtful Adjudication Practices

Jay K. Wilgus and Joan Tabachnick

Introduction

Over the last 30 years, numerous studies have explored what is known about victims and survivors of sexual harassment, sexual assault, sexual violence, and other forms of sexual misconduct (e.g., Fisher, Cullen, & Turner, 2000; Krebs, Lindquist, Warner, Fisher, & Martin, 2007). These studies also provided insight into victim/survivor experiences and the prevalence of sexual assault in the college environment (e.g., Campbell, Dworkin, & Cabral, 2009; Fedina, Holmes, & Backes, 2016). The courage of victims/survivors, along with their willingness to share the pain and turmoil created by a wide range of harmful sexual behaviors, has brought this issue to the public and garnered the media's attention. What the research and these stories demonstrate is that the majority of sex crimes are perpetrated by someone the victim knows. Among adult female victims/survivors of rape and sexual assault, 51% report being victimized by an intimate partner and 41% by an acquaintance (Black et al., 2011). Criminal justice reports and surveys consistently identify males as the primary perpetrators of sexual violence, although women also commit sexual abuse and males are also victims/survivors of sexual aggression.

We fully acknowledge the pain experienced by victims/survivors, the possible lifelong impact that can be caused by harmful sexual behaviors and crimes, and the need for accountability for a broad range of sexual misconduct. We believe these issues are fully addressed in other chapters throughout this book. This chapter, though, delves into how campuses can improve response, adjudication, and prevention efforts by further incorporating what is known about students accused of and found responsible for sexual misconduct. We understand it may be difficult for some readers, especially those who have been harmed directly or indirectly by sexual violence, to hear the concerns, thoughts, or perspectives of individuals accused of sexual misconduct. In the realm of sexual violence, the emotions and consequences involved naturally create some level of polarization between the parties involved and those who support them. To make sense of things, it can be tempting to oversimplify perspectives, apply generalized labels, frame choices in absolutes, or reduce complex experiences into competing "sides." One common reduction suggests there are those who support victims/survivors and those who do not. Another reduction suggests that all students who engage in sexual misconduct are serial offenders who should be immediately expelled from the campus community, while others dismiss these sexual behaviors as drunken campus misunderstandings. Neither extreme is helpful nor consistently accurate, yet this chapter, and the campus adjudication processes to which it pertains, exist within this milieu. As one leading authority in student conduct administration frequently reminds audiences, "Judges must 'hear cases before they decide them'" (Pavela, 2014). Readers of this chapter are encouraged to do the same.

To help institutions improve their overall response to student sexual misconduct, as well as their prevention programming, this chapter invites readers to consider research about and perspectives from students accused of sexual misconduct (**respondents**), including those who accept responsibility for the reported behavior and those who are found responsible for it following an appropriate adjudication process (collectively, **responsible persons**). To make it accessible and useful, this chapter gravitates—as often as possible—toward center, toward a balance of perspectives, toward an integration of interests, and toward a common goal: offering support and closure for victims/survivors, holding responsible persons accountable for their behavior, and doing everything possible to ensure they never engage in similar behavior in the future.

The chapter begins with three principal goals: (a) convey information that sheds light on areas for improvement in campus adjudication efforts; (b) provide insight about those who cause harm that further informs campus prevention and response efforts, including sanctioning processes; and (c) offer practical suggestions to address the most significant tensions in campus disciplinary processes related to student sexual misconduct with the hope of creating safer communities, on campus and off. The first section briefly traces the evolution of campus adjudication processes for student sexual misconduct before outlining various due process concerns with the current framework, as expressed by respondents. The second section explores the impact of an accusation on students accused of sexual misconduct, including those who take responsibility for their actions, those who are found responsible but who remain unwilling to accept responsibility, and those who may not be responsible for the reported behavior. The third section shares research about students who engage in sexual misconduct (again, responsible persons) and offers insights into the wide heterogeneity of these students beyond the one-size-fits-all image of serial offenders. And finally, the fourth section offers thoughts on the path forward, paying special attention to options that seem to address interests expressed by victims/survivors, respondents, and responsible persons.

Campus Adjudication Framework

Much of the current campus framework for adjudicating student sexual misconduct matters stems from now-recalled 2011 guidance from the U.S. Department of Education's Office for Civil Rights (OCR). The guidance was issued in response to institutional cultures that exacerbated the epidemic of sexual misconduct by not taking victim complaints seriously enough, by dissuading victims/survivors from reporting, and by causing victims/survivors to prepare and present their complaint in a hearing-based process where they were likely to come in direct contact with the individual who harmed them. The 2011 Dear Colleague Letter reminded institutions receiving federal funding that sexual harassment is a form of sex-based discrimination under Title IX and required them to adjudicate sexual misconduct matters in fairly specific ways (Ali, 2011). With the possibility of compliance investigations, the potential loss of federal funding, and the fear of damaging the important campus reputation, most institutions sought immediate compliance with OCR's guidance. This shifted campuses from hearing-based systems that mirrored the civil litigation model in some basic respects, yet were intentionally distinguishable from the criminal process (e.g., Stoner & Lowery, 2004), to "best practice" investigative models more often used in civil rights matters (e.g., Bennett, Gregory, Loschiavo, & Waller, 2014). Many applauded OCR for focusing the spotlight on the long-ignored harm experienced by victims/survivors of sexual misconduct (e.g., Baker, Brake, & Cantalupo, 2016). Others argued that the guidance went too far by moving institutions further away from important due process protections provided in criminal proceedings (e.g., Bartholet et al., 2014; Rudovsky et al., 2015).

Although OCR's 2011 Dear Colleague Letter was formally withdrawn in 2017 (Jackson, 2017), many of the strengths and critiques raised by students, parents, lawyers, advocates, and academics following its issuance remain relevant to the national discourse and ongoing policy development processes concerning student sexual misconduct. This is true as institutions await new regulations proposed by the U.S. Department of Education and will likely remain true following any future enactment of the proposed regulations. This section provides a sample of the due process concerns related to students accused of sexual misconduct and highlights how these align with or differ from concerns raised by victims/survivors.

In the era of #MeToo, it is nearly impossible to escape the exponentially growing number of individual voices describing what happened to them. Those subjected to all forms of sexual misconduct, from sexual harassment to rape, are demanding accountability for the harm that was done to them. A number of powerful figures in business, media, politics, and education have been forced to confront their prior behavior, while being held accountable, at least in some respects, for their actions. In response, there has been increased attention paid to the forums in which accountability is possible and a call for increased due process protections for anyone accused—regardless of sex, gender identity, gender expression, or sexual orientation.

Two of the earliest and most publicized critiques of campus policy concerning student sexual misconduct came from law professors at both Harvard College and the University of Pennsylvania. In October 2014, 28 members of the Harvard Law School faculty published a statement in the *Boston Globe* objecting to a newly adopted university-wide policy on student sexual misconduct at Harvard (Bartholet et al., 2014). Among other things, they expressed concern with the placement of investigative, fact-finding, and appellate functions in one office and, more specifically, an office dedicated to Title IX compliance. Doing so, they argued, presents a structural conflict of interest because it gives one office undue influence over the disposition and because that office, by design, must protect the institution itself from Title IX violations. In February 2015, 16 members of the University of Pennsylvania Law School faculty published an open letter expressing similar concerns. Advocating for impartial hearing processes with appropriate checks and balances, they said, "It should not be forgotten that these proceedings are conducted in the shadow of threats of a U.S. Department of Education investigation for failure to properly investigate and sanction students for alleged misconduct. The threat of loss of federal funding risks coloring the proceedings, particularly because a hearing panel may not feel free to acquit without repercussions" (Rudovsky et al., 2015, p. 4). Although penned with accused students in mind, concerns related to conflict of interest, undue influence, and due process have been expressed by some victims/survivors and victim advocates as well. Institutions, they argue, sweep accusations under the rug to maintain a positive public image and are sometimes inappropriately beholden to revenue streams, including athletic programs and wealthy donors.

Further complicating the environment, critics argue, are cultures that gravitate toward believing one party over the other. Students accused of sexual misconduct argue that victim-centered cultures cause institutions to believe and support victims/survivors at the expense of students accused. They note, for example, that trauma-informed training related to investigation or adjudication often focuses on the trauma of being victimized and does not address historic trauma that may be experienced by either or both parties. Some respondents also argue that their institutions are biased against males more generally, even going so far as to claim sex-based discrimination under Title IX (e.g., *Doe v. Columbia University*, 2016). Victims/survivors, in contrast, note that institutions have long-ignored the sexual violence primarily impacting women and, in doing so, have violated Title IX. Suffice it to say, concerns related to bias are shared by students who experience sexual misconduct and those they accuse of committing it.

Additional concern has been raised by respondents about the lack of opportunity for cross-examination. Some commentators have called it "the most important procedure in reaching a fair and reliable determination of disputed facts" (Rudovsky et al., 2015, p. 4), which may be part of the reason why it was proposed in the regulations published by the U.S. Department of Education in late 2018. In a recent case requiring the University of Michigan to permit some form of cross-examination in sexual misconduct cases, the Sixth Circuit Court of Appeals called cross-examination "'the greatest legal engine ever invented' for uncovering the truth" (*Doe v. Baum et al.*, 2018, p. 6).

Not only does cross-examination allow the accused to identify inconsistencies in the other side's story, but it also gives the factfinder an opportunity to assess a witness's demeanor and determine who can be trusted. So if a university is faced with competing narratives about potential misconduct, the administration must facilitate some form of cross-examination in order to satisfy due process (*Doe v. Baum et al.*, 2018, p. 6).

According to the Sixth Circuit, due process in sexual misconduct cases requires a hearing with the opportunity to conduct cross examination whenever a case hinges on questions of credibility because of the substantial interests at stake and the minimal burden the institution would bear by allowing cross-examination (*Doe v. Baum et al.*, 2018).

Recognizing the important and countervailing interests of victims/survivors who seek to avoid the secondary trauma that cross-examination could produce, the Sixth Circuit concluded that the cross-examination process need not be identical to that of a criminal proceeding. As an alternative, the majority in *Doe v. Baum et al.* suggested institutions could allow an accused student's agent to conduct cross-examination on his or her behalf. This approach was largely adopted in the regulations proposed by the U.S. Department of Education despite the concurring opinion in *Doe v. Baum et al.*, which suggested it travels "a bridge too far" (p. 18), and that allowing parties to submit questions to each other or witnesses through the factfinder is sufficient. Although commonly viewed as a ruling in favor of accused students, a circumscribed form of cross-examination could—if it provided adequate protections that avoided secondary victimization—benefit students who experience sexual misconduct as well. In some cases, the complainant may have an interest in testing the veracity of the respondent's statements or examining the credibility of witnesses.

Observers have also expressed support and concern with the evidentiary standard often applied in campus sexual misconduct cases (i.e., preponderance of the evidence; see also chapter 7). Although no longer required to use this standard by OCR, many campuses have chosen to maintain it. For some, that decision is simply a matter of aligning the evidentiary standard for sexual misconduct matters with the preponderance standard most often used in other student conduct matters. For victim advocates and many others, the preponderance standard is viewed as essential to supporting and encouraging victims/survivors to report what happened to them and to creating an opportunity for early intervention with students who may be at risk for further harming behaviors. Critics argue that using the preponderance standard for sexual misconduct matters subjects the most serious campus offenses to the least exacting evidentiary standard. According to these critics, a clear and convincing evidentiary standard would serve as a "more durable safeguard against wrongful 'convictions'" (Rudovsky et al., 2015, p. 5). Critics also suggest that absent a higher evidentiary standard, institutions could decrease the risk of inappropriate findings of responsibility by requiring a unanimous decision from a well-trained, impartial, multimember hearing panel that uses the lower preponderance of the evidence standard (Rudovsky et al., 2015)—an approach that may also result in fewer students being found responsible overall. Regardless of the level of evidence required, there is general consensus that the surrounding procedures should be "scrupulously fair" (Rudovsky et al., 2015, p. 5) to protect both the complainant and the student accused of sexual misconduct from any unintended consequences.

Additional concern has been raised by students accused of sexual misconduct about the timing and type of notice provided prior to an institutional investigation into the reported behavior, the restricted role of legal counsel, vague or imprecise findings and conclusions that limit their ability to appeal an adverse ruling, an expansion of the victim's right to appeal, the potential for self-incrimination in any contemporaneous or subsequent criminal proceeding, and what is viewed as an expanded definition of sexual misconduct that infringes on free speech rights and that deviates from the standard articulated by the U.S. Supreme Court in *Davis v. Monroe County Board of Education* (1999) (see e.g., Alexander et al., 2016; Boutros et al., 2017; Mackey, et al., 2017). In response, some argue that raising these concerns amounts to "conflating the extensive procedural protections rightly afforded to criminal defendants with 'fundamental fairness' in the context of a school disciplinary proceeding" (Turner, 2015, para. 1).

In reviewing the totality of due process concerns, the complexity of these issues begins to fully emerge, and it suggests that students, courts, administrative agencies, and institutions are likely to be grappling with various tensions for years to come as they seek solutions that address multiple interests. As they do, it will be important to consider how proposed solutions impact all students involved, including the perspective of those who have been harmed, their peers, those who are accused of sexual misconduct, and those who are responsible for committing it.

The Impact of Being Accused

This section focuses on the impact an accusation has on students accused of sexual misconduct. In discussing the impact on students accused of sexual misconduct, we acknowledge that the experiences of a student who has been harmed and a student who has been accused of harm are incomparable. A deeper examination of a respondent's experience, however, can provide essential information to help improve campus prevention, response, adjudication, and sanctioning processes. This exploration of respondents' experiences does not excuse their behaviors nor does it discount, diminish, or distract from the significant victim/survivor impacts discussed in other chapters. As with the rest of the chapter, the respondent's perspective can be helpful if it is understood in context, as one necessary reference point among many needed to end sexual misconduct in all of its forms.

Unlike the victim/survivor experience, the respondent's experience following an accusation of sexual misconduct has not been widely discussed in research literature. Their experiences, however, have been revealed in other ways, including some initial studies; individual stories shared with friends, colleagues, and media outlets; staff members at campuses that provide respondent support services; and organizations dedicated to supporting students accused of sexual misconduct. Drawing from those sources, it is clear that students accused of sexual misconduct can find the experience tense, difficult, upsetting, and stressful. Common themes from the stories available indicate that an accusation throws the respondent's life into uncertainty and that the impact of it often intensifies as the accusation becomes more formal and more public in nature. The concerns voiced by many respondents include, but are not limited to the following:

- Criminal repercussions, including possible arrest, jailing, criminal conviction, and lifetime registration/notification requirements
- Campus repercussions, including the following possible interim measures: temporary separation from campus; exclusion (officially or unofficially by peers in the "cancel culture") from campus groups, events, classes, or facilities; stay-away/no-contact orders; changes to class schedules; relocation within a residence hall
- Social and familial repercussions, including rejection and stigmatization via public disclosure of the incident
- Other repercussions, including legal fees, if the accused student decides to hire counsel to assist with the defense; the shame or isolation that may evolve for the respondent during this process; and the physical, mental, and emotional distress associated with all of the above.

Respondents also report experiencing uncertainty in process and timing, as well as conflicting advice (e.g., from attorneys who recommend saying nothing at all versus friends or family who seek all aspects of the story). All of this occurs prior to any finding of responsibility and can be felt by the respondent's family, friends, and anyone closely associated with the respondent.

Numerous students accused of sexual misconduct have shared their stories about the impact of the accusation on their lives. Some students have taken responsibility for their actions with or without the formal adjudication process (e.g., Lepp, 2018). Others speak of being falsely accused, of lives ruined, and reputations destroyed (e.g., Witt, 2014; Zheng, 2015). They sometimes speak as victims of an unfair process or one that was biased against them. Given what's known about the low rate of false reporting (estimated in the range of 2–10%, according to the National Sexual Violence Resource Center, 2012), scenarios in which the student accused of sexual misconduct has done nothing wrong are likely quite rare. They are nevertheless important to acknowledge and consider in the adjudication processes. A long-held maxim of criminal law is that it is better to let the crime of a guilty person go unpunished than to inappropriately condemn the innocent (see e.g., Halvorsen, 2004). The fundamental worry in a criminal setting is that an innocent person will be sent to jail and, for sexual crimes, placed on the sex offender registry for a crime they did not commit. The registry, in turn, will impact where that person can live and work. To protect against the consequences of wrongful conviction, criminal law affords defendants a presumption of innocence, which must be overcome by the prosecution and utilizes the "beyond a reasonable doubt" evidentiary standard. In the campus context, there are similar worries, but consequences on a different scale (e.g., expulsion or transcript notations that could impact enrollment at other institutions or future career choices). Advocates for respondents are also concerned that an accusation alone is enough to create turmoil regardless of any protective procedural presumption.

To adequately address the long history of sexual misconduct on college campuses, which includes innumerable victims/survivors who were not given the chance to speak, were rarely heard, and were not provided the support and resources they needed to address the harm, it may be inescapable that students accused of sexual misconduct will experience some form of condemnation, whether public or private, whether found responsible or not. Campuses, after all, must take reports of sexual misconduct seriously, investigate them exhaustively before making a final determination, and adequately address the impacts on victims/survivors in both the short and long term. The challenge for campus administrators is to minimize, whenever possible, unintended impacts of the process itself on all students involved as they pursue a final result, while also creating an environment that encourages reporting through victim-centered approaches.

What Is Known About Students Who Commit Sexual Misconduct

In contrast to research about victims/survivors, there is a paucity of research about the individuals who perpetrate various forms of sexual misconduct. Most of the research about individuals who have sexually harmed is based on a small percentage who have been reported, apprehended, and convicted in a criminal setting. However, there is a small and growing body of research within a community, campus, or military setting about a wider range of sexually aggressive behaviors. These studies suggest that sexual harassment and sexual coercion exist along a continuum with similar variables (i.e., high sexualization and hostile sexuality) (Knight, Longpre, & Guay, 2018). This research continues to find that those who commit some form of sexual harassment, sexual assault, or sexual violence are a diverse and heterogeneous population—with differing frequencies of behavior, for varying reasons, and different levels of risk for future sexually aggressive behaviors (Breiding, Smith, Basile, Walters, Chen & Merrick, 2011; Hanson, Bourgon, Helmus & Hodgson, 2009; Hanson, Harris, Helmus & Thornton, 2014; Hanson & Morton-Bourgon, 2004; Harris & Hanson, 2004). These findings are consistent with victims/survivors who report being harmed in a variety of ways by a wide variety of individuals, including friends, strangers, acquaintances, intimate partners, family members, colleagues, employers, clergy, and others. This section shares more of what is known about the behaviors, those who commit them, and the various trajectories of campus rape behavior to further inform campus efforts related to prevention, adjudication, and the sanctioning of students found responsible for sexual misconduct.

Variety of Sexual Misconduct Behaviors

In the college and university environment, there is a wide range of behaviors that fall under the widely used umbrella term **sexual misconduct**. One recent examination suggested as many as 42 distinct behaviors that are referred to as sexual misconduct (Koss, Wilgus, & Williamsen, 2014). Those behaviors include contact offenses and non-contact offenses. They include negative coercion, escalated coercion, incapacitation, threats of bodily harm, and physical force. They encompass social and romantic relationships, as well as behaviors that arise in the learning environment and workplace. And they range from verbal sexual harassment to nonconsensual penetration of the vagina, mouth, or anus involving threats of bodily harm or direct physical force. Exhibitionism, voyeurism, disclosures of sexually explicit material/images/information, verbal sexual harassment, forced kissing, groping, forced sex, attempted rape, drug-facilitated and incapacitated sexual assault, attempted rape, and completed rape are all included under this rubric. Some of these behaviors are criminal in nature; some are not.

Heterogeneity of Individuals Who Commit Sexual Misconduct

The wide range of the behaviors described are not perpetrated by a single type of student, but rather a broad diversity of students perpetrating a variety of behaviors, for a variety of motivations, with various levels of cognitive development, and under a variety of environmental conditions. Understanding the heterogeneity of students who commit sexual misconduct and the causes of their behaviors can help institutions manage and mitigate risk of harm more effectively. While this chapter will not delve deeply into research on the etiology of this behavior, it is instructive to note that there is a wealth of information available based on adults and adolescents who have committed a sexual offense and the studies that examine a broader range of sexually aggressive behaviors. Among this population, there is consensus that a number of different factors contribute to sexual assault and that there is no single "type" of individual who engages in sexually offensive behavior.

There is also a growing body of research that shows that while the legal end of adolescence is 18, adolescence as measured by brain development continues until the age of 25 or 26. As "emerging adults," traditional-age college students (18–23 years old) are legally adults, yet developmentally similar to adolescents. They have some of the same "psychosocial, psychosexual, cognitive and neurocognitive immaturity of juveniles, with all of the predictable sequelae of risk taking, impulsivity, poor decision-making, increased proneness to breaking the law, and intense, often poorly managed emotions" (Lamade, Lopez, Koss, Prentky, & Brereton, 2018, p. 5). As such, the research that can offer insights about them are mostly from older adolescents or young adults. The risk factors associated with sexually aggressive behavior in this population include anti-social orientation, self-regulation problems, non-criminal sexual behaviors, and sexual drive/sexual preoccupation/sexual deviance (Lamade et al., 2018).

Among male college students who engage in sexually aggressive behavior, one widely accepted model suggests sexually aggressive behavior stems from the "confluence" of three synergistic pathways involving promiscuous/impersonal sex, hostile masculinity (which involves dominating and controlling personality traits), and the influence of a high-dominance, low-nurturance approach to interpersonal relationships, among other factors (Dean & Malamuth, 1997; Hunter, Figuerado, Malamuth, & Becker, 2003; Malamuth, Sockloskie, Koss, & Tanaka, 1991). There is well-developed research on the assessment of these factors, which could be useful to administrators as they determine their responses to various individuals, behaviors, and circumstances. The campus context is further complicated by environmental characteristics that create a "perfect storm" of risk-converging factors, including opportunities for social engagement, the presence of alcohol, and coercion-supporting peer groups (Lamade et al., 2018). It is also complicated by varying levels of cognitive development and understanding.

Few campuses have developed systems and protocols to address the growing number of students who have been accused of sexual misconduct and also identified as having an intellectual or developmental disability. In cases involving these students, institutions must consider both the impact on the victim as well as the cognitive understanding/development (and need for a different response) of the student who has caused the harm. For example, in a case involving stalking, a student on the autism spectrum may think they are pursuing a friendship, while the victim experiences significant trauma linked to the other student's failure to recognize indirect social cues that neurotypical students would likely interpret as "no." Understanding these developmental differences expands an institution's ability to effectively address these behaviors, provide processes and sanctions that ensure the safety of students involved and the surrounding campus community, and promote ongoing growth, healthy behaviors, and healthy relationships.

Multiple Trajectories for Individuals Who Commit Campus Rape

Sexual misconduct on college campuses includes a wide range of behaviors, yet a great deal of discussion focuses on one behavior: rape. One widely discussed study suggested that a small number of men perpetrate the great majority of rapes on a college campus (Lisak & Miller, 2002). According to that study, which examined the impact of "undetected rapists" on college campuses, these men commit, on average, 5.8 rapes each during their college years. These statistics informed a generation (or more) of campus administrators and galvanized the conviction of all who believe and support victims/survivors of sexual violence that it must be a priority to identify and expel those who cause so much harm on college campuses. A more recent study, however, suggests greater heterogeneity among students who commit rape (Swartout, Koss, White, Thompson, Abbey, & Bellis, 2015). That study outlines three distinct trajectories for the likelihood that a student will commit rape: (a) consistently low or time limited; (b) decreasing; and (c) increasing. It goes on to say that the majority of those who commit rape during their high school or college years fall into the low/time-limited or decreasing categories. According to Swartout and colleagues (2015), there are young men who perpetrate rape across multiple college years, but focusing exclusively on them may cause campus administrators responsible for prevention programs and adjudication processes to overlook the larger number of men who rape, but who do so in low, time-limited, or decreasing frequencies. These findings echo results from current research on known sex offenders about the heterogeneity of this population (Sex Offender Management, Assessment, and Planning Initiative [SOMAPI], 2019) and, more recently, desistance patterns (Farmer, McAlinden, & Maruna, 2015; Harris, 2014; Robbe, Mann, Maruna, & Thornton, 2015). They also reinforce the need for more complex campus prevention programs and adjudication processes that match the heterogeneity of the population.

Although research related to college students who engage in sexual misconduct continues to evolve, current findings indicate that it is essential to understand the context, the behaviors, the motivations, the developmental stages, and the cognitive abilities of the student involved (Andrews, Bonta, & Wormith, 2011; Hanson et al., 2009). Doing so increases an institution's ability to respond flexibly, proportionately, and appropriately to each situation and each student.

The Path Forward

In the current climate, it may be difficult to imagine any path forward that would adequately address the needs of the growing number of students coming forward to report sexual misconduct, much less a path forward that also adequately addresses concerns raised by students accused of sexual misconduct and what is known about students who commit sexual misconduct. That being said, there seem to be various opportunities worth pursuing that could help address persistent tensions and improve campus efforts to prevent and respond to reported sexual misconduct. Those opportunities include, among other things, establishing and implementing adjudication processes that all parties perceive as fair, disaggregating the individuals involved and the behaviors that create harm to permit more specialized interventions, training college and university staff members to manage heterogeneous populations, providing equitable support to all parties involved that adequately addresses their unique needs, and expanding the options available to more fully address the complex realities of campus sexual misconduct.

Establishing Informed Adjudication Processes

With the proposed regulatory revisions to Title IX, local, national, and institutional leaders have an opportunity to update the current framework in a way that incorporates multiple perspectives and addresses various concerns. Although it is beyond the scope of this chapter to suggest specific ways to address each concern, stakeholders may benefit from keeping in mind that providing all parties with a fair and adequate process is not only legally essential, it is vital to campus prevention efforts and the educational mission of higher education more broadly. There is a growing body of evidence indicating that a student's perception of procedural fairness is critically linked to his or her acceptance of the outcome (Mackey et al., 2017). If a student accepts the result, it decreases the risk of litigation, which means the institution avoids expending valuable resources that would be better allocated to prevention efforts related to student sexual misconduct. Moreover, a student's perception of procedural fairness is directly linked to the educational value received from the disciplinary process (King, 2012). When a student perceives the process as fair, their perception of the educational value offered by the process increases. When a student perceives the process as unfair, educational value decreases.

Disaggregating the Students and the Behaviors

Students accused of sexual misconduct are often discussed or referred to in ways that discount other aspects of their identity or potential (e.g., predators, perps, perpetrators, rapists, offenders, sex offenders) and that lump all types of offenses into one concept, typically rape. This approach ignores important distinctions between the individuals and their behaviors and assumes they need to be identified with a label because their sexually inappropriate behavior will persist over time. Students who are subjected to sexual misconduct (victims/survivors) are similarly reduced to a label and repeatedly characterized in terms that suggest they are, or were, somehow responsible for the harm they experienced and will always be identified by that harm. Neither characterization is consistently useful in efforts to confront the realities and complexities of student sexual misconduct, to help the students heal, and to create a safer community.

Given what is known about the heterogeneity of individuals who sexually harm, the wide variety of behaviors in which they engage, and the varied trajectories of campus rape specifically, disaggregating the students involved and their behaviors provides an opportunity to more directly target sexually aggressive behavior in all of its forms, to intervene earlier to prevent harm in the first place, and to reduce the risk of re-offense. Studies have shown that changes in dynamic risk factors correspond with the trajectories of sexual aggression (Thompson, Kingree, Zinzow, & Swartout, 2015). This means it is possible to alter the trajectory of sexual aggression by targeting appropriate **criminogenic needs** (e.g., impulsivity, hostile attitudes toward women, rape supportive beliefs, perceptions of peer approval of forced sex, sexual compulsivity, and perceptions of peer pressure to have sex with many different women). To do so, however, it is critical to treat each student uniquely.

Providing Specialized Training

Faced with the complexity of student sexual misconduct, campuses clearly benefit from unique areas of specialization. One area that warrants greater attention relates to managing the full range of sexually aggressive behaviors. In a 2014 survey, student conduct professionals reported a strong desire for additional training about the diversity of individuals who commit acts of sexual misconduct and research-informed approaches to sanctioning students found responsible for sexual misconduct (University of Michigan, Office of Student Conflict Resolution, Association for Student Conduct Administration, & Center for Effective Public Policy, 2014). As demonstrated in this chapter, the risk factors associated with sexual aggression are complex. Addressing them in a holistic manner has implications for campus prevention efforts, student group advising strategies, campus counseling services, adjudication processes, and more. One recent initiative focused on the sanctioning process specifically and provided specialized training to select pilot sites interested in using risk assessment and treatment interventions (including both cognitive behavioral therapy and psychoeducation) designed for college students found responsible for sexual misconduct (Lamade et al., 2018). As campus prevention and response efforts related to sexual misconduct continue to develop, it will become increasingly important to make sure appropriate staff members have the necessary training and it may become necessary for institutions to look outside higher education for assistance. Although campus adjudication processes are relatively new to confronting problematic sexual behavior and the diversity of individuals who engage in this behavior, there are many professionals who have been addressing it within criminally adjudicated populations (both adult and juvenile) for decades (see e.g., resources available from the Association for the Treatment of Sexual Abusers). There is much to be learned from them.

Creating Equitable Support Services

As campuses broadly consider the question of equitable services in the context of Title IX, it becomes clear there are considerable resources offered to support victims/survivors of sexual misconduct and relatively few parallel support services for students accused of sexual misconduct. Those institutions that do offer "Respondent Support Services" may not provide specialized confidential support (e.g., University of New Mexico, Dean of Students Office, n.d.), as is customary with victim support services. Without equitable services, students accused of sexual misconduct may lack the support they need to navigate complex emotions, consider their past behaviors, and, if appropriate, accept responsibility via formal or informal processes. Although some students can access a campus counseling center for general support, campus counselors are rarely given the training necessary to provide specialized counseling to students with problematic sexual behaviors. In addition, campus counseling staff are not typically trained or positioned to provide advice on how students accused of sexual misconduct ought to navigate the campus adjudication process. Consequently, many students turn to outside legal counsel for advice (frequently defense counsel), which increases the feeling of litigiousness in already intense situations. They may also turn to external clinicians for support with their mental health needs. Having equitable on-campus support services or the ability to make specialized referrals to off-campus providers may not eliminate a respondent's desire (or need) for external support, but it could reduce the feeling of bias that some students express and create additional options for reporting and/or resolving sexual misconduct matters.

Expanding Options

It has been well documented that most campus sexual misconduct is never reported to the institution or law enforcement (Cantor, Fisher, Chibnall, Townsend, Lee, Bruce, & Thomas, 2017). Although most victims/survivors say they did not report the incident because they did not consider it "serious enough," others say they felt too embarrassed or ashamed to report, or that they did not believe anything would be done about it (Cantor et al., 2017, p. 36). These decisions may also have something to do with the limited number of options available for resolving reported sexual misconduct. Some victims/survivors, for example, express a desire to be heard by respondents outside traditional adjudication practices (McGlynn, Westmarland, & Godden, 2012). This corresponds with a desire among some who have been accused to take ownership for their actions (e.g., Lepp, 2015). This subset of respondents faces a unique quandary. They may know they did something wrong and want to acknowledge their behaviors, but feel unable to do so for multiple reasons. If their behavior reaches the level of a criminal offense, they may fear that admitting to some behaviors will be used against them in a criminal proceeding. Even if the behavior was non-criminal in nature, they may fear that accepting responsibility will trigger one or more of the campus-based impacts described previously. If they have talked with an attorney, they are likely to receive the advice to say nothing to anyone about the situation.

This is the essential conundrum and opportunity behind efforts to integrate restorative justice practices into campus procedures for addressing sexual misconduct (see e.g., Campus PRISM, 2016; Koss, Wilgus, & Williamsen, 2014; and chapter 11 of this book). Described as an expansion of the campus adjudication framework, restorative justice practices offer an opportunity to address the harm with a focus on healing and accountability, rather than punishment alone. By accepting responsibility for their behavior in a restorative justice process, students who engaged in sexual misconduct are given an opportunity to repair the harm they created and victims/survivors are offered closure that meets their needs without the turmoil of an adjudication process. The student who engaged in sexual misconduct may still face significant accountability measures, including temporary or permanent separation from the institution. That accountability, however, stems from a willingness to accept responsibility for their behavior and the harm it created, rather than a formal adjudication process designed to determine what the respondent already knows (i.e., that they did it). Campus adjudication processes ought not underestimate the willingness of some respondents to take full responsibility for their actions, or the interest among some victims/survivors to participate with the respondent in a restorative process that allows them to share the impact of the respondent's behavior with the respondent directly, articulate what they need from the respondent to repair the harm they created, and formalize a redress plan that requires the respondent to follow through. Likewise, campuses ought not ignore the very real conundrum faced by these students (i.e., traditional campus adjudication practices do not satisfy their needs). Efforts to adequately address these student interests and concerns under any new regulations that may be issued by the U.S. Department of Education or under the existing framework could open the window to significant reform in cycles and cultures of sexual misconduct.

Another way to expand the options and deepen the impact of campus prevention and response efforts relates to sanctioning processes. The diversity of behaviors and students involved requires sanctioning options that match the complexity of the individual, the behavior, and the environment. Current options are quite limited and frequently only involve one or more of the following: no-contact orders; housing and class restrictions; educational interventions (e.g., readings, reflection papers, lectures, movie viewings); referrals to specialized training (e.g., regarding consent, sexual harassment, or Title IX); periods of probation or suspension; and, when necessary, expulsion, which may or may not be noted on a student's transcript (see also chapter 10). According to a recent study, student conduct professionals very rarely utilize findings from research-informed, sexual abuser-specific risk assessment instruments to inform their sanctioning decisions (University of Michigan, Office of Student Conflict Resolution, Association for Student Conduct Administration, & Center for Effective Public Policy, 2014). They also rarely include referrals to specialized clinicians for treatment specific to sexual misconduct (see e.g., Lamade et al., 2018, describing a specialized treatment program for college students found responsible for sexual misconduct) as an element of typical sanctioning packages. Any referrals to treatment that do exist are generally to campus counselors or external clinicians who are more equipped to manage typical mental health issues among students (e.g., depression, anxiety) than problematic sexual behaviors among heterogeneous offending populations. Without options that are responsive to the granularity that exists among students, behaviors, and harms, campus administrators frequently resort to past precedent when deciding what sanction(s) to apply in a given case (University of Michigan, Office of Student Conflict Resolution, Association for Student Conduct Administration, & Center for Effective Public Policy, 2014). This approach, although common, is not rooted in what is known about students who commit sexual misconduct and what can be done to reduce their likelihood of engaging in similar behavior in the future. Moreover, it does not address whether the sanction was helpful to the victim.

Conclusion

In the changing landscape of campus sexual harassment, sexual assault, and sexual violence, this chapter addressed the numerous ways in which institutions could improve current prevention, response, and adjudication efforts by incorporating what is known about respondents and their perspectives. This chapter explored due process concerns articulated by respondents and noted instances in which victims/survivors may share their concern; it provided a window into the impact of an accusation on students accused of sexual misconduct; it addressed what is known from current research about students who engage in sexually aggressive behavior; and it encouraged respondents' perspectives to be viewed as an addition to victims/survivors' perspectives rather than oppositional to them. The chapter challenges colleges and universities to move beyond a one-size-fits-all approach to develop more complex and comprehensive responses that match the complexity of these situations and the individuals involved. Colleges and universities can build stronger prevention, intervention, and adjudication processes by paying attention to what we know and what we are learning about *all* individuals involved: the student harmed, the student who caused the harm, their peers, and their support people. Given the focus of this chapter, institutions can begin this process by evaluating their current adjudication practices to ensure that they address a wide range of sexual behaviors among a heterogeneous population, while considering how their processes affect all parties involved. In some cases, their review may call for multiple approaches that honor the unique lives, bodies, experiences, perspectives, and future potential of students who experience sexual misconduct, students accused of sexual misconduct, and students responsible for sexual misconduct. This more complex approach addresses the goal of Title IX (i.e., sustaining educational environments free of sex-based discrimination) while supporting the institution's primary educational mission: providing a safe and healthy environment where students can learn and grow.

KEY TERMS

Criminogenic needs: Traits, characteristics, and behaviors that are directly related to offending behavior. They are changeable and, when changed, reduce the likelihood that an individual will reoffend.

Respondent: The individual accused of engaging in sex discrimination.

Responsible person: A student who has been found responsible for sexual misconduct through a campus adjudication process or one who has accepted responsibility for the reported behavior outside the traditional adjudication framework.

Sexual misconduct: A phrase widely used to describe the behaviors prohibited by Title IX, some of which are criminal in nature (e.g., rape, sexual assault), and others which are illegal, but not criminal in nature (e.g., discrimination).

DISCUSSION QUESTIONS

1. What assumptions have you made about students who commit sexual misconduct and how do those assumptions impact how you think about campus adjudication processes?
2. What labels or processes are used on your campus that limit the number of choices available to students who experience or engage in sexual misconduct?
3. How might expanding the number of choices for how to deal with a student found responsible for sexual misconduct impact a victim's choice to report?
4. What is being done on your campus to address students who have engaged in sexual misconduct but who have not been formally reported to your institution? Similarly, what is being done to address students who recognize they have done something wrong but who have not been reported for doing so?

References

Alexander, L., Bibas, S., Barnhizer, D., Caine, B., Bartholet, E., Candeub, D. … & Wilmarth, A. E., Jr. (2016, June 1). *Law professors' open letter regarding campus free speech and sexual assault*. Retrieved from http://www.saveservices.org/wp-content/uploads/Law-Professor-Open-Letter-May-16-2016.pdf

Ali, R. (2011, April 4). Dear Colleague Letter. Washington, DC: U.S. Department of Education, Office for Civil Rights.

Andrews, D. A., Bonta, J., & Wormith, J. S. (2011). The risk-need-responsivity (RNR) model: Does adding the good lives model contribute to effective crime prevention. *Criminal Justice and Behavior, 38*(7), 735–755.

Baker, K., Brake, D., Cantalupo, N., Abramovsky, A., Abrams, A., Ahlers, G. … & Yung, C. (2016, August 4). *Title IX and the preponderance of the evidence: A white paper*. Retrieved from http://www.feministlawprofessors.com/wp-content/uploads/2017/07/Title-IX-Preponderance-White-Paper-signed-7.18.17-2.pdf

Bartholet, E., Brewer, S., Clark, R., Dershowitz, A., Desan, C., Donahue, C., … & Wilkins, D. (2014, October 15). Rethink Harvard's sexual harassment policy. *Boston Globe*. Retrieved from https://www.bostonglobe.com/opinion/2014/10/14/rethink-harvard-sexual-harassment-policy/HFDDiZN7nU2UwuUuWMnqbM/story.html

Bennett, L., Gregory, M., Loschiavo, C., & Waller, J. (2014). *Student conduct administration and Title IX: Gold standard practices for resolution of allegations of sexual misconduct on college campuses*. College Station, TX: Association for Student Conduct Administration. Retrieved from https://www.theasca.org/files/Publications/ASCA%202014%20Gold%20Standard.pdf

Black, M. C., Basile, K. C., Breiding, M. J., Smith, S. G., Walters, M. L., Merrick, M. T., Chen, J., & Stevens, M. R. (2011). *The National Intimate Partner and Sexual Violence Survey (NISVS): 2010 summary report*. Atlanta, GA: Centers for Disease Control and Prevention, National Center for Injury Prevention and Control.

Boutros, A. S., Rice Lave, T., Bernard, P. J., Bettinger-Lopez, C., Cary, R. M., Dunn, L. L., ... & Smith, B.V. (2017, June). *ABA criminal justice section task force on college due process rights and victim protections: Recommendations for colleges and universities in resolving allegations of campus sexual misconduct* (Rep.). Retrieved from https://www.americanbar.org/content/dam/aba/publications/criminaljustice/2017/ABA-Due-Process-Task-Force-Recommendations-and-Report.authcheckdam.pdf

Breiding, M. J., Smith, S. G., Basile, K. C., Walters, M. L., Chen, J. & Merrick, M. T. (2011). Prevalence and characteristics of sexual violence, stalking, and intimate partner violence victimization – National Intimate Partner and Sexual Violence Survey, United States. *Morbidity and Mortality Weekly Report: Surveillance Summaries, 63*(8).

Campbell, R., Dworkin, E., & Cabral, G. (2009). An ecological model of the impact of sexual assault on women's mental health. *Trauma, Violence, & Abuse, 10*(3), 225–246.

Campus PRISM. (2016). *A report on promoting restorative initiatives for sexual misconduct on college campuses.* Retrieved from https://www.skidmore.edu/campusrj/documents/Campus_PRISM__Report_2016.pdf

Cantor, D., Fisher, B., Chibnall, S., Townsend, R., Lee, H., Bruce, C., & Thomas, G. (2017). *Report on the AAU Campus Climate Survey on Sexual Assault and Sexual Misconduct.* Rockville, MD: Westat.

Davis v. Monroe County Board of Education, 526 U.S. 629 (1999)

Dean, K. E., & Malamuth, N. M. (1997). Characteristics of men who aggress sexually and of men who imagine aggressing: Risk and moderating variables. *Journal of Personality and Social Psychology, 72*(2), 449–455.

Doe v. Baum et al., No. 17-2213 (6th Cir. 2018). Retrieved from http://www.opn.ca6.uscourts.gov/opinions.pdf/18a0200p-06.pdf

Doe v. Columbia University, The Trustees of Columbia University, No. 15-1536 (2nd Cir. 2016). Retrieved from https://law.justia.com/cases/federal/appellate-courts/ca2/15-1536/15-1536-2016-07-29.html

Farmer, M., McAlinden, A. M., & Maruna, S. (2015). Understanding desistance from sexual offending: A thematic review of research findings. *Probation Journal, 62*(4), 320–335.

Fedina, L., Holmes, J. L., & Backes, B. L. (2016). Campus sexual assault: A systematic review of prevalence research from 2000 to 2015. *Trauma, Violence, & Abuse, 19*(1), 76–93.

Fisher, B. S., Cullen, F. T., & Turner, M. G. (2000). *The sexual victimization of college women.* Washington, DC: U.S. Department of Justice.

Halvorsen, V. (2004). Is it better that ten guilty persons go free than that one innocent person be convicted? *Criminal Justice Ethics, 23*(2), 3–13.

Hanson, R. K., Bourgon, G., Helmus, L., & Hodgson, S. (2009). The principles of effective correctional treatment also apply to sexual offenders: A meta-analysis. *Criminal Justice and Behavior, 36*(9), 865–891.

Hanson, R. K., Harris, A. J., Helmus, L., & Thornton, D. (2014). High-risk sex offenders may not be high risk forever. *Journal of Interpersonal Violence, 29*(15), 2792–2813.

Hanson, R. K. & Morton-Bourgon, K. (2004). *Predictors of sexual recidivism: An updated meta-analysis.* Ottawa, Canada: Public Safety and Emergency Preparedness Canada.

Harris, A. J. R., & Hanson, R. K. (2004). *Sex offender recidivism: A simple question.* Ottawa, Canada: Public Safety and Emergency Preparedness Canada.

Harris, D. A. (2014). Desistance from sexual offending: Findings from 21 life history narratives. *Journal of Interpersonal Violence, 29*(9), 1554–1578.

Hunter, J. A. Figueredo, A. J., Malamuth, N. M., & Becker, J. (2003). Juvenile sex offenders: Toward the development of a typology. *Sexual Abuse: A Journal of Research and Treatment, 15*(1), 27–48.

Jackson, C. (2017, September 22). *Dear Colleague Letter.* Washington, DC: U.S. Department of Education, Office for Civil Rights.

King, R. H. (2012). Student conduct administration: How students perceive the educational value and procedural fairness of their disciplinary experiences. *Journal of College Student Development, 53*(4), 563–580.

Knight, R., Longpre, N., & Guay, J. (2018, October). *The structure and covariates of sexual harassment and coercion*. Paper presented at Association for the Treatment of Sexual Abusers Annual Conference, Vancouver, British Columbia, Canada.

Koss, M. P., Wilgus, J. K., & Williamsen, K. M. (2014). Campus sexual misconduct: Restorative justice approaches to enhance compliance with Title IX guidance. *Trauma, Violence, & Abuse, 15*(3), 242–257.

Krebs, C. P., Lindquist, C. H., Warner, T. D., Fisher, B. S., & Martin, S. L. (2007). *The Campus Sexual Assault (CSA) study*. Washington, DC: National Institute of Justice, U.S. Department of Justice.

Lamade, R. V., Lopez, E., Koss, M. P., Prentky, R., & Brereton, A. (2018). Developing and implementing a treatment intervention for college students found responsible for sexual misconduct. *Journal of Aggression, Conflict and Peace Research, 10*(2), 134–144.

Lepp, S. (Host). (2018, December 3). A survivor and her perpetrator find justice [Audio podcast]. Retrieved from http://www.reckonings.show/episodes/21

Lisak, D., & Miller, P. M. (2002). Repeat rape and multiple offending among undetected rapists. *Violence and Victims, 17*(1), 73–84.

Mackey, P. R., Berger, R. E., Mulvey, E. N., Silbert, E. J., Sparks A.G., III, & American College of Trial Lawyers. (2017). *White paper on campus sexual assault investigations*. Irvine, CA.

Malamuth, N., Sockloskie, R., Koss, M., & Tanaka, J. (1991). The characteristics of aggressors against women: Testing a model using a national sample of college students. *Journal of Consulting and Clinical Psychology, 59*(5), 670–681.

McGlynn, C., Westmarland, N., & Godden, N. (2012). "I just wanted him to hear me": Sexual violence and the possibilities of restorative justice. *Journal of Law and Society, 39*(2), 213–240.

National Sexual Violence Resource Center. (n.d.). *False reporting: Overview*. Retrieved from https://www.nsvrc.org/sites/default/files/Publications_NSVRC_Overview_False-Reporting.pdf

Pavela, G. (2014, September 15). In sexual-misconduct cases, hear the facts. *Chronicle of Higher Education*. Retrieved from https://www.chronicle.com/article/In-Sexual-Misconduct-Cases/148783

Robbe, M., Mann, R.E., Maruna, S., & Thorton, D. (2015). An exploration of protective factors supporting desistance from sexual offending. *Sexual Abuse, 27*(1), 16–33.

Rudovsky, D., Bibas, S., Balganesh, S., Berman, M., Burbank, S. B., Fisch, J. E., … & Wax, A. (2015, February 18). Open letter from members of the Penn Law School faculty. Sexual assault complaints: Protecting complainants and the accused students at universities [Letter]. Philadelphia, PA: University of Pennsylvania Law School.

Sex Offender Management, Assessment, and Planning Initiative (SOMAPI). Retrieved from https://smart.gov/SOMAPI/index.html

Stoner, E. N., & Lowery, J. W. (2004). Navigating past the "spirit of insubordination": A twenty-first century model student code with a model hearing script. *Journal of College and University Law, 31*(1). Retrieved from https://learn.uvm.edu/wordpress_3_4b/wp-content/uploads/stoner___lowery_JCUL_2004_cropped.pdf

Swartout, K. M., Koss, M. P., White, J. W., Thompson, M. P., Abbey, A., & Bellis, A. L. (2015). Trajectory analysis of the campus serial rapist assumption. *JAMA Pediatrics, 169*(12), 1148–1154.

Thompson, M. P., Kingree, J. B., Zinzow, H., & Swartout, K. (2015). Time-varying risk factors and sexual aggression perpetration among male college students. *Journal of Adolescent Health, 57*(6), 637–642.

Turner, E. (2015, February 25). Guest column by Emily Turner: Response to "Open Letter" from members of the Penn Law School faculty. *Daily Pennsylvanian*. Retrieved from https://www.thedp.com/article/2015/02/response-letter-penn-law-school-faculty

University of Michigan, Office of Student Conflict Resolution, Association for Student Conduct Administration, & Center for Effective Public Policy (2014). *National survey of sanctioning practices for student sexual misconduct at institutions of higher education*. Retrieved from https://www2.ed.gov/policy/highered/reg/hearulemaking/2012/vawa-sanctioningpractices.pdf

University of New Mexico, Dean of Students Office. (n.d.). *Respondent support services*. Retrieved from https://dos.unm.edu/services/respondent-advocacy.html

Witt, P. (2014, November 3). A sexual harassment policy that nearly ruined my life. *Boston Globe*. Retrieved from https://www.bostonglobe.com/opinion/2014/11/03/sexual-harassment-policy-that-nearly-ruined-life/hY3XrZrOdXjvX2SSvuciPN/story.html

Zheng, V. (2015, March 30). ZHENG: A false accusation off-campus. *The Cavalier Daily*. Retrieved from https://www.cavalierdaily.com/article/2015/03/zheng-a-false-accusation-off-campus

V Hearing Outcomes

CHAPTER NINE

College Students' Perceptions of Justice in Campus Sexual Assault Cases

Diane R. Follingstad, Claire M. Renzetti, and Jaspreet K. Chahal

Introduction

The adjudication of campus sexual assault cases has been a flashpoint for universities in recent years, with many aspects of the disciplinary process for these cases critiqued and commented on by the media, higher education institutions, national agencies, sexual assault organizations, and the legal profession. While legislation, university regulations, and the U.S. Department of Education guidance have all weighed in on the expected adjudication processes of sexual misconduct cases in postsecondary institutions, little is known about the perspectives of college students themselves. This significant group of stakeholders comprising the peer group of the complainants and respondents in these cases at one time were typically members of hearing panels for all disciplinary infractions, with similar rights and responsibilities as the faculty and staff members with whom they served (Wilson, 1996). However, many institutions of higher education (IHEs) over the years have removed students specifically from panels involving sexual misconduct cases (Brown, 2018). Several reasons have been offered for this. As Cantalupo points out in chapter 5 of this volume, most IHEs now exclude students from sexual misconduct hearing panels due to the serious problems, such as invasions of privacy, risks to confidentiality, and psychological harm, that may arise from students having to disclose highly personal information and evidence (e.g., evidence collected through a "rape kit") to fellow students.

A second reason IHEs may exclude students from hearing panels in sexual misconduct cases is a concern that students may be too closely connected in age and life circumstances to both the complainants and the accused so that they cannot objectively assess those cases. For example, one study found that students used more information external to cases at hand than faculty or administrators when deciding sanctions (Janosik, 1995). Although we would expect that college students would be most cognizant of the current sexual culture at their institution and in their community, this would not necessarily ensure that they have fully matured judgment around issues such as consent or the impact of alcohol on decision making. Some IHEs, therefore, may fear that students may consider the described behavior in a sexual misconduct case as similar to what they see regularly happening on campus, which could lead them to make a judgment based on perceived normative actions, rather than on basic moral implications of consent. And there is a body of literature that generally challenges the assumption that research done with college students can be generalized to U.S. adults (e.g., Carter, Brandon, & Goldman, 2010; Peterson, 2001), suggesting that young adulthood may be a developmental stage not representative of the "adult" population (see also chapter 8).

A third, related reason IHEs may choose to restrict panel members to older individuals or employees of the university in sexual misconduct cases is a concern that students may choose relatively minor sanctions for egregious behavior (e.g., Janosik, 1995). In other words, the concern is that students might empathize with the plight of another accused student, which may result in a student on a hearing panel being unable to imagine ruining the career of a same-age peer, and thus not impose justifiably harsh sanctions. Conversely, IHEs may worry that students may react too strongly to sexual assault cases, thus choosing the harshest sanctions without considering mitigating circumstances. If college students are thought to be more skewed in their judgments in evaluating campus sexual assault cases, IHEs may worry that students would not be able to engage in the subtle nuances of handling disciplinary functions related to Title IX to rectify "sex discrimination" while providing an educational environment that ameliorates harm for the person experiencing that discrimination. College students may view disciplinary systems in their institutions as similar to criminal justice models that identify wrongs, find wrongdoers "guilty," and apply appropriate punishments. Thus, they might be unlikely to consider, for appropriate cases, whether lesser sanctions or less "punishing" sanctions for the respondent would be more beneficial long term for both the complainant and the respondent. For example, chapter 11 suggests that with certain guidelines, the restorative justice model applied to a subset of sexual misconduct cases may potentially produce better healing for the victim/survivor and greater understanding by and impact on the respondent's future behavior than a sanction such as expulsion (see also chapter 8).[1]

Thus, students are now typically kept at arm's length from adjudication of sexual misconduct cases at the same time that their views of and judgments in these cases involving their peers are relatively unknown. There is, in fact, limited research regarding college students' views on appropriate sanctions in cases of campus sexual misconduct, particularly in terms of whether specific characteristics of the complainant, the respondent, and the context of the misconduct influence their judgments. Research examining mock jurors' deliberations in sexual assault cases have shown that their judgments are influenced by characteristics of both victims and offenders (e.g., Davies, Pollard, & Archer, 2001; Foley, Evancic, Karnik, King, & Parks, 1995; van der Bruggen & Grubb, 2014), as well as the context of the offense (e.g., Castello, Coomer, Stillwell, & Cate, 2006; Grubb & Harrower, 2008; Grubb & Turner, 2012). Scholars conducting meta-analyses (Hockett, Smith, Klausing, & Saucier, 2016; Pollard, 1992; Whatley, 1996) of these findings have concluded that mock jurors view victims negatively when the circumstances of their attack do not appear consistent with the stereotype of what constitutes a "real rape" (i.e., an attack by a stranger in a public place on a sober victim who suffers injuries in her physical defense of herself), thus relying on **rape myths** to guide their reactions (see also chapter 7). Consequently, it would not be surprising if college samples also demonstrated some reactivity to variations in scenarios depicting sexual assaults. However, in recent years, college students have been exposed to considerable information about sexual misconduct and assault through campus prevention programs and media, making an assessment of their susceptibility to modifying their judgments based on characteristics of persons involved or assault characteristics clearly warranted. Specifically, there is virtually no research assessing college students' views as to appropriate sanctions, either across cases with varying characteristics or in response to those case characteristics. We are also lacking knowledge as to whether college students' preformed attitudes are proximally or distally related to campus sexual assault cases. From such information, future research should compare college students' perceptions of justice with non-student populations, including their peers not enrolled in college as well as older adults both inside and outside the university community, especially regarding cases involving prototypical *campus* sexual assaults. Results from research projects involving general community samples reacting to what they believe are more prototypical criminal justice sexual assault cases (e.g., a stranger attacks a sober woman in an outdoor setting where she fought back) cannot be considered equivalent in comparison with the types of person and incident characteristics more likely to be associated with college sexual assault cases.

A better understanding of college students' perceptions of justice for campus sexual misconduct/assault cases should contribute to more evidence-based decisions about the inclusion of students on hearing panels for these cases. More importantly perhaps, understanding students' perspectives regarding these cases may also assist in the development of better prevention and intervention programming on campuses. If we wish to encourage students to report incidents of sexual misconduct and to act as bystanders to prevent or intervene in potential sexual misconduct/assault incidents, we need to better understand their perceptions of guilt, responsibility, and just outcomes in these cases. As well, continued research in this area will also add to the body of literature regarding how members of various social groups react to and make judgments about sexual assault, especially when research findings on the criminal justice model versus campus disciplinary systems may diverge.

An Exploratory Study Assessing College Students' Perceptions of Justice in Campus Sexual Assault Cases

To begin to examine college students' perceptions of justice in campus sexual assault cases, we designed an exploratory study that asked a sample of female and male undergraduates at a large, public university in the southeastern United States to assign relative guilt and responsibility to the victim and an accused student in various sexual assault scenarios, and to recommend what they perceived to be a just sanction for the offender. In this chapter, we discuss some of the details of the methodology of the study and share some of the findings.

Methodology

One of our major goals in the exploratory study was to assess whether external and/or internal factors might affect students' judgments of guilt, responsibility, and just sanctions in cases of campus sexual assault. To do this, we developed vignettes that described sexual assault incidents involving age-similar college students as the complainants and respondents and applied prototypical college lifestyle issues (e.g., alcohol use, types of consequences for the victim). We sought to understand the type and severity of sanctions students would apply to various scenarios of sexual assault and, as a way to potentially understand the judgments they applied, we also assessed their attributions of guilt (**blame**) and **responsibility** to both the complainant and the respondent.

Study participants were recruited through the university's psychology participant pool, who, after consenting to participate, completed a questionnaire online. The final sample had 248 male students (29%) and 597 female students (71%), with an age range of 18–46 (median age = 19). The majority of participants identified as White/Caucasian (80%), with 10% identifying as Black/African American, 5% Hispanic, 2% Asian, and three identifying with another racial/ethnic group (response category "other"); approximately 1% were international students. Two-thirds of the participants were first-year students, but analyses comparing their responses with other undergraduates who participated determined that separate groupings were not necessary for analyses.

Our review of the research literature led us to identify 14 factors as especially pertinent for campus sexual assault cases. These factors include victim characteristics, offender characteristics, and characteristics of the sexual assault, including consequences of the assault for the victim (Pollard, 1992; Whatley, 1996) (see Table 9.1 for the 14 factors and the levels for each that we measured). To reduce confounds *within* a factor, vignettes used identical stories except for the language that delineated the different levels of a specific factor. To reduce confounds *across* the 14 factors, the same generic scenario was used that (a) employed names of the victim and offender that were unlikely to be construed as implying race (except for the factor that explicitly varied the race of both victim and offender); (b) implied the victim was not using poor judgment in attending the event where the sexual assault occurred (i.e., the victim was invited to a party off campus at a residence where her friends knew the students giving the party); (c) the victim had initial benign contact with the offender; (d) the victim reported the assault in a timely way (i.e., the next morning; and (e) clearly described that a sexual assault had occurred (i.e., the victim did not consent to sex with the respondent, with the exception of the factor in which the male's response to the woman's claim of sexual assault varied regarding admission to the assault). All instances involved heterosexual contact with the exception of one indicating a gay man sexually assaulted a male victim, where sexual orientation is intentionally varied.

Thirty-two vignettes were developed, each representing one level of a factor from the selected 14 factors. The vignettes were distributed across four versions of the survey, each with eight vignettes, to prevent participants from responding to more than one level of a factor and to reduce survey fatigue. We attempted to assign vignettes to the versions based on expected severity of the sanctions to avoid any version being weighted toward greater or lighter sanctions. Preliminary analyses indicated that the demographic characteristics of participants were not significantly different across the four versions, thereby eliminating the need to make adjustments in the later analyses based on participant characteristics.

After reading each case vignette, participants rated the degree to which they believed the offender (stated by name) had committed a violation deserving of a sanction. Participants next chose the sanction they thought should apply in the case from a list of hierarchically ranked sanctions (see Table 9.2). To understand the students' perceptions as to the severity of the sanction they chose, they rated their sanction choice as mild, moderate, or severe. They were also asked in an open-ended format to explain why they imposed a particular sanction. This allowed us to explore their rationales and thinking processes.

TABLE 9.1 Factor Descriptions and Levels

	Name of factor	Levels	Description of each level and version of survey on which it appeared
Victim characteristics	1. Reason for victim's incapacitation leading to sexual assault (Angelone, Mitchell, & Pilafova, 2007; Girard & Senn, 2008; Grubb & Turner, 2012; Hammock & Richardson, 1997)	3	1. Victim slipped a drug without her knowledge (V3) 2. Victim slipped extra liquor without her knowledge (V2) 3. Victim was voluntarily drinking a lot (V4)
	6. Sexual orientation of male victim (Sleath & Bull, 2010; Wakelin & Long, 2003; White & Kurpius, 2002)	3	1. Straight man sexually assaulted by gay man (V1) 2. Gay virgin man sexually assaulted by gay man (V3) 3. Gay man sexually assaulted by gay man (V4)
	11. Level of attractiveness of victim (Calhoun, Selby, Cann, & Keller, 1978; Gerdes, Dammann, & Heilig, 1988; Ryckman, Graham, Thornton, Gold, & Linder, 1998)	2	1. Petite and cute victim (V1) 2. Larger and less attractive victim (V2)
	14. Initial level of sexual interest indicated by the victim (Kowalski, 1992; Schult & Schneider, 1991)	2	1. Woman very interested in sexual activity initially but then decides she does not want to have intercourse (V2) 2. Woman only mildly responsive to man and states at the onset she does not want to have intercourse (V4)
Offender characteristics	5. Accused's reaction varied as to discrepancy with the victim's account	3	1. Accused admits to sexual assault (V1) 2. Accused expressed surprise and said he must have misunderstood victim's reactions (V4) 3. Accused had a very discrepant story from victim claiming her consent (V3)
	9. Offender as high-status student on campus	2	1. Intercourse forced on woman by star basketball player (V4) 2. Intercourse forced on woman by student with no status (V1)
	10. Sexual assault offender was fraternity member (Jozkowski & Wiersma-Mosley, 2017)	2	1. Forced intercourse by a member of a fraternity (V2) 2. Forced intercourse by an individual with no fraternity membership (V4)
	12. Gender of offender in heterosexual sexual assault (Ballman, Leheney, Miller, Simmons & Wilson, 2016)	2	1. Female forces oral sex on male (V3) 2. Male forces oral sex on woman (V1)

Sexual assault characteristics	2. Physical injury resulting from sexual assault (Cohn, Dupuis, & Brown, 2009)	2	1. Physical injuries resulted from the sexual assault (V4) 2. Victim did not incur any physical injuries from the sexual assault (V1)
	3. Medical consequences from the sexual assault	3	1. Victim contracted a STI from the sexual assault (V1) 2. Victim became pregnant from the sexual assault (V4) 3. No STI or pregnancy occurred (V2)
	4. Psychological sequelae resulting from the sexual assault (Omata, 2013; Pickel & Gentry, 2017)	2	1. Victim had serious psychological sequelae from the sexual assault (V2) 2. Victim did not have psychological sequelae from the sexual assault (V4)
	7. Type of forced sex	4	1. Man forces oral sex (cunnilingus) on woman (V1) 2. Man forces woman to perform oral sex (fellatio) on him (V2) 3. Man forces anal sex on woman (V3) 4. Man forces vaginal intercourse on woman (V4)
	8. Individual versus multiple offender sexual assault (Shackelford, 2002)	2	1. Forced intercourse by man on a woman (V3) 2. Three men force intercourse on a woman (V4)
	13. Race of victim and offender (George & Martinez, 2002)	4	1. Both victim and offender are African American (V1) 2. Victim is African American and offender is Caucasian (V2) 3. Victim is Caucasian and offender is African American (V3) 4. Both victim and offender are Caucasian (V4)

TABLE 9.2 Mean Scores of Sanction Ratings on a 10-point Scale of Severity

Sanction	Mean score
1. No punishment at all	N/A
2. Verbal warning	1.7
3. Written assignment about the violation	3.0
4. Community service related to the violation	3.1
5. Written disciplinary reprimand in student's record	3.3
6. Educational program about the violation	3.6
7. Mandatory psychological counseling	3.7
8. Fines/restitution for damages	4.3
9. Mediation session that includes the victim and offender to determine reasonable outcome that the victim approves	4.7
10. Social suspension from presence on campus and campus activities (except classes)	5.6
11. Withhold degree until sanctions completed	6.5
12. Admission or degree revoked	7.9
13. Permanent expulsion from university	8.8

Note: The list of sanctions used for assigning sanctions was compiled from universities' general options that can be applied following disciplinary hearings and was pilot tested to determine a hierarchical ranking based on severity. An introductory sociology course fulfilling general educational requirements was utilized because students enroll from a large range of majors and across class rankings. Students rated (1 as a very mild form of punishment to 10 as a very severe form of punishment) 12 possible sanctions as to their impression of severity if those options were applied as sanctions at campus disciplinary hearings. Students in the pilot testing did not participate in the current study.

To help understand participants' sanction choice as their best option to see justice served, we included two additional judgments for each case they read. Most literature on sexual assault cases (e.g., Grubb & Harrower, 2008; Persson, Dhingra, & Grogan, 2018; Süssenbach, Eyssel, Rees, & Bohner, 2017; van der Bruggen & Grubb, 2014) assesses the degree of guilt/blame that respondents place on the complainant and the accused, and we therefore required participants to assign proportional guilt to the two parties involved (i.e., participants assigned a percentage of guilt to each that had to add to a total of 100%). In addition, prior literature (e.g., Hine & Murphy, 2019; Li, Kim, & O'Boyle, 2017; Qi, Starfelt, & White, 2016) has asked observers to determine whether sexual assault victims bore any responsibility for what happened. The distinction between "blame" and "responsibility" was investigated conceptually in the 1980s (e.g., Brewin & Antaki, 1987; Hamilton, 1980; Shaver & Drown, 1986; Shultz & Schleifer, 1983) with the research findings leading to the conclusion that blame distinctly implies liability for a person's actions, whereas a judgment of responsibility determines whether an individual had a role or was accountable in some way for an event's occurrence (Bradbury & Fincham, 1990). The distinction for ratings in these cases appears significant in that Hockett, Smith, Klausing and Saucier (2016) concluded that observers use different case information for determining guilt versus responsibility. Thus, participants in our study assigned a level of responsibility separately to the victim and offender on a 5-point Likert scale as to "the extent the person could have influenced or changed the likelihood of the situation happening as it did."

After rendering their judgments in the vignettes, participants completed several measures of variables that prior research has shown are associated with observers' perceptions of justice in sexual assault cases: (a) the Rape Myth Acceptance Scale (McMahon & Farmer, 2011) comprised of four subscales (She Asked for It; It Wasn't Really Sexual Assault; He Didn't Mean To; and She Lied); (b) four additional rape myth items that thematically assessed downplaying the significance of sexual assault because of the belief that victims and feminists have exaggerated their claims (Stoll, Lilley & Pinter, 2017); (c) an 11-item sexism scale (Gender-Blind Sexism Inventory) (Stoll, Lilley & Pinter, 2017); (d) a six-item version of the Just World Scale (Loo, 2002) measuring perceptions of fairness in the world; and (e) a short version of the Right Wing Authoritarianism Scale (Zakrisson, 2005), measuring one's orientation regarding punitive responses toward people who do not adhere to societal conventions or norms. To assess social desirability, participants also completed a shortened version (Bobbio & Manganelli, 2011) of Paulhus's (1988) Balanced Inventory of Desirable Responding.

Findings Related to External Conditions (Manipulated Factors)

Even though 13 of the 14 factors clearly indicated that a sexual assault had taken place, participants selected sanctions from almost the entire range of options. Across the 32 vignettes, students' responses significantly differed in that they viewed some of the scenarios as warranting more lenient or more severe sanctions. Despite this variability, however, the modal choice for the sanction for 10 of the 14 factors was the most severe option, suggesting students tended to strongly agree that offenders in the vignettes they evaluated had engaged in a violation that should result in harsh sanctions.[2]

Interestingly, college students did not view all of the factors that we had identified differently when comparing the levels of the factors, such that their assignment of the severity of the sanction, their assignment of guilt, and their assignment of responsibility were not affected by the factor levels. In fact, four of the 14 factors demonstrated *no* differences. First, there were no differences in the scenario depicting whether a victim experienced physical injury as a result of the sexual assault; across the levels of this factor, college students viewed the sexual assault as rape and deserving of serious sanctions. Prior literature in the criminal justice arena suggested that "proof" of a sexual assault was often predicated on the presence of physical injury, indicating adherence to the myth that a woman must show that she aggressively physically fought against the offender to demonstrate her lack of consent. Thus, our finding suggests that, at least with a college-student population, this myth may be disappearing and there is greater understanding of the reality of most sexual assaults.

Second, there were no differences for determinations of justice when students read that the offender was a high-status campus figure (i.e., star basketball player) than when the offender did not have high status (i.e., a student who "helped" with the team). It is possible that media reporting of high-profile cases involving the treatment of offending athletes at universities has sensitized students to not differentiate offenders along this dimension and to not excuse a student's sexual misconduct because of their elevated status on campus.

Third, it is encouraging to note that varying the level of attractiveness of the victim did not result in stronger sanctions for the offender. The sanctions imposed by participants in our study did not differ when the victim was described as petite and "cute" relative to when she was not described this way. This finding suggests that college students are not influenced by the superficial characteristic of victim attractiveness when assigning sanctions, guilt, and responsibility in sexual assault cases.

Finally, varying the race of the victim and offender did not produce differences in assigning guilt/responsibility to the victims, or in applying sanctions to offenders. More specifically, regardless of the race of the victim and offender depicted in the vignette (e.g., White/Caucasian victim and offender; Black/African American victim and offender; Black/African American victim and White/Caucasian offender; or White/Caucasian victim and Black/African American offender), the participants in our study found the offenders deserving of equally severe sanctions and as bearing equal responsibility.

The other 10 factors examined in the study produced significantly different ratings by college students (three victim characteristics, three offender characteristics, and four sexual assault context characteristics). However, judgments made by students were not always consistent within a factor; for example, students might choose different sanctions for levels of a factor, but not rate guilt and/or responsibility differently for those levels.

What distinguished three of the factors from others that produced significant differences in ratings was that *all* the outcome variables were viewed differently across the levels of the factors. These were (a) the factor varying the number of offenders (individual versus multiple); (b) the factor varying whether the female victim had acted flirtatiously toward the offender; and (c) the factor varying the offender's reaction/story in response to the victim's report of sexual assault (admitted he committed the assault, expressed surprised at the accusation and was sorry he "misinterpreted" the situation, or claimed consensual sex). It is perhaps easy to understand why sexual assault by multiple offenders was viewed as deserving stronger sanctions, and assignments of guilt and responsibility to the victim were rated significantly lower than those assigned to the victim who was assaulted by one man. Less understandable, but indicative of support for specific rape myths, were students' ratings in the vignette in which an offender forced sex on a woman who was highly flirtatious initially but who then decided not to have intercourse versus an offender who forced sex on a mildly sexually interested woman who made the same decision not to proceed to intercourse. Students believed the offender with the highly flirtatious victim should receive more lenient sanctions and was less guilty and less responsible for the sexual assault than the offender who forced sex on the mildly sexually interested woman.

Students' judgments for the vignette in which we varied the reaction of the accused man to the woman's claim of sexual assault are more puzzling. The ratings for the offenders in the three levels of the factor were quite distinguishable from each other. This was the only factor in which the vignettes did not state clearly that the young man forced the victim, so explanations for differences for this factor could range from serious concern that a woman claiming rape would be so quickly doubted versus appreciating the ability of college students to wish to be more cautionary if the evidence is unclear. One interesting finding for this factor is that even though the offender who admitted the sexual assault was judged more harshly than the two comparison offenders, the mean ratings of assigned sanctions, guilt, and responsibility were not as high as those of many of the other 13 factors we tested. Thus, it appears participants felt that his admission warranted some reduction in the severity of his punishment. However, in the condition in which the accused male student presents a contradictory story to the woman's claim of sexual assault in the vignettes and claims the sexual encounter was consensual, ratings for assigned sanctions, guilt, and responsibility change significantly. Although some students still believed that a sexual assault occurred, many students quickly moved away from believing the victim's story and were more likely to suggest that the two parties should meet with a mediator to work things out because of their discrepant accounts. This is often the *last* option a victim wants because the victim does not want to face the perpetrator, and because mediation typically assumes that the parties just viewed events differently rather than starting with the assumption that the victim was assaulted. It may be that students in the study share the idea that it was "all just a big misunderstanding" and that is why they assigned the most lenient sanctions to the accused student who stated he engaged in consensual sex. But they also judged him as less guilty and less responsible, even compared with the student who claimed he must have misunderstood the woman's cues. These findings beg for further exploration, since campus sexual assault cases frequently involve situations in which the complainant's and the respondent's accounts differ with regard to consent. The qualitative explanations student participants provided will hopefully elucidate their thinking in this regard.

The other seven factors produced significant rating differences by participants but not consistently across the outcome variables. For example, for the vignette in which the victim experienced psychological problems following the assault, participants assessed more serious sanctions on the offender, but they did not view guilt or responsibility for the offender or victim differently for the two conditions. Similarly, the type of sexual activity forced on a victim influenced participants' assignment of sanctions to the offender: The offender who performed oral sex on the victim (cunnilingus) was given less severe sanctions compared to the offenders who forced intercourse, fellatio, or anal sex, but students did not rate guilt or responsibility differently across conditions in this vignette.

Mixed significant findings were evident for the rest of the factors as well. For instance, a woman being incapacitated from substances when she was sexually assaulted influenced participants' judgment. Not surprisingly, the woman who was slipped a drug was considered least responsible or guilty for the sexual assault. An offender who slipped a victim either a drug or extra alcohol was viewed as more *deserving* of a sanction than the condition in which a woman voluntarily drank until she was incapacitated. Surprisingly, however, the actual sanction assigned across these three conditions was not significantly different. Students' judgments also varied somewhat when the gender of the assaulting offender in a heterosexual assault was varied. Participants believed the male offender was more deserving of a sanction than the female offender was, but the sanctions they imposed were not different for male and female offenders. Interestingly, for this particular vignette, participants viewed the male victim of forced fellatio as more responsible for the assault than the female victim of forced cunnilingus. Sexual orientation of a male victim sexually assaulted by a gay man only produced differences in ratings of responsibility by the participants. Although presented exactly the same as to how the sexual assaults came about, the heterosexual man was viewed as having less responsibility for what occurred compared with a gay male victim and a male victim who was a gay virgin. The offender's status as a fraternity member or not also only demonstrated significant differences in ratings for responsibility of the victim. The female victim of a fraternity member was viewed as less responsible for the sexual assault, which may indicate that students have come to see fraternities as supportive of a "rape culture" on campuses (DeSantis, 2007; Jozkowski & Wiersma-Mosley, 2017). And the factor varying medical consequences for the victim from the sexual assault (none, contracted a STI, became pregnant) also yielded some significant findings: Although participants assigned similar sanctions across these conditions, they assigned greater responsibility and guilt to the woman who became pregnant. Again, analysis of the student participants' explanations for their responses will hopefully shed some light on their thinking with regard to guilt and responsibility as well as just sanctions in such cases.

Findings Related to Internal Factors (Preformed Attitudes)

Social desirability as a response style had negligible influence on the students' responses for the cases they read and so was *not* considered a confounding variable or potential covariate for incorporation into further analyses. Because we were interested in assessing whether preformed attitudes were influential across sexual assault scenarios, we calculated students' average ratings on the dependent variables across the eight vignettes they read and rated. Ratings of the students participating in each of the four versions of the survey were compared, resulting in some significant differences; that is, some versions produced higher average scores than others, suggesting the valence for the cases for the four versions may not have been equal. Therefore, the associations between attitude variables and students' ratings on the dependent variables were analyzed separately for each of the four versions of the survey as well as overall results.

Even when analyzing the impact of preformed attitudes separately for the four survey versions, a consistent pattern emerged. Rape myth acceptance, downplaying the significance of rape, and sexism were the most frequently and strongly associated attitudes with students' assignments of sanctions, guilt, and responsibility. The more strongly students adhered to rape myths and downplayed the significance of sexual assault, the more likely they were to choose less punitive sanctions for an offender and assign more guilt and responsibility to the victim. The same pattern also emerged with regard to sexism (i.e., attitudes that discriminate against or denigrate women), with more lenient sanctions imposed on offenders and more guilt/responsibility assigned to victims. Right-wing authoritarianism was only weakly correlated with greater assignment of guilt to victims on one version and weakly correlated on another version with assignment of responsibility to victims and lesser sanctions for offenders. Just world beliefs were infrequently and inconsistently associated with the dependent variables.

College Students' Perceptions of Justice in Sexual Misconduct Cases

It is important to remember that in our exploratory study *all* levels for *all* factors except one described a sexual assault of one college student by another. It would not be unreasonable, therefore, to expect that student participants' judgments would be quite consistent within a factor as well as across factors. Even though the students often chose to mete out harsher sanctions from the list of hierarchically ranked disciplinary outcomes available at universities, it appears that external characteristics of the cases and internal belief systems impacted students' judgments for many of the cases they read. We were not expecting to find large effect sizes because almost every level of every factor described a sexual assault, so the fact that 10 of the 14 factors still demonstrated different ratings by college students for at least some of the dependent variables is important.

Although the sanctions imposed tended to be rather severe, when comparing levels of factors and when contrasting factors, sanctions were not consistently applied, even correcting for multiple analyses. In addition, and possibly helpful for explaining students' variation in the application of sanctions, students often demonstrated some variability when assigning guilt and responsibility to the victim and offender for those factors.

The three factors that yielded consistent differences across levels for all dependent variables were (a) similarity versus discrepancy of the victim's and offender's accounts of the incident, (b) the initial level of sexual interest shown by the victim, and (c) a single offender versus multiple offenders. It was surprising how quickly any discrepancy between the victim's and offender's accounts (both when the offender reported he had misunderstood or when the offender denied the assault and claimed consensual sex) resulted in reduced sanctions for the offender and increased guilt and responsibility applied to the victim. If the offender denied the assault, he received milder sanctions than the offender who claimed to have misunderstood the victim's intentions who, in turn, received milder sanctions than the offender who admitted wrongdoing. Therefore, the offender who immediately contradicted the victim's account was given significant latitude rather than being viewed with skepticism, and the victim's account was placed in doubt with nothing in the scenario to suggest the woman was not truthful. While this might be explained by the difference between certainty (admission) versus lack of certainty (denial), it does appear to support the rape myth that a woman's accusation of rape should immediately be doubted if there is *any* reason to do so, because women cannot be trusted to tell the truth about being raped.

Rape myths may also help explain the consistent lowering of sanctions for the offender along with increased guilt and responsibility applied to the victim when the victim's initial level of sexual interest varied. The scenario was identical in stating there was a clear point at which the victim declared she did not want to have intercourse after which the sexual assault occurred; the only difference in the two vignettes was the woman's initial behavior. Activated rape myths for this scenario might suggest the man was teased by the flirtatious woman beyond his ability to contain himself, thus excusing/explaining his forced sexual assault, or that the flirtatious victim no longer had the right to refuse intercourse if she acted interested in sexual activity up to that point.

Do characteristics of the victim and offender influence college students' application of sanctions and assignments of guilt and responsibility for campus sexual assault cases? Of the eight factors that varied characteristics of the offender or the victim, six demonstrated significant differences among the levels on at least one of the dependent variables, although only three of them resulted in the application of significantly different *sanctions*. It is encouraging that students' judgments of appropriate sanctions, guilt, and responsibility were not swayed by the high status of offenders or the reported attractiveness of the victim. However, the findings do support prior research (e.g., Davies, Pollard, & Archer, 2001; White & Yamawaki, 2009) that showed sexual orientation of the victim influences perceptions of justice in that in this study, gay men who were sexually assaulted (whether a virgin or level of sexual experience not specified) were assigned more responsibility for the assault than a straight male victim. It is difficult to know why being gay would result in more responsibility being placed on a male victim, but it may be that participants hold stereotypes of gay men as promiscuous, or they may apply rape myths similar to those historically applied to women, which blame them for a sexual assault if they voluntarily go with a man when they should have known not to, or for "sending the wrong signals" to a man. But college students appear to draw on victim-blaming rape myths when a woman's incapacitated rape was a result of her voluntary drinking, when a woman acted flirtatiously and sexy when initially interacting with a man, and when her account of the sexual assault was contradicted by the accused man.

It also appears that characteristics of the assault as well as consequences for victims influence college students' application of sanctions and assignment of guilt and responsibility in campus sexual assault cases. In our study, for example, four of the six factors that varied characteristics or consequences of the assault appeared to influence students' judgments. When responding to vignettes that varied potential consequences for assault victims, students did not rate incidents differently whether a physical injury had resulted, which may suggest that the stereotypical view that a woman needs to demonstrate injuries to prove she was forced may now be less prevalent in college populations. However, evidence of significant psychological symptoms subsequent to the assault impacted assigned *sanctions* for the offender, while evidence of medical consequences did not. It is somewhat surprising that medical consequences would not be viewed parallel to psychological consequences, suggesting further research is needed to understand this discrepancy. What might be important, however, is to better understand when participants assess the severity of the actions by the offender based on the severity of consequences to the victim. A sexual assault is no less reprehensible when the victim happens to be a woman with excellent resilience and coping skills in the face of adversity than when the victim is more psychologically vulnerable.

Students mostly did not make distinctions regarding the four types of forced sex included for this factor when applying sanctions to sexual assault offenders. The exception was that participants gave more severe sanctions to offenders forcing anal sex than offenders who forced women to *receive* oral sex from them, although all other paired comparisons did not indicate the application of different levels of sanction severity. Interestingly, students believed they were assigning stronger sanctions to offenders who forced fellatio on a woman compared with offenders who forced cunnilingus on a woman, although the sanctions applied were not actually different in severity. These distinctions also require further study. At this point we can only speculate that perhaps students are again applying a rape myth (i.e., that forced cunnilingus is not "harmful" or "that bad" because it doesn't involve penetration). Similarly, students were more lenient when the offender was a woman who performed oral sex on the male victim. This judgment may also reflect students' adherence to the rape myth than men cannot be victims of sexual assault involving fellatio or intercourse because both acts require them to be sexually aroused and achieve an erection, which many erroneously believe would be impossible if they were nonconsenting.

College students' preexisting attitudes also appear to be associated with their application of sanctions and assignments of guilt and responsibility for campus sexual assault cases. In our study, rape myth acceptance, downplaying the significance of rape, and sexism were most frequently and significantly related to students' assignments of sanctions, guilt, and responsibility. More specifically, stronger negatively discriminating beliefs about women and rationalizations for a sexual assault were related to more lenient sanctions for offenders, less certainty that the offender should be punished, and more liability and culpability being placed on the victim. As anticipated, the more closely an assessed attitudinal construct related to campus sexual assault, the stronger its relationship to the students' judgments in the cases. As constructs became broader, requiring more inference to understand how that construct might predict ratings in this particular study, their impact was weaker and less consistent. Thus, the strongest associations between the measured attitudes and ratings of judgments in these campus sexual assault cases were with the Rape Myth Acceptance subscales. The sexism measure, a step removed from direct assessment of attitudes toward sexual assault, showed somewhat more variability, but appeared most strongly related to assigning increased responsibility to the victim and decreased responsibility to the offender. The more distant concepts we hypothesized as related to judgments in campus sexual assault cases were right-wing authoritarianism (RWA), a view consistent with demanding procedural justice for wrongdoing, and just world beliefs, which is the expectation that bad things only happen to bad people; these did not result in significant or consistent associations. RWA did not impact sanctions for offenders and was only weakly related to assignments of guilt and responsibility. When we did find small correlations, the direction indicated that high authoritarian students applied more guilt and responsibility to the victim than low authoritarian students. In the overall analyses, just world beliefs were not related to students' judgments.

Conclusions and Implications

Similar to community samples of research participants who were asked to make judgments about sexual assault cases in the criminal justice system, college students also appear to be influenced by characteristics of the sexual assault, the offender, and the victim—some fairly significantly, and quite a few to some degree. In addition, preformed attitudes that are closely related to ideas regarding the legitimacy of claims of sexual assault or victim blaming appear associated with college students' judgments, similar to prior studies using community respondents. Direct comparisons of judgments by students versus community samples on the same materials regarding campus sexual assault are needed, however, to determine the degree of similarity or difference between them. If similar, a case could be made that students tend to make judgments about these cases on par with representative groups of community adults. If different, students may be deemed as a group to potentially hold more or less biased views regarding sexual assault, based on the direction of the assessed differences. However, because there are obvious within-group differences, the approach of many universities to educate potential hearing panel members regarding rape myths prior to their participation in actual hearings appears designed to address such biases if they exist.

Even though IHEs typically pride themselves on promoting more enlightened attitudes based on "facts" or evidence grounded in empirical research, it is unknown whether faculty and staff of IHEs hold views and beliefs consistent with their general community, or whether university faculty and staff might potentially hold relatively bias-free attitudes regarding sexual assault compared with community adults. If the latter were the case, then it would be important to conduct investigations to compare beliefs and attitudes of faculty/staff with university students to assess the similarities and differences between the two groups. Once again, it would be important to know if, as a group, students compared favorably (or better) with those currently designated as decision makers for campus sexual assault cases, thus providing more information about the viability of including students on these disciplinary panels.

It is encouraging to see that at least some of the characteristics that have negatively influenced research participants in the past when evaluating sexual assault cases are less influential with younger generations of college students. Specifically, not showing leniency toward a high-status student, not demonstrating differential judgments depending on a victim's attractiveness, similar ratings regardless of the race of the victim and offender (especially with a sample of mostly White/Caucasian students at a southeastern university), and the apparent absence of the requirement that victims prove their lack of consent, all seem to be positive signs that particular stereotypes influencing judgments of sexual assault cases may have decreased among younger populations.

The case factors that still appear to influence college students' judgments remain significant for educational, prevention, and intervention purposes. Trainings for individuals selected to be on college disciplinary panels that include sexual misconduct cases would be remiss if they did not include sensitization to factors that may skew perceptions from focusing on the fact that a sexual assault occurred to blaming the victim or using extraneous factors to assess case severity. For example, how a victim becomes incapacitated due to substances has no bearing on whether an offender used the victim's incapacitation to force a sexual act. An investigator might use the information that the offender deliberately put a drug or extra alcohol into a person's drink as evidence of intentionality, but persons who voluntarily drink to incapacitation should not be considered responsible for a sexual act that occurred when they were unable to consent. The factors that still appear to affect some college students' judgments need to be included in prevention and education programs on campuses, first to help correct potential misjudgments of students toward their peers, but also so that potential victims do not use misjudgments on themselves, which may impact their personal well-being and influence their decision to report the incident.

Once again, the acceptance of rape myths and sexism have demonstrated the strong connection to behaviors exhibited when judgments are made about sexual assault. How to impact these attitudinal systems is a question that does not have an easy answer. Simply informing people that their set of beliefs are erroneous and that we have data to prove it is unlikely to change them. People collect their own "data" daily, often selectively and in confirmation of their existing beliefs. Educational programs might start at earlier ages where hopefully certain beliefs do not have strong roots. But awareness of these attitude clusters and their relationship to evaluations of cases may be most important in the disciplinary sphere, where sensitization through training prior to participation as a student or an employee of a university on hearing panels appears to be warranted.

KEY TERMS

Blame: Liability for one's actions.

Rape myths: Attitudes and beliefs about sexual assault that are generally false but are widely and persistently held and that serve to preserve and defend the status quo of sexual violence.

Responsibility: The extent to which an individual had a role or was potentially accountable in some way for an event's occurrence.

Sexism: Attitudes that discriminate against or denigrate one sex, typically women, relative to another, typically men.

DISCUSSION QUESTIONS

1. In light of the findings of the study discussed in this chapter, do you think students should be included on hearing panels for campus sexual misconduct/assault cases? Why or why not?
2. Some of the findings from the study discussed in this chapter are puzzling. How would you explain, for example, the finding that students assigned more guilt and responsibility to the female victim who became pregnant as a result of the assault? How would you explain the finding that the female victim who was assaulted after voluntarily overconsuming alcohol was assigned more guilt and responsibility than the victims who were slipped a drug or extra alcohol by the offender before the assault?

3. The study discussed in this chapter explored a relatively large number of factors that might influence students' judgments of blame, responsibility, and sanctions in campus sexual assault cases. Can you think of other factors (e.g., other characteristics of victims, offenders, or the context of the assault) that might influence students' judgments in such cases? What about additional factors pertaining to the students making the judgments; for instance, do you think it would make a difference in the assignment of blame, responsibility, and assignment of sanctions if the student making the judgment has been the victim of some type of sexual misconduct or had ever been accused of sexual misconduct?

Notes

1 It has also been suggested that the seriousness of sexual misconduct/assault allegations may be one reason for keeping decision making in the hands of faculty and staff, thus protecting students from having to make potentially life-altering decisions regarding sanctions to be imposed on their peers for sexual misconduct. But if that is the rationale for excluding students, the fact that students make judgments in other cases involving serious infractions that may involve severe sanctions (e.g., expulsion for a physical assault on another student) appears to contradict this explanation.

2 For all analyses, we adjusted our significance level to require a more stringent level of significance to prevent error that might result from multiple analyses.

References

Angelone, D. J., Mitchell, D., & Pilafova, A. (2007). Club drug use and intentionality in perceptions of rape victims. *Sex Roles, 57*(3), 283–292.

Ballman, A. D., Leheney, E. K., Miller, K. E., Simmons, B. L., & Wilson, L. C. (2016). Bystander perceptions of same-gender versus mixed-gender rape: A pilot study. *Journal of Aggression, Maltreatment & Trauma, 25*(10), 1079–1096.

Bobbio, A., & Manganelli, A.M. (2011). Measuring social desirability responding. A short version of Paulhus' BIDR-6. *Testing, Psychometrics, Methodology in Applied Psychology, 18*(2), 117–135.

Bradbury, T. N., & Fincham, F. D. (1990). Attributions in marriage: Review and critique. *Psychological Bulletin, 107*(1), 3–33.

Brewin, C., & Antaki, C. (1987). An analysis of ordinary explanations in clinical attribution research. *Journal of Social and Clinical Psychology, 5*(1), 79–98.

Brown, S. (2018, January 21). Making sexual assault hearings fair. *Chronicle of Higher Education.* Retrieved from https://www.chronicle.com/article/Making-Sexual-Assault-Hearings/242291

Calhoun, L. G., Selby, J. W., Cann, A., & Keller, G. T. (1978). The effects of victim attractiveness and sex of respondent on social reactions to victims of rape. *British Journal of Social and Clinical Psychology, 17*, 191–192.

Carter, A. C., Brandon, K. O., & Goldman, M. S. (2010). The college and noncollege experience: A review of the factors that influence drinking behavior in young adulthood. *Journal of Studies on Alcohol and Drugs, 71*(5), 742–750.

Castello, J., Coomer, C., Stillwell, J., & Cate, K. L. (2006). The attribution of responsibility in acquaintance rape involving ecstasy. *North American Journal of Psychology, 8*(3), 411–420.

Cohn, E. S., Dupuis, E. C., & Brown, T. M. (2009). In the eye of the beholder: Do behavior and character affect victim and perpetrator responsibility for acquaintance rape? *Journal of Applied Social Psychology, 39*(7), 1513–1535.

Davies, M., Pollard, P., & Archer, J. (2001). The influence of victim gender and sexual orientation on judgments of the victim in a depicted stranger rape. *Violence and Victims, 16*(6), 607–619.

DeSantis, A. D. (2007). Inside Greek U: Fraternities, sororities, and the pursuit of pleasure, power, and prestige. *Higher Education, 16*. Retrieved from https://uknowledge.uky.edu/upk_higher_education/16

Foley, L. A., Evancic, C., Karnik, K., King, J., & Parks, A. (1995). Date rape: Effects of race of assailant and victim and gender of subjects on perceptions. *Journal of Black Psychology, 21*(1), 6–18.

George, W. H., & Martinez, L. J. (2002). Victim blaming in rape: Effects of victim and perpetrator race, type of rape, and participant racism. *Psychology of Women Quarterly, 26*(2), 110–119.

Gerdes, E. P., Dammann, E. J., & Heilig, K. E. (1988). Perceptions of rape victims and assailants: Effects of physical attractiveness, acquaintance, and subject gender. *Sex Roles, 19*(3–4), 141–153.

Girard, A. L., & Senn, C. Y. (2008). The role of the new "date rape drugs" in attributions about date rape. *Journal of Interpersonal Violence, 23*(1), 3–20.

Grubb, A. R. & Harrower, J. (2008). Attribution of blame in cases of sexual assault: An analysis of participant gender, type of sexual assault, and perceived similarity to the victim. *Aggression and Violent Behavior, 13*(5), 396–405.

Grubb, A.R., & Turner, E. (2012). Attribution of blame in rape cases: A review of the impact of rape myth acceptance, gender role conformity, and substance use on victim blaming. *Aggression and Violent Behavior, 17*, 443–452.

Hamilton, V. L. (1980). Intuitive psychologist or intuitive lawyer? Alternative models of the attribution process. *Journal of Personality and Social Psychology, 39*(5), 767–772.

Hammock, G., & Richardson, D. R. (1997). Perceptions of rape: The influence of closeness of relationship, intoxication and sex of participant. *Violence and Victims, 12*(3), 237–246.

Hine, B., & Murphy, A. (2019). The influence of "high" vs. "low" rape myth acceptance on police officers' judgements of victim and perpetrator responsibility, and rape authenticity. *Journal of Criminal Justice, 60*, 100–107.

Hockett, J. M., Smith, S. J., Klausing, C. D., & Saucier, D. A. (2016). Rape myth consistency and gender differences in perceiving rape victims: A meta-analysis. *Violence Against Women, 22*(2), 139–167.

Janosik, S. M. (1995). Judicial decision-making and sanctioning: Agreement among students, faculty, and administrators. *NASPA Journal, 32*(2), 138–144.

Jozkowski, K. N., & Wiersma-Mosley, J. D. (2017). The Greek system: How gender inequality and class privilege perpetuate rape culture. *Family Relations, 66*(1), 89–103.

Kowalski, R. M. (1992). Nonverbal behaviors and perceptions of sexual intentions: Effects of sexual connotativeness, verbal response, and rape outcome. *Basic and Applied Social Psychology, 13*(4), 427–445.

Li, J., Kim, S., & O'Boyle, J. (2017). "I believe what I see": College students' use of media, issue engagement, and perceived responsibility regarding campus sexual assault. *Journal of Health Communication, 22*(9), 772–782.

Loo, R. (2002). Belief in a just world: Support for independent just world and unjust world dimensions. *Personality and Individual Differences, 33*(5), 703–712. doi:10.1016/S0191-8869(01)00185-4

McMahon, S., & Farmer, G. L. (2011). An updated measure for assessing subtle sexual assault myths. *Social Work Research, 35*(2), 71–80.

Omata, K. (2013). Factors affecting bystanders' blame of a sex-crime victim and assessment of psychological damage: Reputation of victims and prejudice about women's desire for violent sex. *Japanese Journal of Social Psychology, 29*(1), 1–10.

Paulhus, D. L. (1988). *Assessing self-deception and impression management in self-reports: The Balanced Inventory of Desirable Responding.* Vancouver, Canada: University of British Columbia.

Persson, S., Dhingra, K., & Grogan, S. (2018). Attributions of victim blame in stranger and acquaintance rape: A quantitative study. *Journal of Clinical Nursing, 27*(13–14), 2640–2649.

Peterson, R. A. (2001). On the use of college students in social science research: Insights from a second-order meta-analysis. *Journal of Consumer Research, 28*(3), 450–461.

Pickel, K. L., & Gentry, R. H. (2017). Mock jurors' expectations regarding the psychological harm experienced by rape victims as a function of rape prototypicality. *Psychology, Crime & Law, 23*(3), 254–273.

Pollard, P. (1992). Judgments about victims and attackers in depicted rapes: A review. *British Journal of Social Psychology, 31*(4), 307–326.

Qi, S. J., Starfelt, L .C., & White, K.M. (2016). Attributions of responsibility, blame and justifiability to a perpetrator and victim in an acquaintance rape scenario: The influence of marijuana intoxication. *Journal of Sexual Aggression, 22*(1), 20–35.

Ryckman, R. M., Graham, S. S., Thornton, B., Gold, J. A., & Linder, M. A. (1998). Physical size stereotyping as a mediator of attributions of responsibility in an alleged date-rape situation. *Journal of Applied Social Psychology, 28*, 1876–1888.

Schult, D. G., & Schneider, L. J. (1991). The role of sexual provocativeness, rape history, and observer gender in perceptions of blame in sexual assault. *Journal of Interpersonal Violence, 6*(1), 94–101.

Shackelford, T. K. (2002). Risk of multiple-offender rape-murder varies with female age. *Journal of Criminal Justice, 30*(2), 135–141.

Shaver, K. G., & Drown, D. (1986). On causality, responsibility, and self-blame: A theoretical note. *Journal of Personality and Social Psychology, 50*(4), 697–702.

Shultz, T. R., & Schleifer, M. (1983). Towards a refinement of attribution concepts. In J. Jaspars, F. D. Fincham, & M. Hewstone (Eds.), *Attribution theory and research: Conceptual, developmental, and social dimensions* (pp. 37–62). New York, NY: Academic Press.

Sleath, E., & Bull, R. (2010). Male rape victim and perpetrator blaming. *Journal of Interpersonal Violence, 25*(6), 969–988.

Stoll, L. C., Lilley, T. G., & Pinter, K. (2017). Gender-blind sexism and sexual assault myth acceptance. *Violence Against Women, 23*(1), 28–45.

Süssenbach, P., Eyssel, F., Rees, J., Bohner, G. (2017). Looking for blame: Rape myth acceptance and attention to victim and perpetrator. *Journal of Interpersonal Violence, 32*(15), 2323–2344.

van der Bruggen, M., & Grubb, A. (2014). A review of the literature relating to sexual assault victim blaming: An analysis of the impact of observer and victim characteristics on attribution of blame in sexual assault cases. *Aggression and Violent Behavior, 19*(5), 523–531.

Wakelin, A., & Long, K. M. (2003). Effects of victim gender and sexuality on attributions of blame to rape victims. *Sex Roles, 49*(9–10), 477–487.

Whatley, M. A. (1996). Victim characteristics influencing attributions of responsibility to rape victims: A meta-analysis. *Aggression and Violent Behavior, 1*(2), 81–95.

White, B. H., & Kurpius, S. E. R. (2002). Effects of victim sex and sexual orientation on perceptions of rape. *Sex Roles 46*(5–6), 191–200.

White, S., & Yamawaki, N. (2009). The moderating influence of homophobia and gender-role traditionality on perceptions of male rape victims. *Journal of Applied Social Psychology, 39*(5), 1116–1136.

Wilson, J. M. (1996). Processes for resolving student disciplinary matters. *New Directions for Student Services, 73*, 35–52.

Zakrisson, I. (2005). Construction of a short version of the Right-Wing Authoritarianism (RWA) scale. *Personality and Individual Differences, 39*(5), 863–872.

CHAPTER TEN

The Sanctioning Process and Notations in Adjudication of Campus Sexual Misconduct Cases

Valerie Simons, Regina Tirella, and Kristi Wold-McCormick

For the foreseeable future, the adjudication of sexual misconduct cases on college campuses, including the imposition of a sanction following a finding of responsibility, will remain in flux. The courts will eventually land on and agree, either through consensus or, potentially, U.S. Supreme Court review, as to what constitutional due process requires in this area. It is also likely—in fact, probable at this point—that by the time this book is published the U.S. Department of Education will issue new regulations implementing Title IX.[1] The goal of this chapter, therefore, is not to predict the future or navigate the current seas of uncertainty, but rather to set forth the basic components of fundamental fairness, promptness, and equity that universities and colleges should afford to all students involved in a sexual misconduct sanctioning process based on decades of historical precedent that has developed from the courts,[2] federal agencies,[3] and on-the-ground experience of practitioners.

A General Overview of the Sanctioning Process

As an initial matter, it is important to define what we mean by the term "sanction." For example, is a sanction a punishment or an educational tool, particularly in the context of sexual misconduct on a college campus? The Association of Title IX Administrators (ATIXA) notes in its *Guide to Sanctioning Student Sexual Misconduct Violations* (2018) that this a false dichotomy. While sanctions should always be consistent with a university's overall mission as an institute of higher learning, they are typically on a continuum that will more often than not include components that are educational, preventative, rehabilitative, as well as punitive.

Consider the following scenario. The university receives an allegation of sexual assault involving two students. The student alleged to have been assaulted is often called the complainant, while the student alleged to have committed the sexual assault is called the respondent. If the respondent is found responsible for the assault following an investigation and/or hearing process, the university's sanction could include the following requirements for the respondent:

- Complete a sexual behavior evaluation and treatment
- Not communicate with the complainant, which in the university context is referred to as a no-contact order
- Be academically "removed" from the campus for a fixed length of time, which is called a suspension and
- Be geographically barred from entering the campus for a fixed length of time, which is called an exclusion.

These terms or requirements included in this single sanction could be considered both educational and punitive, or, from a respondent's point of view, all punitive. However, from the perspective of a university, "All sanctions can and should be educative, and all have a punitive element of some kind; on a continuum, some will feel (or are intended to be) more educative than punitive, or vice versa" (ATIXA, 2018, p. 4). The characterization is not as important as what the sanction is designed to address. That determination will always depend on the specific facts of the case.

Those facts are developed through the larger adjudication process, of which sanctioning is just one component, that is generally trying to answer two, related questions:

1. Is the respondent—the student accused of sexual misconduct—responsible or not?
2. And, if so, what consequences should occur given the circumstances?

The first question is answered through a fair, equitable, and impartial process (investigations and/or hearings, for example) that determines what happened and whether there is a violation of the school's policy and/or student code of conduct as related to sexual misconduct. The second question, and the focus of this chapter, is answered by determining what sanction or consequence should be imposed on the respondent that is proportionate and rationally related to the particular findings of the case (ATIXA, 2018). Thus, practitioners often refer to a **finding** (whether a policy or code of conduct was violated) as distinct from a **sanction** (the specific consequence imposed). As ATIXA (2018) explains, the "delineation between finding and sanction is one of the most important concepts" for any practitioners in this area (p. 3). Sanctioning considerations are "wholly independent from, and should be made subsequent to, the analysis of whether a student is responsible for violating the sexual misconduct policy or related code of conduct" (ATIXA, 2018, p. 3). Indeed, sanctioning itself constitutes a process with a series of steps prior to the sanctioning decision. This process will be elucidated in this chapter to provide a more sophisticated awareness of what is involved for sanctioning to occur.

Before delving into the process details, however, another important overview consideration is what guides decision makers through the sanctioning process. As the Office for Civil Rights (OCR) has made clear, decision makers should always be asking themselves, "What action should be taken to end the sexual misconduct at issue, eliminate any related hostile environment to the specific complainant or others, and prevent it from reoccurring in the future?" (Office for Civil Rights, 1997, p. 9; 2001 p. 15). For example, to achieve the goals of ending specific incidents of sexual misconduct and eliminating any future sexual misconduct, a university could impose on the respondent a suspension, no-contact order, counseling, and requirements for readmission. To prevent others from following the same path, the school may have training for the larger community to ensure they understand what constitutes sexual misconduct and how the university will respond (Office for Civil Rights, 1997).

As a practical matter, sanctioning is accomplished through written procedures that should be followed for each case for both the complainant and respondent and that are equitable, prompt, and afford due process. With respect to "equity," it is advisable that these written procedures and applicable decision makers provide the same rights and opportunities to the respective parties. That means that what a university or college provides to one party should be provided to the other. And what would that include? A best practices list for Title IX written grievance procedures, which again assumes a delineation between the finding decision and the sanction decision, is as follows:

1. *Written notice of the outcome of the investigation and/or hearing (notice of finding):* This is the first question answered in a formal adjudication about whether an individual student is responsible and sets the stage for answering the second question regarding sanctioning. This written notice is often called a **notice of finding** and should be provided concurrently to the parties and include a determination of responsibility, the specific policy provisions violated, and the facts supporting that finding. It should also identify sanctioning decision maker(s), the status of any temporary safety measures implemented at the beginning of the investigation and/or hearing and whether they are still in place, and a brief description of the sanctioning process and applicable time frames.

2. *Sharing of information:* Each party should have the opportunity to provide information to the sanction decision maker, including either an in-person meeting with the decision maker and/or submission of written statements and other relevant information. This is an important step, as will be explained later, as the factors and information pertinent to a sanctioning decision are unique to those pertinent to whether a student violated a policy or code of conduct provision.
3. *Advisors:* Similar to the investigative and/or hearing process, each party should have the opportunity to utilize advisors throughout the process, including but not limited to lawyers, confidential advocates/counselors, parents, and/or other support persons.
4. *Sanctioning factors:* These are the criteria on which a sanction will be decided, including the use of so-called **mitigating** and **aggravating factors**, which can either decrease or increase the severity of a sanction.
5. *Types of sanctions:* This is a list that identifies and defines all the potential types of sanctions applicable to sexual misconduct, such as classes, trainings, temporary or permanent removal from residential housing and/or the university as a whole, or part or whole exclusions from university property, and the ranges, which from a punitive standpoint can go from a warning all the way to an expulsion.
6. *Written notice of the sanctioning outcome (notice of sanction):* This is the second question answered in a formal adjudication about what consequences are appropriate for a specific student and the facts of the case. This written notice is often called a **notice of sanction.** This document identifies the policy provisions violated (which should match what was identified in the notice of finding), the sanction(s) imposed (including applicable time frames and conditions for readmission, if applicable), and the availability of any appeal.
7. *Time frames:* Like all stages in a formal adjudication, there should be relatively prompt time frames for the sanctioning phase. For example, if the parties have an opportunity to meet or submit information to the sanction decision maker, there should be a time frame in which to do so (5 business days, for example). As always, time frames should be flexible enough to allow extensions for "good cause," which can mean either one or both parties need more time to prepare or gather information or consult with their advisors, or decision makers need additional time to review the case that is more complex and/or includes a more voluminous record.

In terms of how these rights can be applied in practice, each party receives the written outcome from the investigation or hearing (notice of finding) and has a set amount of time to provide aggravating or mitigating factors to the decision maker, either through written submission or in person. The information provided to the decision maker should be relevant to a sanction and should not attempt to re-adjudicate the finding of sexual misconduct. Parties should be permitted to have advisors accompany them as requested, but the institution should always retain discretion to set reasonable limits in terms of time and scope of submissions and meetings, particularly to ensure a prompt process.

The decision maker then carefully reviews all the applicable information (including documentation from the underlying investigation and/or hearing and submitted information during the sanctioning process); consults with investigators or hearing officers as needed; applies any applicable sanctioning criteria as identified in their written procedures; and finally, reviews any historical, comparative cases to ensure institutional consistency and that similarly situated respondents receive comparable treatment. This last requirement regarding consistency and treating similarly situated respondents in the same manner is truly a civil rights obligation. The sanctioning guide (ATIXA, 2018) notes that "[consistency] encompasses the added obligation of equitable sanctioning imposed by Title IX" (p. 2). Sanctions for similarly situated respondents should not vary based on sex or gender pursuant to Title IX, but also should not vary based on any other protected classes as recognized under state and federal law, including but not limited to, race, color, national original, or disability, for example. Indeed, sanctioning factors or rubrics, as described in the guide, are designed to improve consistency and avoid inequitable sanctioning. Once the decision makers apply the factors or rubrics and identify a comprehensive sanction, they can send the parties written, concurrent notice of the sanction.

Once notice of the sanction has been sent to the parties, schools must then follow internal procedures to ensure notification to university departments with a "legitimate need to know" consistent with the Family Educational Rights and Privacy Act (FERPA) about the sanction. As related to suspension or expulsion specifically, notification may encompass a student's school or college, university housing (particularly if a housing contract has been terminated), office of the registrar (for transcript notations, if applicable, and databases for student discipline and "holds"), police departments (to enforce a physical exclusion from a portion or all of university property) and any other shared university campuses (by agreement or as part of a university system).

The final stage is to have a process and have personnel for monitoring one or both parties after a discipline decision depending on their enrollment status and for monitoring conditions of readmission as applicable.

With this overview, we explore specific sanctioning issues in the sections that follow.

Decision Maker: Who Should Sanction?

While there has been a wealth of federal and state court opinion and federal regulatory guidance about who should and who should not investigate or conduct hearings in sexual misconduct cases and how these processes should be conducted (see, for example, chapters 5 and 6), there has been little guidance about who should sanction following a sexual misconduct policy violation. For example, OCR (2017) says that "the decision maker as to any disciplinary sanction imposed after the finding of responsibility may be the *same or different* from the decision maker who made the finding of responsibility" (p. 6). While this question has not typically raised concerns, there are legitimate questions as to whether a *single* decision maker for all stages would comport with principles of fairness and equity. Ideally, the sanction decision maker would not be the original decision maker on responsibility so as to provide a more robust process on balance, particularly in cases involving the potential for suspension or expulsion. Although investigators or hearing officers who made the finding of responsibility are not considered "biased" or "conflicted" because of that finding, if universities and colleges have adequate staffing, it would be advisable to have a separate sanction decision maker to ensure a multi-tiered review process and a clearer delineation between decision making regarding a finding versus a sanction pursuant to ATIXA guidance. On the other hand, if the sanction decision maker is a distinct individual from the person or persons deciding the finding of responsibility, it is imperative that they have fully reviewed and analyzed all the pertinent information from the investigation or hearing to ensure that the sanction is truly tailored and proportionate to the individual facts of the case.

Another issue that schools have to consider is whether to have a single decision maker for sanctions or to use an advisory panel or sanctioning board model. Consistent with the previous discussion, a board or panel (again, who are not the decision makers on responsibility) as opposed to a single individual does provide a more comprehensive review, particularly for serious sanctions. More important, however, is what types of experience, expertise, and training the sanction decision maker has. As with investigators and hearing officers, it is imperative that decision maker(s), whether one or many, have the specialized background that is essential and required for sanctioning sexual misconduct cases. Recently, many universities have moved sexual assault adjudications, including but not limited to sanctioning, away from traditional student conduct offices and into stand-alone "Title IX offices" or general civil rights offices, which are staffed with personnel who have legal training or a similar type of formal, investigative experience.

The upside of these civil rights offices is that they are staffed with personnel who have the specialized experience and training in resolving and remediating civil rights complaints that is the purview of regulating agencies such as OCR. The downside is that they may lose the "student perspective" that is the core of more traditional student conduct offices, where staff have expertise and training in student development and success. As the Association for Student Conduct Administrators (ASCA, 2014) cautions, we can never forget that college campuses are "learning-centered" and the field of student conduct is focused on ensuring that "individual students' rights are upheld as they are engaged in an educational process about the behavioral (and sometimes academic) standards of the campus community" (p. 1; see also ATIXA, 2018, p. 2). Thus, some universities and colleges have returned sexual misconduct cases for sanctioning from their civil rights or equity offices to their student conduct offices for sanction decision making, while others have used a "hybrid" approach with a panel or board with staff from both the civil rights office and the student conduct office.

Determining the Specific Sanction: Application of Factors

As discussed, a sanction must be proportionate and tailored to the facts of each case. But what is the process for determining that sanction, particularly given the severe educational impact that is likely to be felt by both parties? As OCR (2017) noted, "Disciplinary sanction decisions must be made for the purpose of deciding how best to enforce the school's code of conduct while considering the impact of separating a student from her or his education" (p. 6). One way to do this is to have "mandatory sanctions" for a specific policy violation. While in theory you would meet the goal of consistency on its face for particular policy violations and could argue that a severe case of sexual assault should always result in expulsion, it is more likely that proportionality will not be achieved given the wide variety of fact patterns in sexual misconduct cases on college campuses. Although it is true that many cases involve the interplay between consent and incapacitation (however those terms are defined by each institution), there is still such variability in facts that mandatory sanctioning potentially poses more problems than it solves. It also eliminates the consideration of mitigating and aggravating factors that are often new to the adjudication as a whole because they were not relevant to the consideration of whether there was a policy violation. Overall, there is a real risk that applying a simple grid would either over-discipline or under-discipline, thereby failing the requirement of proportionality.

A better approach is to create and utilize sanctioning criteria or factors that can be applied to each case. "Proper sanctioning for sexual misconduct violations requires careful review of numerous different factors and circumstances. ... Colleges and universities must assess these considerations in light of the obligation to stop, prevent, and remedy incidents of [sexual misconduct]" (ATIXA, 2018, p. 6). If well designed, the factors can be used as a vehicle for achieving a sanction that will eliminate the misconduct at issue and prevent its recurrence. Examples of such factors—and the applicable questions—may include the following:

1. Severity of conduct and whether it escalated during the incident: How egregious was the violation? Did it intensify as the incident went on?
2. Whether the complainant was incapacitated (alcohol or other drugs, sleep, and/or disability) at the time: Was the complainant aware of what was occurring or able to respond? Was the respondent responsible for the incapacitation of the complainant?
3. Whether there was force/violence, weapons, or threats of force/violence: Was there physical violence or force to gain sexual access?
4. Any prior history of related criminal or policy violations: Does the respondent have prior policy violations that may be cause for a more severe sanction or demonstrate a pattern of behavior? ATIXA (2108) explains that even though conduct history is not typically part of an investigation, it is highly relevant to the sanctioning phase. As explained later, this history can serve as what is called an "aggravating factor," which could increase the sanctioning range. On the other hand, a decision maker must determine whether any prior conduct violations are related to the present sexual misconduct violation. Prior violations for drug use or academic dishonesty would not be relevant to a sanction on sexual misconduct.
5. Impact of separating a student from their education: How will the sanction impact the complainant and ensure continuing access? Similarly, what will it mean for the respondent facing potential suspension or expulsion, particularly if they are about to graduate? While this has always been an implicit factor, OCR (2017) made it an explicit factor.
6. Acceptance of responsibility by the respondent: Did the responding party credibly understand and accept the policy violation and are they committed to making a change? Another way to characterize this factor is the respondent's attitude regarding a violation. ATIXA (2018) cautions that there is a difference between respondents' right to defend

themselves or remain silent and a "brazen refusal to acknowledge and take responsibility for a clear violation of policy" (p. 12).

7. Ongoing safety risk to the complainant and/or the community: Based on the available information, how does the respondent potentially pose a risk to either the complainant and/or the community in general?

The application of these factors will necessarily be informed and shaped by any specific mitigating or aggravating factors presented by the parties or that are available to the sanction decision maker. For example, "severity of conduct" may be increased or decreased depending on new information submitted by the parties that did not come up in the underlying investigation or hearing because it was not relevant to a determination of whether there was a policy violation.

In addition, to achieve consistency—which would have been achieved by mandatory sanctioning—it is imperative that the sanction decision makers identify any past "comparator cases" to inform the institution's response in the specific circumstance. According to ATIXA (2018), "Ultimately, the goal of developing an institution-specific sanction guide is to promote proportionality and consistency, so students who violate the same policy under similar circumstances face the same base sanctioning range, at least a starting point before aggravating, mitigating, and/or compounding factors are considered" (p. 14). While consistency is important to ensure that similarly situated respondents receive similar sanctions, the ultimate requirement is that the sanction for each case is designed to remedy the specific, factual misconduct at issue.

Range of Sanctions

Once the factors have been reviewed, the question then becomes, "What type of sanction—and for how long, if applicable—will proportionately address the violation and the mitigating and aggravating factors presented?" As ATIXA (2018) explains and as is common practice, there remains a wide variety of options, ranging from low to high impact:

Warning/written reprimand: A written statement explaining how the behavior was inappropriate and that more serious action will be taken should subsequent infractions occur.

Educational programs/trainings: A requirement that students attend a program, class (e.g., alcohol or anger management classes) or a specific training on issues such as consent or incapacitation.

Assessments/evaluations: A requirement that the student be evaluated by an expert in the area of concern (psychosexual or forensic risk, for example). The expert would (a) review the nature, duration, and severity of any risk posed; (b) assess the probability of any threat to occur; and (c) advise any applicable recommendations that could effectively reduce the risk and likelihood of any identified threat from occurring. The student would then be required to submit to the evaluation in full, including recommendations. The recommendations would need to be complete before the final sanction would be decided.

Residence hall reassignment: A requirement that the student who resides in a residence hall be assigned to a different residence hall on campus.

Residence hall termination: A termination of the student's residence hall agreement through the adjudication process and a prohibition from residing in any university residence hall on either a permanent or temporary basis. Specific exclusion from the residence halls may also be imposed. Termination may occur in cases where a student appears to be involved in violations of university policies and the behavior or pattern of behavior has a significant negative impact on a person's living community.

Probation: A period of time in which a student is on a "warning status," with or without conditions, and any further violations of policies or the conditions of probation committed during the probationary period could result in further disciplinary action. A probation notation typically does not appear on the student's transcript.

Restriction or denial of university services: A restriction from using or a denial of specified university services, including participation in university activities.

Delayed conferral of degree: A delay in awarding a student's diploma for a specified period of time.

Suspension: An academic removal where the student is required to leave the university for a specific period of time and a suspension notation can appear on the student's transcript (as explained further later). After the period of suspension has expired, if there was a transcript notation, it may be removed. The student may be required to apply for readmission to the university after the suspension period. Suspension from the university often includes a physical exclusion from university property during the period of suspension.

Exclusion: A requirement that the student may not physically access all or a portion of university property. When a student is excluded from university property that student may be permitted on university property for limited periods and specific activities with permission. Should the student enter university property without permission, action may be taken by the police for trespassing.

Expulsion: A permanent, academic removal from the university (on one campus or system wide, as applicable) and typically also involves an exclusion from university property. At many institutions, a notation of expulsion remains permanently on the student's transcript.

Transcript Notations

Without a doubt, the most critical and sensitive work in misconduct cases occurs during the adjudication process. However, campus policies and procedures on what happens after sanctioning occurs also are important because of the short- and long-term impacts they have on both students and institutions. Having clear policies and protocols helps campuses foster a culture of accountability, safety, and fairness.

It is not uncommon for institutions to impose sanctions of suspension, dismissal, or expulsion on students found responsible for sexual misconduct. These formal separations from a campus are almost always recorded, in some manner, in student record systems, and often coincide with holds that prevent future registration at the institution. What is less consistent across campuses nationally are recording practices, or "notations" of sanctions, on student academic transcripts. Inconsistencies range from whether a notation appears on a transcript to the verbiage of a notation, to the permanence of the notation. Without formal and published policies and practices with respect to notations and record impacts, higher education institutions run the risk of inequitable treatment of students found in violation of campus conduct codes, including with respect to sexual misconduct.

This section provides a historical overview of recommendations and standards related to disciplinary notations on transcripts as published by various higher education professional associations, but primarily the American Association of Collegiate Registrars and Admissions Officers (AACRAO). It also includes a summary of related legislative and advocacy activity to date and offers guidance and considerations related to disciplinary notations or notifications.

Historical Overview

The transcript has long been the outward-facing official record of a student's *academic* history, progress, and standing at an institution from the time of matriculation to separation. It typically includes a chronological history of academic coursework, grades, credits, degrees and credentials earned, as well as notations about academic standing and honors. It has also been a common document on which to record instances of suspension or dismissal due to substandard academic performance.

There are longstanding and commonly adopted standards for recording academic activities and standing on transcripts. This does not hold true, however, for recording practices of disciplinary sanctions. Over the past several decades, registrars, enrollment managers, and student conduct professionals have had shifting viewpoints and practices with respect to recording and reporting student disciplinary records. Much of the historical research, including articles and publications on disciplinary notations on academic records, has been produced by the American Association of Collegiate Registrars and Admissions Officers (AACRAO).

In 1953, a publication titled *A Guide to Good Practices in the Recording and Reporting of Student Disciplinary Records* was jointly published by AACRAO, the American College Personnel Association (ACPA), the National Association of Deans of Women (NADW), and the National Association of Student Personnel Administrators (NASPA). The four associations agreed on a common practice of noting disciplinary actions on transcripts. General support for recording disciplinary sanctions appears in professional publications of these associations for approximately the two decades following its publication.

In 1965, AACRAO differentiated between a student's primary disciplinary file, the official educational record, and the transcript. Though considered separate records, its authors stated, "Entries on the official education record showing currently effective disciplinary actions which suspend or dismiss the student or restrict, limit, or condition the student's eligibility to return or re-enroll in the college, automatically become a part of the transcript" (pp. 19–20).

Many of the questions and concerns raised in the 1960s are the same as those being discussed today, more than a half century later. These include when and to whom transcripts may be released without student consent, the difference between transcripts used for educational versus employment purposes, and standardization of transcript terminology related to the statuses of dismissal, suspension, and probation. A recommendation from the 1965 AACRAO guide was to record academic status resulting from low standing with unsatisfactory grades as *academic dismissal* and to label the same status for conduct disciplinary action taken as *disciplinary dismissal*. Alternate language for other reasons for institutional separation was offered, including *involuntary withdrawal* and *disqualification*.

A gradual shift away from displaying disciplinary notations on transcripts began to occur later that decade. The 1969 record and transcript guide provided less specific guidance and simply stated, "Each institution of higher education should have a carefully considered policy regarding the information which becomes a part of a student's permanent education record and governing the conditions of its disclosure. This policy should reflect a reasonable balance between the obligation of the institution for the growth and welfare of the student and its responsibilities to society" (AACRAO, 1969, p. 18). The publication's authors clarified, "Transcripts of educational records should contain only information about academic status, except that disciplinary action which affects the student's eligibility to re-register should be recorded if in accordance with institutional policy. If it is the institution's policy not to record such actions, however, this policy should be indicated on the transcript (legend)" (AACRAO, 1969, p. 18).

In 1977, 3 years after the passage of FERPA, the guide's authors, Dala and colleagues, exclusively focused their attention on institutional separations for student failure to maintain academic standards. Askins, Demitroff, Mack, Meerzo, Poulsen, and Redrick contended in the 1984 guide published by AACRAO that "[d]isciplinary actions should not be a part of the academic record or transcript" (p. 8). During this era, courts had been reluctant to interfere with college proceedings on internal discipline. The 1988 case of *Schulman v. Franklin and Marshall College* ruled that each college is unique and must self-govern because of different standards, attitudes, and values concerning misconduct.

By 1996, AACRAO included an entire chapter in its guide on "Not Recording Disciplinary Actions on Transcripts." Aucoin and colleagues (1996) claimed "a number of questions have been raised regarding the shift in social behaviors and the responsibility that institutions have to document and report those behaviors. ... Divergent views about recording aberrant behavior has created an environment for inconsistent and subjective practices" (p. 25). The authors provided the option for institutions to use a statement, such as "Student is eligible to return unless otherwise noted" on transcripts (Aucoin et al., 1996, pp. 25–26).

Aucoin and colleagues (1996) referenced a 1992 inter-association task force that endorsed and reaffirmed a 1967 joint statement on student rights and freedoms. That joint statement advocated that institutions maintain separate academic and disciplinary records, that the transcript only contain information about academic status, and that information from disciplinary files not be available to anyone off campus without the express consent of the student, except under legal compulsion or where safety is concerned.

In opposition to the 1996 guidance, Quann and Ratcliff (1997) argued in support of a 1969 National Association of Student Personnel Administrators' (NASPA) determination of when disciplinary notations may appear on transcripts. They stated, "Disciplinary suspension or dismissal relates precisely to a student's ability to re-enroll, and it is here that the distinction between 'academic' and 'disciplinary' record fades" (Quann & Ratcliff, 1997, p. 6). They recommended that AACRAO, the Association of Student Judicial Affairs (ASJA), ACPA, and NASPA appoint a joint task force to study the issues and formulate a uniform policy on the notation of disciplinary suspension and dismissal on student transcripts.

In 1999, such a task force was formed and, in 2001, it published the *Position Paper of the Interassociation Task Force on Disciplinary Dismissals and Student Transcripts* (Mercer et al., 2001). The task force recommended that "the student's academic transcript should include a notation indicating that student is ineligible to return to the institution when the student may not be re-enrolled at the institution." Through 2011, however, AACRAO remained consistent in its recommendation *against* recording disciplinary actions on the official transcript. Divergent terminology used by campuses, inconsistent institutional policies about recording practices, insufficient or unclear information contained in transcript notations, and varying interpretations and applications of sanctions for behavioral misconduct across colleges and universities reinforced this stance. In addition, there were records professionals who believed—and some still do—that the transcript should exclusively represent a student's academic experience at an institution and it should not include non-academic information.

High-profile cases of student sexual misconduct, coupled with increasing support for more transparency related to student standing at an institution, resulted in AACRAO changing its stance in 2016. The latest edition of the guide states that "disciplinary suspension" or "ineligibility to re-enroll" are *essential* components in an institution's database and *optional* on the transcript, unless otherwise mandated by state law. Further, AACRAO defined *good standing* as a "student's eligibility to continue enrollment or re-enroll" (AACRAO, 2016, p. 112). Actions and sanctions that reverse a student's good standing and eligibility for continuous enrollment are noteworthy on an academic transcript.

Finally, other higher education professional associations have published position statements in recent years regarding transcript notations. Both the Association for Student Conduct Administration (ASCA) and ATIXA have recommended that all institutions place notations of expulsion and suspension on academic transcripts if a student is ineligible to re-enroll as a result of a serious disciplinary action.

Legislation

At the time of this writing, New York, Texas and Virginia have passed legislation requiring public and private institutions to place specific notations on transcripts for students who are suspended or dismissed for certain disciplinary violations. New York law requires transcript notations for students found responsible for crimes that meet the reporting requirements pursuant to the federal Clery Act, including but not limited to sexual violence. Virginia law requires transcript notations for students found responsible for crimes involving sexual violence, which is defined as physical sexual acts perpetrated against a person's will or against a person incapable of giving consent. Texas law, approved in 2019, stipulates that if a students is suspended or expelled from an institution for any reason, the institution shall include on the student's transcript a disciplinary notation.

Laws in New York and Virginia require notations for students who withdraw while under investigation for violations meeting those criteria or pending a disciplinary hearing. Each state includes language on the retention or removal of such notations. For example, per the Code of Virginia, an institution shall remove suspension notations from a student's academic transcript if the student completed the term and conditions of the suspension and the student is determined to be in good standing according to the institution's code, rules, or standards. Texas institutions may remove disciplinary notations, upon student request, if the institutions determine that each condition of the suspension has been fulfilled, if applicable, or if good cause exists to remove the notation.

In December 2016, U.S. Congresswoman Jackie Speier (D-CA) introduced a federal bill to amend FERPA and require the notification by educational agencies and institutions of public safety concerns. The Safe Transfer Act called for the withholding of federal funds to any educational agency or institution that fails to disclose, via the transcript, to an official of another educational institution or agency in which the student seeks or intends to enroll, the results of a disciplinary proceeding that finds a student in violation of any crime of violence. The proposed legislation mandated a 5-year minimum for such notations to be included on the transcript and included specific language related to transcript notations and notifications for pending disciplinary proceedings related to alleged acts of violence. Speier's proposed legislation died with the 2016 Congress.

Student Data Privacy

Under FERPA, disciplinary records are considered part of the education record. As such, FERPA permits colleges and universities to provide education records, including disciplinary information, to other education institutions under three scenarios:

1. When a student seeks or intends to enroll, or is enrolled, at another institution. Unless the disclosure is initiated by the student (e.g., via a transcript request), the institution must either make a reasonable attempt to notify the student of this information release or describe such releases as their standard business practice in their FERPA annual notice.
2. When an appropriate professional at an institution feels there is a legitimate "health or safety" threat to the student or other individuals, including at another institution, such a release and the rationale for it must be recorded in the student's record.
3. When a student has been found in violation of a crime of violence or non-forcible sex offense in an institutional disciplinary proceeding, the release can include only the name of the accused student, the violation committed, and the sanction imposed.

With respect to health and safety emergencies, FERPA (§99.36) specifically permits educational institutions to do the following:

1. Include in the education records of a student appropriate information concerning disciplinary action taken against the student for conduct that posed a significant risk to the safety or well-being of that student, other students, or other members of the school community
2. Disclose appropriate information to school officials within the institution who have legitimate educational interests in the behavior of the student
3. Disclose appropriate information to school officials at other schools who have been determined to have legitimate educational interests in the behavior of the student

Determining who has "legitimate educational interest" or who is a "school official" are not specified in FERPA, but rather are left to institutions based on their own criteria, procedures, and policies. However, legitimate educational interest may generally be defined as the "demonstrated 'need to know' by those officials of an institution who act in students' educational interest, including faculty, administration, clerical and professional employees, and other persons who manage student record information including student employees or agents" (Rooker & Falkner, 2012, p. 10).

While FERPA allows for such disclosure, it does not require disciplinary information to be released, nor does it specify the manner in which information may be disclosed. Those decisions and details are made according to institutional discretion. These varying institutional interpretations and applications of FERPA have led, in part, to inconsistent policies and practices across campuses.

Current Guidance

After AACRAO changed its stance in 2016 to notations being optional on student transcripts, many registrars were left with questions and uncertainty regarding best practices. Later that year, AACRAO formed a work group made up of members of varying institution types and roles to research and develop guidance on disciplinary notations. The guidelines, published in 2017, affirmed that the use of disciplinary notations (or suitable alternatives) were an appropriate and responsible practice. The work group based its conclusions on the assertion that institutions have a responsibility to notify other institutions of potential threats to their communities from students they have suspended or expelled for serious behavioral misconduct, including, but not limited to, that defined by the Clery Act.

The AACRAO work group published several recommendations related to transcript notations. The determination that laid the foundation for all the others is that misconduct that results in the involuntary separation of the student from an institution may indicate a pattern of behavior that might be repeated at a subsequent institution. As such, a key recommendation of the work group is that *some form of notice* should be provided to a receiving institution when a student has committed serious behavioral misconduct (e.g., including, but not limited to, that defined by the Clery Act).

The work group determined that the academic transcript is *an* appropriate means to support communication about serious student misconduct but may not be the only means of notification. Alternatives might include supplemental documents to the official transcript, such as a student conduct transcript, a dean's certification letter, or a transcript insert that there is a conduct record on file with the university and whom to contact for additional information.

Institutions are advised to align as closely as possible in their use of standardized terms and definitions for various student sanctions or penalties for misconduct when including notations on transcripts. These include terms such as expulsion or dismissal for cases of permanent separations from the institution, and suspension for temporary separations from the institution when there is the option of a possible future return. In addition, it is recommended that transcript notations include verbiage as to the *general* type of infraction, such as behavioral or disciplinary, as well as the department or committee responsible for issuing the student separation from the institution (e.g., Office of Student Conduct), and the effective date or date/term range of student separation from the institution.

Institutions may record a statement on transcripts while an investigation or hearing is planned or underway. A special notation also may be placed on the transcript when a student is permitted to withdraw while an investigation is underway. Standard suspension and expulsion language should replace temporary notations if a student ultimately is found in violation of the code and removed if the student is found not to be in violation. Institutions may also use a hold to block the release of an official transcript until the investigation concludes.

In its report, the AACRAO work group also recommended that transcript notations be placed at the end of the term in which the sanction occurs. Transcript legends (keys) should offer further explanation, as needed, and provide the reader with instructions on how and where to obtain additional information.

While the focus of notations and notifications historically has been on the institution that imposes the sanction, there is increased attention and advocacy on admissions policies and procedures when receiving institutions are informed of an applicant's misconduct record at a prior institution. AACRAO recommends that institutions not automatically deny students entry based on disciplinary notations without seeking or considering additional information.

Conclusion

At all stages of a sanctioning process—whether during the practical imposition of a sanction that is tailored and proportionate, or how that sanction will be reflected on a transcript—it is essential that students are afforded equity, fairness, and transparency. Higher education officials bear the responsibility to ensure campus safety for students on their own campuses through appropriate sanctioning to remediate the effects of sexual misconduct and to provide adequate notice to other campuses where students suspended for behavioral reasons may seek to enroll. To ensure that all students are treated in a consistent and just manner, campuses should develop and maintain thorough and transparent written procedures on both the sanctioning process and the disclosure of behavioral misconduct to other institutions.

KEY TERMS

Aggravating factor: Relevant circumstances accompanying the commission of misconduct or occurring prior to the misconduct that could add to its seriousness.

Assessments/Evaluations: When the university would like to have the student evaluated by an expert in the area of concern (psychosexual or forensic risk, for example). The expert would (a) review the nature, duration, and severity of any risk posed; (b) assess the probability of any threat to occur; and (c) advise any applicable recommendations that could effectively reduce the risk and likelihood of any identified threat from occurring. The student would then be required to submit the evaluation in full, including recommendations. The recommendations would need to be complete before the sanction would be considered complete.

Delayed conferral of degree: The issuance of a student's diploma is delayed for a specified period of time.

Educational programs/trainings: Requiring students to attend a program, class (e.g., alcohol or anger management classes) or a specific training on issues such as consent or incapacitation.

Exclusion: A student is denied access to all or a portion of university property. When a student is excluded from university property that student may be permitted onto university property for limited periods and specific activities with permission. Should the student enter university property without permission, action may be taken by the police for trespassing.

Expulsion: The student is required to permanently leave the university. A notation of expulsion remains permanently on the student's transcript and keeps the incident on file with the university permanently. Expulsion from the university includes an automatic exclusion from university property. Sometimes an expulsion decision results in the student being expelled from all campuses of the university, if there are multiple.

Mitigating factor: Relevant circumstances accompanying the commission of misconduct or occurring prior to the misconduct that could decrease its seriousness.

Notice of finding: Identifies policy provisions violated (as identical to original notice or amended notice) from a hearing and/or investigation, basic factual premise for each, identity of sanctioning decision maker(s), status of any interim remedial and/or protective measures, and brief description of sanctioning process and applicable time frames.

Notice of sanction: Identifies policy provisions violated, sanction(s) imposed (including applicable time frames and conditions for readmission, if applicable) and availability of any appeal.

Probation: Period of time in which a student is on a "warning status" with or without conditions and any further violations of policies or the conditions of probation committed during the probationary period could result in further disciplinary action.

Residence hall reassignment: A student who resides in a residence hall is assigned to a different residence hall on campus.

Residence hall termination: A student's residence hall agreement is terminated through the adjudication process and the student is prohibited from residing in any university residence hall on either a permanent or temporary basis. Specific exclusion from the residence halls may also be imposed. Termination may occur in cases where a student appears to be involved in violation of university policies and the behavior or pattern of behavior has a significant negative impact on a person's living community.

Restriction or denial of university services: The student is restricted from using or is denied specified university services, including participation in university activities.

Suspension: The student is required to leave the university for a specific period of time. A suspension notation appears on the student's transcript. After the period of suspension has expired, the transcript notation may be removed. The student may be required to apply for readmission to the university after the suspension period. Suspension from the university may include an exclusion from university property during the period of suspension.

Warning/written reprimand: A written statement explaining how the behavior was inappropriate and that more serious action will be taken should subsequent infractions occur.

Withholding of official transcript: The transcript is withheld for a specified time frame for those students who have already graduated.

DISCUSSION QUESTIONS

1. What are the components of a sanctioning process that ensures fundamental fairness and equity to both parties in a sexual misconduct case?
2. How have transcript notations changed over time? How are transcript notations part of the process of sanctioning incidents of sexual misconduct? Where do you stand on the question of transcript notations in cases of sexual misconduct?
3. What role does collaboration between university offices have in the sanctioning process? Does such collaboration make the sanctioning process more consistent? More fair or equitable? Or do you think such collaboration has the opposite effects?

Notes

1 Title IX is the federal statute that provides, in relevant part, that "no person ... shall, on the basis of sex, be excluded from participation in, be denied the benefits of, or be subjected to discrimination under any education program or activity receiving Federal financial assistance" (20 U.S.C. § 1681(a)).

2 The primary cases from the 1990s on Title IX include *Davis v. Monroe City Board of Education* (1999), recognizing student-on-student cases of sexual misconduct and establishing a "severe, pervasive and objectively offensive" requirement for a finding; *Gebser v. Lago Vista Independent School District* (1998), requiring "notice" and "deliberate indifference" standards in private actions under Title IX; and *Franklin v. Gwinnett County Public Schools* (1992), establishing a private right of action under Title IX for harassment of a student by a teacher.

3 The current "sub-regulatory" guidance from the U.S. Department of Education's Office for Civil Rights (OCR) includes "Q&A on Campus Sexual Misconduct" (2017, referred to in this chapter as "Interim Guidance"); "Revised Sexual Harassment Guidance: Harassment of Students by School Employees, Other Students, or Third Parties" (2001); and "Sexual Harassment Guidance" (1997). The U.S. Department of Education released its proposed regulations in November 2018. The proposed regulations are currently in the Federal Register at 34 CFR Part 106.

References

American Association of Collegiate Registrars and Admissions Officers. (1953). *A guide to good practices in the recording and reporting of student disciplinary records.* Washington, DC: Author.

American Association of Collegiate Registrars and Admissions Officers. (1965). *An adequate permanent record and transcript guide.* Washington, DC: Author.

American Association of Collegiate Registrars and Admissions Officers. (1969). *Record and transcript guide.* Washington, DC: Author.

American Association of Collegiate Registrars and Admissions Officers. (2017). *Transcript disciplinary notations: Guidance to AACRAO members.* Washington, DC: Author.

Askins, P., Demitroff, J., Mack, G. S., Meerzo, A. K., Poulsen, L. J., & Redrick, P. L. (1984). *Academic record and transcript guide.* Washington, DC: American Association of Collegiate Registrars and Admissions Officers.

Association for Student Conduct Administration (ASCA). (2013). *Report of the Transcript Notation Task Force.* College Station, TX: Author.

Association for Student Conduct Administration (ASCA) (2014). *Student conduct administration and Title IX: Gold standard practices for resolution of allegations of sexual misconduct on college campuses.* Retrieved from https://www.theasca.org/Files/Publications/ASCA%20 2014%20White%20Paper.pdf

Association of Title IX Administrators. (2015). *ATIXA position statement in favor of notation of expulsion and suspension on college and university transcripts.* Berwyn, PA: Author.

Association of Title IX Administrators (2018). *ATIXA guide to sanctioning student sexual misconduct violations.* Berwyn, PA: Author.

Aucoin, P., Bolli, G. J., Bradley, E. E., Brown, W. O., Mack, G. S., Posey, C. H., Robertson, M. N. & Stewart, J.T. (1996). *Academic record and transcript guide.* Washington, DC: American Association of Collegiate Registrars and Admissions Officers.

Code of Federal Regulations 34 C.F.R. §106.8

Dalla, L. D., Baldwin, H. R., Bullock, B. J., Legoza, R., LeRoy R. O., Nicolai, F. L., Roney III, J. & Benn H. (1977). *Academic record and transcript guide.* Washington, DC: American Association of Collegiate Registrars and Admissions Officers.

Davis v. Monroe City Board of Education, 526 U.S. 629 (1999)

Franklin v. Gwinnett City, Public Schools, 503 U.S. 60 (1992)

Gebser v. Lago Vista Independent School District, 524 U.S. 274 (1998)

Mercer, W., Baldizan, L., Elsinga, L., Finley, L., Kipetz, S., Quann, C. J., & Ratcliff, T. (2001). *Position paper of the Interassociation Task Force on Disciplinary Dismissals and Student Transcript.* Retrieved from Wanda Mercer.

Office for Civil Rights. (1997). *Sexual harassment guidance.* Retrieved from https://www2.ed.gov/about/offices/list/ocr/docs/sexhar01.html

Office for Civil Rights. (2001, January). *Revised sexual harassment guidance: Harassment of students by school employees, other students, or third parties.* Retrieved from https://www2.ed.gov/about/offices/list/ocr/docs/shguide.html

Office for Civil Rights. (2017, September). *Q&A on campus sexual misconduct.* Retrieved from https://www2.ed.gov/about/offices/list/ocr/docs/qa-title-ix-201709.pdf

Quann, C. J., & Ratcliff, T. D. (1997). An argument for and a case study of recording significant disciplinary actions on students' transcripts. *College & University, 73,* 2–6.

Rooker, L., & Falkner, T. (2012). *AACRAO 2012 FERPA guide.* Washington, DC: American Association of Collegiate Registrars and Admissions Officers.

CHAPTER ELEVEN

Restorative Justice for Campus Sexual Misconduct

Elise C. Lopez, Mary P. Koss, David R. Karp, and Jay K. Wilgus

Introduction

In recent years, the discourse on expanding response options for campus sexual misconduct has turned toward **restorative justice (RJ)**. Institutions of higher education (IHEs) seek resolutions that are responsive to victims/survivors of sexual assault, promote opportunities for respondents to take responsibility for causing sexual harm, promote a safe and equitable campus environment, and comply with federal statutes and guidance. RJ is one avenue to meet these goals. In this chapter, we discuss (a) the differences between conventional adversarial justice, RJ, and mediation; (b) the principles of RJ and programs that implement them; (c) RJ applications to sexual harm; (d) evidence of effectiveness of RJ programs for non-sexual student conduct issues at IHEs; and (e) entry points and practical considerations in implementing RJ for sexual misconduct.

Restorative and Adversarial Justice: A Comparison

A **justice mechanism** is defined in the criminal justice literature as "a justice response, process, activity, measure, or practice" (Daly, 2016, p. 18). Daly (2016) differentiates restorative and conventional justice mechanisms. Each category differs in process and achievable outcomes. The primary differentiation between restorative and conventional mechanisms is the absence or presence of a fact-finding component (Daly, 2016). Other differences include adversarial (or not) nature, focus on punitive versus rehabilitative and redress-based sanctions, and focus on offenders versus victims.

Conventional criminal justice (i.e., the court system or criminal justice system) employs opposing attorneys to represent state and defendant interests, discover and present evidence, present alternate narratives of the offense, and create doubt regarding the evidence each side presents. Judges or juries weigh the evidence, assign blame, determine guilt, and then apply primarily punitive sanctions intended to punish the offender (Daly, 2016; Seidman & Pokorak, 2011). The inescapable conclusion is that conventional justice has a fact-finding mechanism that involves an adversarial methodology. In an adversarial system, the incentives for a wrongdoer to take responsibility for committing harm may be a reduced sanction or a personal need to be forgiven. Even when the defendant wishes to express remorse, adjudicated persons often are pressured by counsel to maintain innocence in the interest of preserving appeal rights. A malignant outcome of the adversarial process is that the acts of questioning and undermining evidence reinforce the denial or minimization of a wrongdoing that characterizes many defendants. Adversarial justice is not centered on the restoration of the victim. For example, in a conventional criminal proceeding, the victim is relegated to being a witness and the crime is charged as an offense against the state. Victims do not control whether their cases move forward. Sanctions for a person who is adjudicated or pleads guilty may not consider the victim's wishes.

Institutions of higher education typically use hearing board or investigative models to adjudicate sexual misconduct cases (see chapter 5). Both of these models are adversarial; they differ in how the adversarial process is carried out. A hearing board model is one where the case is presented during a meeting (hearing) to a panel of people from the institution (board), which usually includes a mix of faculty, staff, and students who have undergone some training in weighing evidence, making a finding, and assigning sanctions. The hearing board will come to a determination together about whether to find a student responsible for misconduct. Alternatively, an investigative model uses one or two staff investigators to collect and weigh evidence, make a determination of responsibility, and assign sanctions. IHEs that utilize an investigative model often use a hearing board for appeals.

The way hearing boards and investigative models carry out the adjudication process in IHEs has been shaped in recent years by U.S. Department of Education guidelines to move closer to criminal justice practice. Under hearing-based models, the victim (complainant) may be asked to gather information, present evidence, and appear before a judicial board in the same room as the individual who harmed them (respondent), although the complainant does have the option to request that the respondent/accused student appear via video from another room. As with its criminal justice system counterpart, campus adjudication is concerned with weighing evidence, determining responsibility, and assigning sanctions for those who are found responsible for misconduct. Under investigative models, the victim (complainant) becomes a witness to an allegation of misconduct and, similar to the criminal justice system, in some instances a case can be pursued when it is deemed to meet the needs of an IHE, even if a victim does not desire it. And, likewise, the investigator or a hearing board may assign sanctions that do not necessarily consider the complainant's input on what would be meaningful to them, such as redress or the respondent participating in a rehabilitation program.

The criminal justice system uses the term "restorative" to reference enhancements to the court system that have been adopted to lessen the trauma of conventional justice on both victims and offenders. Enhancements include victim compensation, victim impact statements, and specialized therapeutic courts such as those focusing on drug or domestic violence crimes. Daly (2016) argues that although sorely needed, these approaches are improperly considered RJ because they are embedded in the adversarial process. The processes may be trauma informed to lessen their potential to cause secondary victimization and may be a pathway to receiving therapeutic services, but at the core they are enhancements at the end of an adversarial, fact-finding process that assigns blame. A process that activates contemplation of blame is problematic from the victim perspective because self-blame has been found to be a primary driver of the severity and duration of post-traumatic symptoms (Koss, Figueredo, Bell, Tharan, & Tromp, 1996; Koss, Figueredo, & Prince, 2002).

Restorative justice (RJ), on the other hand, as an overarching philosophy, is best understood as justice achieved by identifying and repairing the harm created by a particular person or persons. The most commonly used RJ definition is from Howard Zehr (2002):

> *Restorative justice is a process to involve, to the extent possible, those who have a stake in a specific offense and to collectively identify and address harms, needs and obligations, in order to heal and put things right as possible.* (p. 37)

RJ is a set of principles rather than one specific practice. It is fundamentally concerned with identifying the ripple effects of harm and creating a mechanism by which the person who committed it can repair harm and rebuild trust. As a justice mechanism for carrying out these principles, RJ is typically conducted through "a meeting (or several meetings) of affected individuals, facilitated by one or more impartial people" (Daly, 2016). There are many forms of RJ meetings; common formats include conferencing, circles, and victim-offender dialogue—all of which can be integrated into the justice system or facilitated by institutions of higher education.

Because RJ is not concerned with fact-finding and determination of guilt (like adversarial justice), RJ processes begin with acceptance of responsibility by the person responsible. Thus, RJ is not routinely used in the U.S. criminal justice system as an alternative to the typical prosecution process, even when a person admits guilt early on. In the following discussion, we will describe the ways that RJ is used to complement the existing criminal justice system.

Overall, RJ program participation requires voluntariness from both the victim/survivor and person responsible. These programs provide opportunities for victims/survivors to voice the impact of the harm; ask questions of the person responsible; and, in RJ programs that take place pre-sentencing/sanctioning, to contribute ideas for reparation that would be meaningful to them (Koss & Achilles, 2008). RJ programs offer the person responsible a chance to accept responsibility and demonstrate a commitment to repairing the harm. By creating a space to safely discuss the harm and its impacts, RJ programs can facilitate the reparation of harm, provide support and a voice to victims/survivors, promote rehabilitation and provide accountability for persons responsible, and address the impact of harm on the community (Koss, 2006).

Typically, what differentiates applications of RJ is their entry point in the temporal sequencing of addressing harm. Two common RJ processes used for prevention and for determining redress after an initial harm has occurred are circles and conferences. **Restorative circles** are convened to express and reduce the impact of individual or multiple incidents of a sexually offensive nature that constitute violations of behavioral codes of conduct (Karp, 2015). Circles can be a one-time event, or multiple circles can take place to have ongoing dialogue. Circles include community members, direct victims, and persons responsible. Circles involve a facilitator to express guidelines and assist in movement of the process, but circles are otherwise non-hierarchical and often involve a symbolic talking piece (e.g., a talking stick, ball, or other item). Whoever is holding the talking piece is the speaker. When they have finished their turn, they hand the talking piece off to someone else. Use of a talking piece helps to ensure that a variety of voices are heard and also helps to minimize interruptions and side conversations. Circles for prevention or risk reduction may involve community members, people at risk of being victimized, and people who may be engaging in behavior that could escalate to harming others. The process involves discussion of the impact of negative social norms and their potentially harmful trajectory. A plan to move forward could involve actions community members can take proactively and may include broadly applicable accountability mechanisms if any identifiable group(s) are responsible. For example, a circle could be used to discuss and come to an agreement on changing a work environment that is conducive to sexual harassment.

RJ conferences are facilitated meetings that include, at a minimum, the harmed person and the person responsible. RJ conferences are enhanced when secondary victims (e.g., family and friends of the harmed person and person responsible) and tertiary victims (e.g., community members) are in attendance so that the full extent of the harm can be heard and addressed. RJ conferences are guided by an agenda, led by a trained facilitator, and result in a redress and accountability plan (Strang, Sherman, Mayo-Wilson, Wood, & Ariel, 2013; Umbreit, Coates, & Vos, 2002). These programs provide opportunities for victims/survivors to voice the impact of the incident, ask questions of the person responsible, and contribute ideas for reparation that would be meaningful to them (Koss & Achilles, 2008). RJ programs offer the person responsible a chance to accept responsibility and demonstrate a commitment to repairing the harm. RJ conferences typically end with agreement on a redress plan and include an accountability mechanism to ensure that the responsible person follows through.

The previous models are designed for resolution of sexual misconduct as an alternative to a judicial process, such as court prosecution. Other models of RJ take place after an adversarial process, including determination of guilt and assignment of punitive sanctions, such as jail time, have taken place. **Victim-offender dialogue (VOD)** (sometimes called victim offender mediation, or VOM) is a form of RJ that brings together victims and typically incarcerated or soon-to-be-released offenders for a facilitated conversation but does not involve development of a redress and accountability plan (Umbreit, 1998). The goal of VOD is to provide a harmed person with an opportunity to voice the impact of the harm and ask questions and to provide an opportunity for an offender to take responsibility and offer answers to the harmed person. One can envision this method used by IHEs following judicial findings of responsibility to permit the victims to express impact in a non-adversarial setting and pose questions that often revolve around "Why me?" Although VOD is often used in the criminal justice system to allow victims to meet with and ask questions of incarcerated offenders, it is not currently used in IHEs.

Circles of support and accountability (COSAs) are implemented after a wrongdoer has completed a court-ordered sanction, such as incarceration, and is reintegrating into the community. COSAs help to prevent recidivism by providing social support to the responsible person, while also providing reassurance to the community that the offender is being closely monitored. A COSA is a support network (e.g., family and friends, community volunteers, service professionals) that convenes to discuss a plan for meeting the returning offender's practical needs (e.g., making connections to social services or counseling if these connections are not already established); provide emotional support to counteract ostracism or stigma; develop strategies to prevent re-offense such as involvement in new, positive peer groups; monitor alcohol/drug use; include bystander intervention should sexual misconduct precursors occur; and put in place accountability protocols, such as regular check-ins with members of the offender's COSA. Formal COSAs are not currently utilized by college campuses for returning students who have been found responsible of sexual misconduct; however, evaluations of COSAs suggest that they are a useful and important model of reintegration (Elliott, Zajac, & Meyer, 2013), and therefore, we believe they should be considered for use at IHEs.

Differentiating RJ From Mediation

RJ and mediation are not synonymous. **Mediation** involves two or more parties (disputants) with a neutral facilitator. The most common form of mediation on campus is conflict resolution, although there are other models. In the campus context, mediation is most often used by residence life professionals to address lifestyle issues such as roommate disputes. RJ is not appropriate in these instances because there is no clear wrongdoer. Conflict resolution takes a neutral stance to the parties without designation of wronged and responsible parties. The goal is to achieve a negotiated settlement of the dispute and the process does not necessarily involve a face-to-face meeting; the mediator may shuttle draft documents between parties. The neutral stance and the emphasis on negotiations mean that a victim would not likely achieve validation as a legitimate victim, and the involvement of the mediator may reduce feelings of procedural fairness by some or all disputants in a mediation process. To emphasize the distinction between RJ and mediation, we recommend that those who promulgate restorative models avoid using the following terms: conflict, mediation, conflict resolution, dispute, disputants, and mediator. As we point out later in this chapter, we strongly agree with the U.S. Department of Education that mediation is inappropriate for sexual misconduct cases and, in fact, poses high risks to safety and re-abuse if applied to sexual misconduct.

Community-Based RJ for Sexual Harm

Scholarly dialogue considering the degree to which RJ could be safely used to address sexual harm began to surface in the late 1990s (Braithwaite & Daly, 1998; Daly, 2006; Hudson, 1998, 2002; Koss, 2000). Proponents argued that RJ had the potential to address some of the major limitations of the conventional justice system in addressing sexual violations. In particular, there were three major concerns related to the impact of the conventional justice system that the addition of RJ was considered to ameliorate (for a review, see Keenan, 2017). First, victims/survivors play an unsatisfactory and often re-traumatizing role in criminal justice cases, where they serve as witnesses in the state's case against the alleged perpetrator. Even with a conviction, victims often feel revictimized and invalidated by the adversarial process. Second, conventional justice lacks sufficient mechanisms to hold offenders accountable for the ripples of harm they inflicted. The impacts of sexual harm on the community, such as feelings of vulnerability and danger, are not reduced, and the process does not extend to repairing social bonds. Third, conventional justice fails to provide mechanisms to successfully rehabilitate and reintegrate offenders into society.

RJ programs for sexual harm that have been developed and implemented alongside criminal justice responses over the years have generally been based on the shared belief that "[n]o crime victim should be forced to confront their perpetrator, but neither should she/he be denied the opportunity if she/he desires it" (Koss, 2000, p. 1338). Empirical studies have demonstrated that victims' reasons for choosing RJ options for sexual harm cases are similar to the reasons victims choose RJ options in non-sexual harm cases: Overall, victims want their voices to be heard, they desire an opportunity to voice the impact of the harm, and they want to have that impact acknowledged by the person responsible (McGlynn, Downes, & Westmarland, 2017; McGlynn, Westmarland, & Godden, 2012). Many victims want to have a voice in sanctions and reparations, and to express their vision of justice, which may be different from the punitive sanctions offered by the conventional justice system. Few victims choose RJ solely to hear an apology; however, many victims do want the opportunity to ask questions of the person responsible, such as, "Why did you do this to me?"

In community settings, it has been found that RJ can be utilized safely and with high satisfaction from RJ participants when the RJ programs are proactively designed to address the victim interests listed. RESTORE, a federally funded restorative justice demonstration project, utilized RJ conferencing for prosecutor-referred misdemeanor and felony sex crimes. The program was a diversion alternative to court adjudication, and cases were chosen for referral to the program by local prosecutors. It was the first program of its kind to be developed, implemented, and empirically evaluated. The program design and evaluation results have been published in peer-reviewed journals (Koss, 2014; Koss, Bachar, Hopkins, & Carlson, 2004), and the program has been replicated in several countries. RESTORE program steps include referral, consent, and intake; a preparation period with case managers and psychosexual assessment of responsible persons; an agenda-driven conference led by a trained facilitator, which includes the victim/survivor, person responsible, secondary victims (family and friends of the victim/survivor and person responsible), and tertiary victims (community representatives). It concludes with a formal redress plan and a 12-month monitored redress and accountability period for the person responsible, including sex offender treatment, stay-away orders, regular contact with a case manager, and meetings before a Community Accountability and Reintegration Board (CARB). The CARB represents the community's interest in safety, and on a quarterly basis would meet with all RESTORE responsible persons to assess progress on redress plans and collectively decide any remediation, including potentially reverting the case back to criminal justice processing, if progress had stalled. The RESTORE program evaluation showed perceived high levels of procedural justice from all parties involved (e.g., parties felt that the process and redress plan were fair) and participant satisfaction (e.g., with the preparation and conference protocols) (Koss, 2014). Process evaluation and mental health assessment of survivors/victims also showed optimistic results that the program was conducted safely. Rates of responsible person program completion were high, and no responsible persons were arrested for new sex crimes during their time in RESTORE.

RJ on Campus

RJ is not new to student conduct administration (Karp & Schachter, 2018). In fact, the first case study on developing an RJ program at the University of Colorado, Boulder was published nearly 20 years ago (Sebok & Goldblum, 1999). By 2004, several additional institutions were integrating RJ responses into student conduct cases such as substance abuse, vandalism, and hazing (Karp & Allena, 2004). Since then, the number of campuses with developed RJ programs or principles incorporated into their student conduct system has continued to grow (Karp & Franks, 2016). These programs continue to expand the cases processed restoratively and now frequently include theft (Karp, 2011), disorderly conduct (Rinker & Jonason, 2014), and even sexual harassment (Llewelyn, MacIsaac, & Mackay, 2015; for a detailed review, see Karp & Schachter, 2018). Institutions of higher education thus are primed, in many ways, to seriously consider avenues to utilize RJ for sexual misconduct.

Non-Sexual Misconduct

Several empirical studies on campus-based RJ have yielded encouraging results. Ahlin, Gibbs, Cavanaugh, and Lee (2017) found that, in a general sample of students at a large public university, most were favorable toward RJ processes. Those most positive identified as women, were further along in their educational career, and were involved in the campus community (e.g., participated in student clubs, attended campus events). Gallagher Dahl, Meagher, and Vander Velde (2014) focused on responsible students who had participated in an RJ conference or dialogue meeting on campus to assess their reasons for participation, satisfaction with the process, and any benefits of participation. This study found that most (92%) were satisfied or very satisfied with the process and felt that meeting with the person(s) they harmed was somewhat to very beneficial (81%). Common reasons that responsible students chose to participate in RJ were both intrinsic/self-motivated (e.g., "remove the offense from my record;" "take responsibility for making things right") and extrinsic/oriented toward the other party ("help the harmed party" or "offer an apology"). Most students (93%) did not feel that they were being pressured to participate in RJ. Studies presented as RJ, but potentially better conceptualized as educational processes include one by McDowell, Crocker, Evett, and Cornerlisson (2014) on peer-facilitated circles to discuss dormitory issues affecting community safety or climate (for example, students feeling uncomfortable/unsafe after an anonymous resident repeatedly drew lude pictures on the dormitory whiteboard). Students who participated were more likely to report that they "attempted to see the perspectives" of others, and "were more willing to listen to the perspectives of others regarding a conflict situation" (McDowell et al., 2014, p. 353). Similarly, Meagher's (2009) study of 19 responsible students reported that they displayed more awareness of how their actions affected others and learned new communication skills to resolve conflicts. Karp and Sacks's (2014) multi-campus study of campus RJ for non-sexual conduct issues demonstrated enhanced student development compared with traditional disciplinary approaches. In a multiple regression analysis, the disciplinary method was the only variable that accounted for increased student learning on a number of variables, including interpersonal competence (e.g., cooperative and inclusive problem solving, ability to communicate remorse, willingness to repair relationships), positive perceptions of community/social group connectedness (including a draw to abide by community/social group standards), and positive perceptions of social ties to the institution.

Entry Points for RJ for Sexual Misconduct in the Student Conduct Process

A delineation of the entry points for RJ in the student conduct process for sexual harm cases, and doing so within federal regulations and guidelines, was first conceptualized in the scholarly literature by Koss, Wilgus, and Williamsen (2014). This concept paper discussed how IHEs could use RJ in place of adversarial adjudication, after a finding of responsibility, and for reintegration. Koss and Lopez (2015) expanded this vision to fit within the 2014 VAWA reauthorization. Support for RJ interventions for campus sexual misconduct has also grown to include professional organizations. The Association for Student Conduct Administration (ASCA) included RJ in its "Gold Standard Practices for Resolution of Allegations of Sexual Misconduct" (ASCA, 2014), and a task force of the American Bar Association (ABA) has also listed RJ in its campus sexual misconduct recommendations report (ABA, 2017). The Campus PRISM (Promoting Restorative Initiatives for Sexual Misconduct) Project, an initiative of the Skidmore College RJ Project, has grown to an active, international collaborative interest group on the topic and has posted a comprehensive review (Karp, Shackford-Bradley, Wilson, & Williamsen, 2016), a briefing paper distinguishing RJ from mediation (Campus PRISM Project, 2016), and a briefing paper on next steps for RJ to address campus sexual misconduct (Karp, 2017).

RJ can be integrated at multiple points in the temporal sequence of campus responses to sexual misconduct. Campuses may begin by assessing where in their campus prevention and disciplinary process it will be easiest to integrate RJ. What follows is an overview of a tiered approach to using RJ to address sexual misconduct in the campus adjudication process, first described by Koss, Wilgus, and Williamsen (2014) and then expanded by the Campus PRISM Project to include an educational dialogue process intended for victims and offenders (Karp, 2017; Karp et al., 2016).

Primary Prevention

It is debatable whether an intervention intended for potential, rather than actual, victims and perpetrators and occurring outside the context of any specific incident qualifies as a justice approach. However, the circles approach to sanctioning and to reintegration has been extended to interactive group dialogue on sexual assault as opposed to the more typical didactic presentation approach to sexual assault prevention used on most college campuses. The circle gatherings adapt methods from RJ circles, including a facilitator and use of a talking piece to avoid maladaptive communication practices such as interruption, cross-talk, and side conversations. The topics discussed include negative peer influences, alcohol use, party culture, and social norms that lead to misconduct; and participants discuss narratives around gender role stereotypes and encourage pro-social behavior such as bystander intervention, all with the intent to build community around these topics. The gatherings have been shown to be successful in creating movement on campus issues such as attitudes about race (Gurin, Nagda, Stephan, & Stephan, 2013) and campus party culture (for a case study, see Karp et al., 2016). The gatherings can be one-time events, or they can be scheduled on a regular basis to facilitate ongoing dialogue. Ideally, prevention circles should be conducted within established communities (e.g., Greek chapter houses and other residential spaces, cultural centers, student groups) to achieve ongoing development and reinforcement of shared norms and values. If guided by competent facilitators conversant with sexual assault prevention, working within established groups can lead to action planning and shared commitments, follow-up and accountability, and cultural shift (Karp & Sacks, 2014).

An Alternative or Supplement to Traditional Investigation and Adjudication

There are instances where the traditional adjudication system is not triggered to intervene, but in which RJ could provide a means of addressing sexual harm. RJ in the form of restorative circles can be used to address incidents of sexual harm that do not rise to the level of a conduct code violation. For example, rape-supportive chants or banners hung on fraternity houses may be protected as free speech. Yet, the speech may have a harmful effect on the campus community, such as negatively affecting women's sense of safety. Although misconduct has not occurred, conducting a restorative community circle that includes individuals who engaged in the offensive behaviors and individuals harmed by it can provide an opportunity to discuss the impact of these behaviors and the social norms that bolster them.

An RJ option could also make logical sense when there is a report of misconduct and the accused student immediately accepts responsibility. Experienced conduct professionals will attest that this scenario is not rare. In these cases, where a respondent has taken responsibility for the harm they caused and seems willing to make amends, a restorative option in lieu of traditional investigation and adjudication can provide an avenue to do so.

Campuses may want to create a restorative conferencing option that could be used in lieu of investigation or judicial hearing methods of resolution. Offering an RJ option after initial fact-finding may encourage complainants to come forward who may not desire a traditional investigation and adjudication process but simply want to safely discuss the respondent's behavior and see a plan put into place to reduce that person's risk of hurting someone else. It is imperative that this option include a mandatory accountability period after the conference in which the responsible person is monitored as they complete a rehabilitation and redress plan. In the absence of an accountability plan, responsible persons who are not truly remorseful may agree to a voluntary conference in order to avoid adjudication and sanctions.

Sanctioning Circles or Conferences

After adjudication has occurred, a circle or conference can be convened specifically with the intent of creating a collaborative process that includes both the complainant and respondent in determining reparative components of a student's sanction plan. Although some institutions may require punitive sanctions as listed in their institutional policy, providing an additional restorative opportunity to discuss the case and the impact of the harm, and to collaboratively determine reparative components for the sanctioning plan could potentially have a positive impact on both the complainant's (victim/survivor) and respondent's (responsible person) sense of procedural justice.

Some IHEs have begun to implement RJ for sexual misconduct, although it is too soon to evaluate the efficacy of such programs. For example, Draper (2018) has presented the experiences from the first nine cases processed at The College of New Jersey. This program facilitates communication between the victim and responsible person through whatever means are deemed mutually acceptable. In spring 2019, the University of Michigan codified in its policies the option to utilize RJ conferences ("facilitated dialogue") in instances where the complainant and respondent voluntarily agree to do so and where the case is deemed eligible by a student conduct professional. The RJ option can be used for a variety of student conduct issues, including some instances of sexual misconduct. The student conduct office has a process in place to document voluntariness, prepare the individuals and conduct the conference, and maintain accountability of the respondent. The university also offers a restorative circles process. At this time, the RJ program is too new to show results of a process or outcomes evaluation; however, information about the program is publicly available on the university's website (University of Michigan, 2019).

Reintegration

COSAs can be used to reintegrate students who are returning to campus after a period of separation. COSAs create a support network and plan for the responsible student and can also help to reassure survivors/victims that something is being done to minimize risks of re-offense by the person responsible. The goal of creating a COSA for reintegrating students is to provide opportunities and support for the person to change their behavior. The success of the model with community-based reintegration shows promise for success on college campuses, and a few institutions are beginning to incorporate COSAs into their policies and procedures. McMahon, Karp, and Mulhern (2019) provide a case study of one COSA for a student returning to a campus after a 1-year suspension for sexual misconduct.

In a campus setting, a COSA should include individuals who are close to the reintegrating student professionally and personally. Campus professionals in the COSA might include student conduct professionals, counselors, coaches, or faculty mentors. Positive personal contacts to help monitor, support, and model pro-social behavior for the reintegrating student on a day-to-day basis include non-offending peers, graduate student mentors, residence advisors, roommates, and club/interest group peers. COSAs can also include trained campus volunteers. Institutional policies or agreements made on a case-by-case basis can determine how often COSAs should meet formally and for what overall length of time (e.g., throughout the first academic year that the student is reintegrating to campus). COSAs can create a support plan for the student, brainstorm pro-social activities to take the place of activities that promote rape-supportive attitudes and develop plans for addressing potential or new transgressions.

Title IX Compliance

As noted earlier, it is essential to differentiate RJ from mediation because under guidance issued by the U.S. Department of Education's Office for Civil Rights (OCR) in 2001 (Cantu, 2001) and 2011 (Ali, 2011), IHEs were forbidden from using mediation to resolve sexual assault on college campuses. Those guidance documents were silent, however, on the role of RJ, which prompted some to argue that RJ was not only permissible but could enhance an institution's compliance with Title IX by offering victims access to an additional form of justice (Koss, Wilgus, & Williamsen, 2014). These guidance documents were rescinded in fall 2017. The interim guidelines (Jackson, 2017a) offered lukewarm encouragement of alternative adjudication methods but failed to explicitly clarify the difference between RJ and mediation. From 2014 to 2017, many IHEs were under federal investigation by OCR for Title IX compliance violations regarding sexual misconduct cases. Thus, although there was evidence from community models that RJ could be used safely with cases involving sexual harm, and many student conduct professionals, such as the Association of Student Conduct Administration, have recommended RJ, many institutions were hesitant to utilize RJ beyond non-sexual harm misconduct for fear that doing so would result in a compliance violation (i.e., OCR would equate RJ with mediation). Despite urging from RJ proponents, including Campus PRISM (see Campus PRISM Project, 2016), the guidelines under revision by OCR at the time of this writing continue to demonstrate ambiguity even though there are clear-cut differences between RJ and mediation.

Practical Considerations

An institution that is ready to begin the journey of developing and implementing an RJ program for sexual misconduct will find that details matter. Developing an RJ program for sexual misconduct must be a conscious and conscientious process with careful attention to best practices. Some practical considerations for developing and carrying out RJ programs follow.

Including Diverse Partners

It is important to gain buy-in and establish partnerships with people at various levels throughout the university who have expertise to inform the program policy, practice, and assessment (Karp, 2017). Engaging the voices of a spectrum of stakeholders is key to promoting acceptance of RJ throughout campus, developing a program that is sensitive to the needs of diverse students, and ensuring that individuals with knowledge of best practices inform the program model and assessment plan. People who would have a vested interest in ensuring programmatic success include student conduct professionals, Title IX administrators, attorneys, counseling center staff, researchers, prevention staff, staff and students from diverse groups and centers (e.g., women's center, centers for students with disabilities, cultural centers, communities of color, LGBTQ), faculty, and respondent and victim services coordinators or advocates.

Training Facilitators

Utilizing RJ for sexual misconduct requires skilled facilitators who have received specialized training in both restorative justice and the dynamics of sexual harm (Keenan, 2018; Lopez & Koss, 2018). There may be individuals on campus who have prior experience with mediation or restorative justice, but mediation or RJ practitioners with foundational training alone cannot be expected to have a deep understanding of the complexities of sexual harm. These cases inherently involve power imbalances and other complex relational dynamics. Basic RJ foundational competency training is necessary but not sufficient to ensure that facilitators, for example, can notice subtle power differential cues between the complainant and respondent, identify and shut down instances of re-abuse, and conduct the conference in such a way that minimizes the myriad ways that a victim/survivor of sexual harm might be retraumatized. Similarly, IHEs are apt to have a variety of professionals on campus who have specialized training in and understanding of sexual violence, but less training in RJ. Training in basic RJ is typically 3–5 days and includes didactic training, facilitated discussion, video or other example material, and experiential practice exercises.

Ensuring Voluntariness

Inherent to RJ is the principle that participation should be voluntary on the part of the victim/survivor and the responsible person. Voluntariness is also critical for Title IX compliance purposes. Complainants and respondents should never be forced or coerced into participating in an RJ process, whether it is a circle process for prevention, RJ conference or dialogue, or a reintegration circle of support and accountability. Although institutions may include in their policies that RJ is voluntary, feelings of coercive pressure on the part of the complainant or respondent are subjective (Karp, 2017). Safeguards to protect voluntariness can include statements to complainants and respondents of their right to freely choose to participate and to consult an advisor before agreeing to participate or pursue another option, and the ability to withdraw from RJ and revert to the conventional process at any time.

Safety

Safety is paramount at every step of the process. Student conduct professionals should utilize a risk-assessment protocol to determine whether it would be safe for a respondent/responsible person to participate in RJ. A respondent/responsible person who has taken responsibility for sexual misconduct and who has agreed to participate in an RJ process with a complainant/victim/survivor should undergo an additional assessment to ensure that they can participate without compromising victim safety. Psychosexual assessment conducted by a mental health professional can help to uncover additional information that would impact the suitability of a person to participate in RJ—for example, whether there are other undisclosed incidents that might indicate a pattern of perpetration behavior, or that the person has not, in fact, taken responsibility for the sexual harm and has opted to participate in RJ simply to "get out of trouble quicker."

Confidentiality

Confidentiality is a key component of RJ, as it allows for greater trust among participants. However, respondents, in particular, may be concerned that information they disclose, such as taking responsibility for the sexual misconduct, could be used against them in other instances (e.g., if the case reverts back to traditional campus adjudication; criminal or civil proceedings). Although it remains that student records can be discoverable in legal proceedings, IHEs can create internal policies to protect against RJ information being shared in other campus settings. For example, the IHE could create a policy, to which the complainant and respondent would sign an agreement, that information shared in the RJ process could not be used if the case reverted to the traditional adjudication process. To limit discoverable information in RJ processes, IHEs can consider the paperwork and documentation strategies used by victim advocates to balance case management needs (e.g., showing the types and numbers of services provided, referrals made) with the privacy of the individual receiving the advocacy services. Notes can be balanced to include minimum items needed to adequately progress a case through the RJ process with the level of detail that, should it be needed, can show institutional commitment to due process and due diligence if challenged later by either party. Some states have laws that recognize the confidential nature of mediation proceedings, and some have language that would include RJ as confidential proceedings. IHEs in these states may be able to make their processes confidential. A strategy utilized with RESTORE that IHEs could employ is to create agreements with local prosecutors that recognize the campus-based RJ processes as useful and in which prosecutors agree to honor those processes as confidential.

Conclusion

Utilization of RJ at institutions of higher education is a question of *when*, not *if*. Models of RJ to address sex crimes in community settings, and to address non-sexual misconduct on college campuses, have been implemented safely and effectively. These models can, and have started to be, adapted to address campus sexual misconduct. Opportunities exist to utilize RJ for prevention, as an alternative to traditional adjudication, in sanctioning and reintegration within Title IX guidelines. Careful attention to detail can make these programs successful at IHEs.

KEY TERMS

Circles of support and accountability (COSAs): A support network for offender reintegration into the community. This mechanism is considered partially restorative.

Conventional criminal justice: An adversarial justice mechanism that employs opposing attorneys to represent state and defendant interests, discover and present evidence, present alternate narratives of the offense, and create doubt regarding the evidence each side presents. Judges or juries weigh the evidence, assign blame, determine guilt, and then apply primarily punitive sanctions.

Justice mechanism: A justice response, process, activity, measure, or practice

Mediation: A conflict resolution process involving two or more parties (disputants) with a neutral facilitator. Mediation takes a neutral stance to the parties without designation of wronged and responsible parties. The goal is negotiated settlement of the dispute.

Restorative circles: Gatherings to discuss the impact of negative social norms or a harmful event and a plan to move forward. When circles are used for prevention, they are considered "partially restorative" because they are not oriented toward restoration after a specific event.

Restorative justice (RJ): A justice mechanism that involves, to the extent possible, those who have a stake in a specific offense and to collectively identify and address harms, needs, and obligations in order to put things as right as possible. RJ only moves forward if an offender takes responsibility for causing harm and is not concerned with fact-finding or determination of guilt.

RJ conferences: Facilitated meetings with the harmed person and the person responsible, secondary victims, and tertiary victims. RJ conferences are considered fully restorative.

Victim-offender dialogue (VOD): A partially restorative form of RJ that brings together victims and typically incarcerated or soon-to-be-released offenders for a facilitated conversation but does not involve development of a redress and accountability plan.

DISCUSSION QUESTIONS

1. What laws exist in your state regarding the confidentiality of mediation or other alternative dispute resolution processes, including restorative justice? How might those laws help or hinder the creation of an RJ program for sexual misconduct on your campus?
2. What are the primary benefits of RJ in responding to campus sexual misconduct cases for complainants, respondents, IHEs, and campus communities? Do you see any potential disadvantages to using RJ instead of a traditional campus adjudication process?
3. What resources are available on your campus or in your community that promote or provide RJ practices? How might you connect with them to deepen your thinking about the role of RJ in addressing campus sexual misconduct?
4. How can an IHE create the conditions that make it possible for someone who caused sexual harm to acknowledge and take responsibility for it?
5. How can an IHE respond to the requests of a survivor for a restorative response while also communicating to the campus community that sexual misconduct will not be tolerated?

References

Ahlin, E. M., Gibbs, J. C., Kavanaugh, P. R., & Lee, J. (2017). Support for restorative justice in a sample of US university students. *International Journal of Offender Therapy and Comparative Criminology, 61*(2), 229–245.

Ali, R. (2011). *Dear Colleague Letter.* Washington, DC: U.S. Department of Education, Office for Civil Rights.

American Bar Association. (2017). *ABA Criminal Justice Section Task Force on College Student Due Process Rights and Victim Protections: Recommendations for colleges and universities in resolving allegations of campus sexual misconduct.* Retrieved from https://www.americanbar.org/content/dam/aba/publications/criminaljustice/2017/ABA-Due-Process-Task-Force-Recommendations-and-Report.authcheckdam.pdf

Association for Student Conduct Administration. (2014). *Student conduct administration and Title IX: Gold standard practices for resolution of allegations of sexual misconduct on college campuses.* Retrieved from https://www.theasca.org/files/Publications/ASCA%20 2014%20Gold%20Standard.pdf

Braithwaite, J., & Daly, K. (1998). Masculinities, violence, and communitarian control. In S. L. Miller (Ed.), *Crime control and women: Feminist implications of criminal justice policy* (pp. 151–172). Newbury Park, CA: Sage.

Campus PRISM Project (2016). *Distinguishing campus restorative justice from mediation.* Saratoga Springs, NY: Skidmore College. Retrieved from https://www.skidmore.edu/campusrj/documents/RJ-vs-Mediation-Brief.pdf

Cantu, N. V. (2001). *Revised sexual harassment guidance: Harassment of students by school employees, other students, or third parties.* Washington, DC: U.S. Department of Education, Office for Civil Rights.

Daly, K. (2006). Restorative justice and sexual assault: An archival study of court and conference cases. *British Journal of Criminology, 46*(2), 334–356.

Daly, K. (2016). What is restorative justice? Fresh answers to a vexed question. *Victims and Offenders, 11*(1), 9–29.

Draper, J. (2018, September). *A college approach to alternative resolution and restorative practices for Title IX.* Presentation to the PISLAP Conference, Washington, DC.

Elliott, I. A., Zajac, G., & Meyer, C. A. (2013). *Evaluability assessments of the circles of support and accountability (COSA) model.* University Park, PA: Penn State Press.

Gallagher Dahl, M., Meagher, P., & Vander Velde, S. (2014). Motivations and outcomes for university students in a restorative justice program. *Journal of Student Affairs, Research, & Practice, 51*(4), 364–379.

Gurin, P., Nagda, B. A., Stephan, C. W., & Stephan, W. G. (2013). Intergroup dialogue: Its role in contemporary society. In P. Gurin, B. A. Nagda, & X. Zúñiga (Eds.) *Dialogue across difference: Practice, theory and research on intergroup dialogue* (pp. 133–170). New York, NY: Russell Sage Foundation.

Hudson, B. (1998). Restorative justice: The challenge of racial and sexual violence. *Journal of Law and Society, 25*(2), 237–256.

Hudson, B. (2002). Restorative justice and gendered violence: Diversion or effective justice? *British Journal of Criminology, 42*(3), 616-634.

Jackson, C. (2017a). *Dear Colleague Letter on sexual violence.* Washington, DC: U.S. Department of Education, Office for Civil Rights.

Jackson, C. (2017b). *Q&A on campus sexual misconduct.* Washington, DC: U.S. Department of Education, Office for Civil Rights.

Karp, D. R. (2011, December 20). Spirit horse and the principles of restorative justice. *Student Affairs eNews.* Retrieved from https://www.skidmore.edu/campusrj/karp-vitae-files/misc-publications/Spirit-Horse.pdf

Karp, D. R. (2015). *Little book of restorative justice for colleges and universities: Revised and updated.* New York, NY: Skyhorse.

Karp, D. R. (2017). Next steps for a restorative justice approach to campus-based sexual and gender-based harassment, including sexual violence. *Campus PRISM Project.* Retrieved from https://www.skidmore.edu/campusrj/documents/Next-Steps-for-RJ-Campus-PRISM.pdf

Karp, D. R. (in press). Restorative justice and responsive regulation in higher education: The complex web of campus sexual assault policy in the United States and a restorative alternative. In G. Burford, V. Braithwaite, & J. Braithwaites (Ed.), *Restorative and responsive human services.* New York, NY: Routledge.

Karp, D. R., & Allena, T. (Eds.). (2004). *Restorative justice on the college campus: Promoting student growth and responsibility, and reawakening the spirit of campus community.* Charles C Thomas Publisher.

Karp, D. R., & Frank, O. (2016). Restorative justice and student development in higher education: Expanding "offender" horizons beyond punishment and rehabilitation to community engagement and personal growth. In T. Gavrielides (Ed.), *Offenders no more: An interdisciplinary restorative justice dialogue* (pp. 141–164). New York, NY: Nova Science Publishers.

Karp, D. R., & Sacks, C. (2014). Student conduct, restorative justice, and student development: Findings from the STARR Project (Student Accountability and Restorative Research Project). *Contemporary Justice Review, 17*(2), 154–172.

Karp, D. R., & Schachter, M. (2018). Restorative justice in universities: Case studies of what works with restorative responses to student misconduct. In T. Gavrieldes (Ed.), *Routledge international handbook of restorative justice* (pp. 247–263). New York, NY: Routledge.

Karp, D. R., Shackford-Bradley, J., Wilson, R. J., & Williamsen, K. M. (2016). *CAMPUS PRISM: A report on promoting restorative initiatives for sexual misconduct on college campuses.*

Retrieved from https://www.skidmore.edu/campusrj/documents/Campus_PRISM__Report_2016.pdf

Keenan, M. (2017). Criminal justice, restorative justice, sexual violence and the rule of law. In E. Zinsstag & M. Keenan (Eds.), *Restorative responses to sexual violence: Legal, social, and therapeutic dimensions* (pp. 64–88). New York, NY: Routledge.

Keenan, M. (2018) Training for restorative justice work in cases of sexual violence. *International Journal of Restorative Justice*, *1*(2), 292–303.

Koss, M. P. (2000). Blame, shame, and community: Justice responses to violence against women. *American Psychologist*, *55*(11), 1332–1343.

Koss, M. P. (2006). Restoring rape survivors: Justice, advocacy, and a call to action. *Annals of the New York Academy of Sciences*, *1087*(1), 206–234.

Koss, M. P. (2014). The RESTORE program of restorative justice for sex crimes: Vision, process, and outcomes. *Journal of Interpersonal Violence*, *29*(9), 1623–1660.

Koss, M. P., & Achilles, M. (2008). Restorative justice responses to sexual assault. Harrisburg, PA: VAWnet: The National Online Resource Center on Violence Against Women.

Koss, M. P., Bachar, K. J., Hopkins, C. Q., & Carlson, C. (2004). Expanding a community's justice response to sex crimes through advocacy, prosecutorial, and public health collaboration: Introducing the RESTORE program. *Journal of Interpersonal Violence*, *19*(12), 1435–1463.

Koss, M. P., Figueredo, A. J., Bell, I., Tharan, M., & Tromp, S. (1996). Traumatic memory characteristics: A cross-validated mediational model of response to rape among employed women. *Journal of Abnormal Psychology*, *105*(3), 421–432.

Koss, M. P., Figueredo, A. J., & Prince, R. J. (2002). Cognitive mediation of rape's mental, physical and social health impact: Tests of four models in cross-sectional data. *Journal of Consulting and Clinical Psychology*, *70*(4), 926–941.

Koss, M. P., & Lopez, E. C. (2014). VAWA after the party: Implementing proposed guidelines on campus sexual assault resolution. *City University of New York Law Review*. Retrieved from http://www.cunylawreview.org/category/vawa/

Koss, M. P., Wilgus, J. K., & Williamsen, K. M. (2014). Campus sexual misconduct: Restorative justice approaches to enhance compliance with Title IX guidance. *Trauma, Violence, & Abuse*, *15*(3), 242–257.

Llewelyn, J. J., MacIsaac, S., & Mackay, M. (2015). *Report from the restorative justice process at the Dalhousie University Faculty of Dentistry*. Halifax, Nova Scotia, Canada: Dalhousie University.

Lopez, E. C., & Koss, M. P. (2018). Training in restorative justice for sex crimes from the perspective of sexual assault specialists. *International Journal of Restorative Justice*, *1*(2), 310–314.

McDowell, L. A., Crocker, V. L., Evett, E. C., & Cornerlisson, D. G. (2014). Perceptions of restorative justice concepts: An evaluation of university housing residents. *Contemporary Justice Review*, *17*(2), 346–361.

McGlynn, C., Downes, J., & Westmarland, N. (2017). Seeking justice for survivors of sexual violence: Recognition, voice and consequences. In E. Zinsstag & M. Keenan (Eds.), *Restorative responses to sexual violence: Legal, social, and therapeutic dimensions* (pp. 179–191). New York, NY: Routledge.

McGlynn, C., Westmarland, N., & Godden, N. (2012). "I just wanted him to hear me": Sexual violence and the possibilities of restorative justice. *Journal of Law and Society*, *39*(2), 213–240.

McMahon, S. M., Karp, D. R., & Mulhern, H. (2019). Addressing individual and community needs in the aftermath of campus sexual misconduct: Restorative justice as a way forward in the re-entry process. *Journal of Sexual Aggression*, *25*(1), 49–59.

Meagher, P. J. (2009). *A phenomenological study of the experience of respondents in campus-based restorative justice programs* (Dissertation). Bowling Green, OH: Bowling Green State University.

Rinker, J. A., & Jonason, C. (2014). Restorative justice as reflective practice and applied pedagogy on college campuses. *Journal of Peace Education, 11*(2), 162–180.

Sebok, T., & Goldblum, A. (1999). Establishing a campus restorative justice program. *California Caucus of College and University Ombuds, 2*, 12–22.

Seidman, I., & Pokorak, J. J. (2011). Justice responses to sexual violence. In M. P. Koss, J. W. White, & A. E. Kazdin (Eds.), *Violence against women and children, Volume 2: Navigating solutions* (pp. 137–157). Washington, DC: American Psychological Association.

Strang, H., Sherman, L. W., Mayo-Wilson, E., Woods, D., & Ariel, B. (2013). Restorative justice conferencing (RJC) using face-to-face meetings of offenders and victims: Effects on offender recidivism and victim satisfaction. A systematic review. *Campbell Systematic Reviews, 12*. Retrieved from http://www.publicsafety.gc.ca

Umbreit, M. (1998). Restorative justice through victim-offender mediation: A multi-site assessment. *Western Criminology Review, 1*(1), 1–29.

Umbreit, M. S., Coates, R. B., & Vos, B. (2002). *The impact of restorative justice conferencing: A review of 63 empirical studies in 5 countries*. Minneapolis: University of Minnesota Center for Restorative Justice and Peacemaking, School of Social Work.

University of Michigan (2019). *Adaptable conflict resolution: ACR*. Retrieved from https://oscr.umich.edu/article/adaptable-conflict-resolution-acr

Wilgus, J. W., & Lowery, J. W. (2018). Adjudicating student sexual misconduct: Parameters, pitfalls, and promising practices. In J. Jessup-Anger & K. Edwards (Eds.), *New directions for student services: Addressing sexual violence on campus* (pp. 83–94). Hoboken, NJ: Wiley.

Zehr, H. (2002). *The little book of restorative justice*. New York, NY: Good Books.

VI

The Future of Campus Sexual Misconduct Adjudication: Best Practices

CHAPTER TWELVE

Best Practices in the Adjudication of Campus Sexual Misconduct Cases

Tara N. Richards

Developing responses to campus **sexual misconduct**—sexual harassment, sexual assault, stalking, dating violence, and domestic violence—is difficult; there are no perfect or easy solutions. As a result, legislation and guidance regarding prevention and response procedures have advanced, and sometimes seemingly regressed, over time. The rights of both students accused of conduct violations and alleged victims must be balanced while also considering the institution of higher education's (IHE) responsibility to the greater campus community. In light of these equally important objectives, the current chapter provides a review of policies and practices aimed at improving the response to campus sexual misconduct. It begins by arguing that compliance with, and enforcement of, existing policies is paramount. Then, suggestions for improvements in data collection and transparency are outlined and some of the essential elements of the investigatory and adjudicatory processes are discussed. The chapter closes with commentary on the limitations of administrative enforcement in responding to sexual misconduct and the importance of prevention programming.

Distinguishing Bad Policy from Bad Compliance

In the 1980s, **sexual harassment** was established as a form of sex discrimination in IHEs under **Title IX of the Education Amendments Act of 1972** through civil case precedent (e.g., *Alexander v. Yale*, 1980), and in 1997, the U.S. Department of Education's Office for Civil Rights (OCR) provided the first in a series of guidance documents regarding an IHE's obligations to respond to sexual harassment under Title IX (U.S. Department of Education,

1997). The 1997 guidance provided the definition of sexual harassment, also known as sexual misconduct, used in administrative enforcement under Title IX, which is still used today. OCR defines sexual harassment as "unwelcome conduct of a sexual nature … that can include unwelcome sexual advances, requests for sexual favors, and other verbal, nonverbal, or physical conduct of a sexual nature including sexual assault (U.S. Department of Education, 1997, p. 2). OCR plainly states that "Title IX protects any 'person' from sex discrimination, and as such both male and female students are protected from sexual harassment … and that Title IX prohibits sexual harassment regardless of the sex of the harasser, as in cases where the harasser and the person being harassed are members of the same sex" (U.S. Department of Education, 1997, p. 2).

While OCR guidance allows institutions some freedom in developing policies to respond to sexual misconduct, it mandates that each institution designate a Title IX coordinator and make the campus community aware of this person and how to contact them; must establish equitable grievance, investigative, and judicial procedures to promptly respond to complaints of sexual harassment; notify complainants about their right to report the sexual assaults to law enforcement; and inform complainants about all available interim remedies, such as housing accommodations, victim advocates and/or legal assistance, academic support, and physical and/or mental health services (U.S. Department of Education, 1997, 2001, 2011).

A new era of Title IX guidance and enforcement began in 2011 when OCR published a Dear Colleague Letter restating schools' obligations to address sexual harassment, including sexual violence, as a form of sex-based discrimination. And in 2014, OCR provided a "Questions and Answers on Title IX and Sexual Violence" document (i.e., answers to frequently asked questions or FAQ), which provided detailed instructions for IHEs regarding compliance with Title IX (U.S. Department of Education, 2014). The FAQ explained that in order to ensure equal educational opportunities, if an alleged victim chooses to file a formal Title IX complaint or the Title IX coordinator believes an allegation is so egregious as to pose a significant risk to the campus community, a fair and impartial investigation must take place: IHEs must provide equal treatment to both the complainant (i.e., alleged victim) and respondent (i.e., alleged perpetrator) (e.g., equal time, equity regarding access to advisors, confidentiality). IHEs must notify complainants about their rights to notify law enforcement, any available interim measures such as changing their academic schedule or campus housing to minimize contact with the respondent, and any sources of support (e.g., advocates). The preponderance of the evidence standard should be used in disciplinary hearings, and if a student is found responsible for violating the IHE's sexual misconduct policy, then the IHE should sanction the student per a written disciplinary policy.

In addition, the Jeanne Clery Disclosure of Campus Security Policy and Campus Crime Statistics Act of 1990 (20 U.S.C.A.§ 1092) (i.e., "Clery Act") mandates that IHEs gather data on crime in the campus community (including forcible and non-forcible sex offenses) and make these data available in an **annual security report (ASR)**. ASRs must be compiled into one document and made accessible to all current and prospective students and employees. The 1992 amendments to Clery instructed IHEs to promote prevention and intervention strategies for sexual assault and added the Sexual Assault Victim's Bill of Rights, which requires that IHEs notify victims about their right to report the assault to law enforcement, provide both the accuser and the accused with the same opportunity to have advisors present, and inform both the accuser and the accused of the outcome of any disciplinary proceeding associated with the assault. Further, the Violence Against Women Reauthorization Act's (VAWA) Campus Sexual Violence Elimination Act (SaVE Act; VAWA of 2013) expanded Clery's reporting provisions beyond sexual violence to include information on domestic violence, dating violence, and stalking in their ASRs. Campus SaVE also required that campus policies inform victims about their right to notify law enforcement or to choose not to notify law enforcement about their assault, as well as their options to pursue no-contact and/or protective orders.

Most recently, in 2017, the U.S. Department of Education withdrew the 2011 Dear Colleague Letter and 2014 guidance on Title IX, noting that neither went through the public "notice and comment period" where all stakeholders, including the public, could provide comments. The U.S. Department of Education issued notice that OCR would begin using the 2001 Revised Sexual Harassment Guidance and the 2006 Dear Colleague Letter on Sexual Harassment for Title IX investigations and enforcement and would seek to make new changes to OCR standards through a future notice and comment period (U.S. Department of Education, 2017a). An interim document provides guidance to IHEs regarding OCR enforcement (U.S. Department of Education, 2017b), and a review of that document in comparison to the withdrawn 2011 and 2014 guidance results in the following "real" changes: (a) Schools are no longer required to use the preponderance of the evidence standard (i.e., the standard commonly used for civil matters) in disciplinary hearings, but can use either the clear and convincing standard or the preponderance of the evidence standard; IHEs must use the same standard for all types of misconduct hearings; (b) schools are no longer encouraged to provide complainants the right to appeal in cases where a respondent is found not responsible; instead, IHEs *can* provide an appeals process to both parties or just the accused student (U.S. Department of Education, 2017b); and, (c) in a departure from the 2001 "Revised Sexual Harassment Guidance," the 2017 guidance from OCR allows schools to use "informal resolutions," such as mediation, at their discretion, presumably even in cases of sexual assault (U.S. Department of Education, 2017b). Comparatively, the 2001 guidance was clear that "in some cases, such as alleged sexual assaults, mediation will not be appropriate even on a voluntary basis" (U.S. Department of Education, 2001, p. 21).

In explaining these changes, the U.S. Department of Education (2017a) argued that "the 2011 and 2014 guidance documents may have been well-intentioned, but those documents have led to the deprivation of rights for many students—both accused students denied fair process and victims denied an adequate resolution of their complaints" (pp. 1–2). The basis of this argument is that it is the guidance, the *policy*, that has led to negative outcomes; however, there has been little analysis or discussion about whether IHEs are complying with policy and the role of noncompliance in IHEs' failure to protect students. As previously discussed, OCR guidance regarding Title IX, as well as mandates from the Clery Act and the Campus SaVe Act (2013), specify a range of policies and protections that IHEs must provide to students regarding sexual misconduct. However, two nationally representative studies—one in 1999 (Karjane, Fisher, & Cullen, 2002) and another in 2015 (Richards, 2016)—found that many IHEs have not implemented a number of these *mandated* provisions. For example, in 2015, 33% of IHEs still failed to identify a Title IX coordinator, 39% did not indicate offering any programs aimed at preventing sexual violence, 30% did not notify students about interim remedies such as academic or housing accommodations, and 23% did not notify students that the IHE would assist them in making a report to law enforcement (Richards, 2016). Further, a 2017 examination of the sexual misconduct polices and disciplinary procedures from the top 50 IHEs, as ranked by *U.S. News and World Report*, found that many procedural safeguards mandated by OCR's Title IX guidance or the Clery Act for sexual misconduct investigations and disciplinary hearings were either insufficient or absent from the policies (Foundation for Individual Rights in Education, 2017).

Additional evidence regarding IHEs' failures to comply with mandates regarding campus sexual misconduct is found in the growing number of civil lawsuits brought by students, both complainants (i.e., alleged victims) and respondents (i.e., alleged perpetrators), against their IHEs. Cantalupo (2014) provides a detailed discussion of eight general categories of actions brought by complainants against IHEs for violations of Title IX, such as IHEs "doing nothing at all" to "taking months or years to investigate" allegations of sexual misconduct. She also notes several six-figure settlements, including the "largest settlement to date," *Simpson v. University of Colorado Boulder* (2007). In *Simpson*, the University of Colorado, Boulder was ordered to pay the plaintiff (the complainant, in Title IX speak) $2.85 million, hire a special Title IX analyst, and fire 13 university officials, including the president and football coach after two female students were gang raped during an "unsupervised football recruiting program" (p. 229). In addition, according to the *Washington Post*, more than 300 students have filed suits against their IHEs for accusations related to sexual misconduct (i.e., respondents) since 2011; the lawsuits often allege violations of due process rights and/or gender discrimination against the accused student by the IHE (*Washington Post* Editorial Board, 2018).

Such evidence highlights the need for caution against mistaking bad implementation of Title IX guidance and related legislation (i.e., Clery, Campus SaVE) for bad policy. Both empirical research and legal case studies suggest that IHEs are failing to comply with guidance regarding protecting students in cases of sexual misconduct; the federal government has not done enough to train IHEs to implement Title IX guidance with fidelity and/or hold IHEs accountable when they fail to do so. As a result, students are turning to the civil court system for recourse.

Increased efforts for training IHEs to implement the mandates outlined in federal guidance are necessary. However, Title IX, the Clery Act, and Campus SaVE are unfunded mandates that require IHEs to employ staff (e.g., a Title IX coordinator) and provide resources to students (e.g., prevention programming) outside of their core educational missions. At the same time, state education budgets are shrinking. More state and federal resources must be expended on combatting sexual misconduct on college campuses. For example, the Campus Accountability and Safety Act (CASA), a bipartisan bill proposed in 2014, includes several provisions that advance the goal of increased training and provide additional resources. Specifically, CASA directs the secretary of education to develop online training materials for training higher education responsible employees, Title IX coordinators, and individuals involved in implementing an IHE's student conduct grievance procedures. CASA also calls for the inclusion of additional resources for training, such as increasing the minimum grant that may be provided to IHEs to combat sexual misconduct on campuses and authorize the use of such grants to train campus stakeholders. It would also amend the Higher Education Act (HEA) to authorize the secretary of education to use funds collected from the HEA's penalty provisions to award competitive grants to IHEs for campus responses to sexual misconduct.

Training on compliance is only the first step; monitoring and accountability are also necessary advancements. Currently, OCR only completes investigations—and civil litigation is only filed—after noncompliance has led to the deprivation of students' rights. More effort must be made to *prevent* noncompliance, and mechanisms for holding IHEs accountable must be strengthened. First, compliance audits must become routine. For example, in 2015, New York passed the landmark "Enough is Enough" law that, among other things, requires all IHEs governed by the state higher education commission to submit documentation regarding their compliance with state and federal policies governing campus sexual misconduct. A multi-agency task force completed a comprehensive review of these policies and procedures and determined whether each IHE included information in their policy on a series of mandated elements (e.g., the IHE identified a Title IX coordinator, provided confidential reporting). IHEs were identified as compliant or not compliant for each element and then given an overall compliance score: (1) "compliant" (i.e., 38.9% of IHEs included mandated information and demonstrated innovative approaches to protecting students, as well as using technology to provide informational resources); (2) "significantly compliant" (i.e., 49.2% of IHEs were found to be mostly compliant but still presented concerns that must be addressed to comply with the Enough is Enough law); and (3) "noncompliant" (i.e., 11.9% of IHEs' policies were found to be deficient across multiple elements). Data identified for each element and the IHE's overall compliance score were also made publicly available on the New York Office of Campus Safety website so that students and other interested stakeholders can utilize the information to see how well individual schools are doing. In addition, a report was released that synthesized the overall compliance of New York IHEs and the state's plan to move IHEs who were missing elements into full compliance. Second, increased penalties for IHEs that demonstrate a pattern of discrimination against students is warranted. Currently, OCR can withhold federal funds from IHEs for failure to comply with Title IX, but IHEs cannot be fined. CASA authorizes the secretary of education to impose civil penalties on IHEs that fail to uphold key provisions of Title IX guidance and amends the Education Amendments Act of 1972 to authorize the secretary of education or the Department of Justice to impose civil penalties on IHEs that violate or fail to carry out Title IX requirements.

Improve Data Collection and Transparency

In addition to better compliance, compliance monitoring, and accountability, data collection and dissemination for incidents of sexual misconduct that are reported to Title IX coordinators must be improved. Currently, the primary avenue for gathering information on reported incidents of sexual misconduct on any given college campus is the IHE's ASR. However, research demonstrates that the number of incidents publicly reported in ASRs is lower than the number internally reported to Title IX coordinators (Krebs, Lindquist, Berzofsky, Shook-Sa, & Peterson, 2016; Richards, 2018; Yung, 2015) or to counseling centers or prevention centers on campuses. For example, Krebs and colleagues (2016) compared the number of rapes students indicated they had reported to campus security authorities with the number of rapes presented in ASRs for nine campuses and found that only 67% of the rapes that students stated they reported to campus officials had been included in their campus crime statistics. Likewise, in a study of all public, private, and independent IHEs in a Mid-Atlantic state (n = 42), Richards (2018) found that ASRs only captured about half of the incidents of sexual assault and about one-third of the "other" sexual misconduct cases (e.g., stalking, dating violence) reported to Title IX coordinators. The sheer number of cases "lost" using only official reporting mechanisms underscores the undercounting of incidents in official statistics. An analogous example could be drawn from comparisons of reports of sexual violence in the data from the Uniform Crime Reports (i.e., law enforcement incident information) and the National Crime Victimization Survey (i.e., reports from victims of crime); the longstanding discrepancies between these two datasets highlight the great informational loss that is attributed to reliance on reports to law enforcement alone to understand sexual violence. Taken together, this research suggests that we need to make aggregate data from Title IX coordinators publicly available, too.

Several states have addressed these limitations by mandating that their institutions report aggregate data on sexual misconduct and make that data publicly available. For example, after legislation in 2015, Maryland now requires their IHEs to report the aggregate data collected under Title IX to the state's higher education commission every 2 years. The higher education commission releases a report that presents the data for the state's IHEs as well as by IHE type (i.e., independent, public 4-year, and community colleges). In addition, New York's IHEs are now required to report their aggregate data on sexual misconduct and the resolution of reports annually to the State Education Department. These data are also publicly available. Legislators in other states including Louisiana, New Jersey, Minnesota, and Pennsylvania have proposed legislation that would lead to similar data reporting strategies, but these bills have been stalled at varying legislative stages (Richards & Kafonek, 2016). Importantly, these state-level strategies focus on data that should already be collected by IHEs under the requirements of OCR. A holistic solution to the dearth of information on reported incidents of sexual misconduct is for the U.S. Department of Education to mandate that IHEs make the aggregate data on sexual misconduct reported to Title IX coordinators available in their ASRs each year.

The utility of ASRs in regard to understanding incidents of reported sexual misconduct on campus could be improved by expanding the types of offenses for which data on "arrests" and "referrals for disciplinary action" are presented to include sex offenses, dating violence, domestic violence, and stalking. Currently, ASRs only present the number of arrests and referrals for disciplinary action associated with incidents of liquor law violations, drug abuse violations, and illegal weapons possessions. The inclusion of such information for incidents of sexual misconduct would provide an additional avenue for transparency regarding the university's response to sexual misconduct as well as an incentive for campus security authorities to take sexual misconduct seriously. Strategies would have to be in place to protect a victim's choice in regard to any "formal" response (i.e., victims have the right to notify or decline to notify law enforcement and file or decline to file a formal Title IX complaint). To this end, ASRs could include an additional data field that presents the number of cases of sexual misconduct where the victim declined formal intervention (via a formal Title IX complaint or the filing of criminal charges).

Some Essential Elements in Investigatory and Adjudicatory Processes

Develop Memorandums of Understanding

Sexual assault continues to be the most underreported of all violent crimes (Langton, Berzofsky, Krebs, & Smiley-McDonald, 2012; Rennison, 2002; Tjaden & Thoennes, 2006). Research also indicates that college student victims specifically are unlikely to report sexual assaults to the police, with studies showing reporting rates of approximately 5–22% (DeKeseredy & Schwartz, 1998; Fisher et al., 2000, 2003; Koss, Dinero, Seibel, & Cox, 1988; Sloan, Fisher, & Cullen, 1997). Further, prior studies suggest that college student victims who were sexually assaulted while incapacitated are less likely to report their assault to police than college student victims who were assaulted using physical force (Fisher et al., 2003; Krebs et al., 2007).

Victims' decisions not to report a sexual assault to law enforcement are probably as diverse as the victims themselves, but studies suggest that there are some primary motivations for victim silence: Victims may feel shame and/or embarrassment about the assault, victims may believe that the assault was not serious enough to report, they may fear that they will not be believed and/or fear that nothing will be done if they report, and they may fear retaliation by the perpetrator or those close to the perpetrator (e.g., friends) (Bachman, 1998; Cantor et al., 2015). While the Campus SaVE Act mandates that student victims of sexual misconduct maintain the right to choose whether they report to law enforcement, better experiences for victims of sexual assault (e.g., being listened to, feeling believed, receiving accurate and timely information, having their choices followed and respected) who do report their assault should be a primary goal for improving the response to campus sexual misconduct. Further, better experiences for victims reporting sexual assault may lead to greater rates of reporting to both law enforcement and service providers (see Campbell, 2006).

More positive victim-law enforcement interactions can be advanced by developing partnerships between law enforcement departments, on-campus officials and advocates, and community-based service providers, and these partnerships can be facilitated by creating **memorandums of understanding (MOUs)**. The 2014 White House Task Force developed sample MOUs for IHEs to utilize in establishing these collaborations. In regard to law enforcement, linkages between IHEs and local law enforcement provide an opportunity for the development of victim-friendly and streamlined reporting strategies for students. Further, given that the Clery Act mandates that IHEs assist students in reporting crime victimization if the student chooses to do so, the IHE has a vested interest in developing a good working relationship with local law enforcement regarding student reporting. At the same time, law enforcement officers are not routinely trained in sensitive interviewing techniques, and a body of research suggests that victims of sexual assault often report negative experiences with the criminal justice system. Terms such as "secondary victimization" (Williams, 1984), the "second assault" (Martin & Powell, 1994), and the "second rape" (Madigan & Gamble, 1991) have been coined to describe the experiences of victims of sexual assault when seeking assistance from the criminal justice system. As such, if no sexual assault response protocol is in place (e.g., a MOU detailing who will take the report, whether an advocate will be accessible), campus officials may be rightly concerned about their students' well-being when they report an assault to law enforcement.

Research suggests that the presence of victim advocates during police interviews has positive effects for victims. For example, advocate assistance is associated with reductions in fear and stress among victims (Ullman, 2010). In addition, Campbell (2006) found that victims who worked with advocates were significantly more likely to have a police report filed and to have their cases investigated than victims who did not have an advocate. As such, partnerships between on-campus (or community-based) victim advocates and local and/or campus law enforcement outlined in MOUs may provide an opportunity to create positive change regarding the reporting and investigatory process. In addition, MOUs with community-based victim service providers allow IHEs that do not have on-campus advocates to provide advocacy to their students. These partnerships may also allow IHEs to expand their service repertoire to include services such as safe housing and/or legal assistance, which are beyond the scope of most IHEs' resources.

Distinguish Title IX Coordinators from Victim Advocates

The distinction between Title IX coordinators and victim advocates is paramount. Every IHE that is a Title IV participant and federal fund recipient is required to comply with federal legislation such as Title IX and must designate at least one Title IX coordinator. According to OCR, "A Title IX coordinator's core responsibilities include overseeing the school's response to Title IX reports and complaints and identifying and addressing any patterns or systemic problems revealed by such reports and complaints" (U.S. Department of Education, 2014, p. 19). Title IX coordinators are often tasked with coordinating student and staff training and prevention programs and developing grievance policies and procedures. Title IX coordinators must also be notified of every alleged violation of the IHE's antidiscrimination policy, including allegations of sexual misconduct (U.S. Department of Education, 2014).

While OCR does not specify which IHE employees should serve as Title IX coordinators, OCR guidance is clear that employees with any potential conflicts of interest (e.g., general counsel, athletics staff, judicial hearing staff) should not serve in this role (U.S. Department of Education, 2014). One potential conflict is that of taking on both the role of Title IX coordinator and victim advocate, either overtly or unintentionally. The Title IX coordinator's data collection, programming, and administrative responsibilities require them to be an objective finder of fact and preclude them from "being on the victim's side" (Richards, 2016, p. 22). As such, it is imperative that IHEs employ on-campus advocates, coordinate with off-campus service providers, or both, to provide support services for victims. Given that Title IX coordinators are notified of all allegations of sexual misconduct, the vast majority of complainants will have direct contact with the Title IX coordinator and will be asked to share their allegations with the coordinator. The process of disclosing a victimization experience can be quite traumatic, and victims benefit from having access to an advocate during the disclosure process (Campbell, 2006); however, Title IX coordinators cannot serve in this role. The availability of an advocate ensures that someone is looking out for the victim, while the Title IX coordinator focuses on compliance with the mandates of Title IX—a fair and impartial investigation and the mitigation of any hostile environments. Further, the presence of an advocate can provide clarity to the victim from the beginning of the process as to the distinct role of the Title IX coordinator and that of the advocate.

Obtain Victim Consent Before Reporting to Law Enforcement

As previously discussed, sexual assault, among both collegiate and non-collegiate victims, continues to be significantly underreported to law enforcement (Langton et al., 2012). At the same time, there have long been murmurings about whether IHEs actually make good-faith efforts to assist students with reporting to law enforcement or whether IHEs attempt to quash victims' reports out of fear of liability and to prevent damage to the university's reputation. Further, some have argued that IHEs have no business investigating allegations of sexual misconduct at all—Title IX be damned—and believe that reports of sexual assault fall under the sole jurisdiction of law enforcement. As such, there has been a trend in some state legislatures to propose and/or pass legislation mandating that law enforcement receive information when any student reports an incident of sexual misconduct to a Title IX coordinator (i.e., mandated reporting) (Richards & Kafonek, 2015). Setting aside the fact that mandated reporting to law enforcement plainly violates the Campus SaVE Act (which specifies that students have the right to decide whether to notify law enforcement), the mere fact that so many victims fail to report to law enforcement suggests that mandated reporting to law enforcement will reduce victim reporting to campus officials. The concern then becomes an associated reduction in campus services and interim measures afforded to victims under Title IX, the Clery Act, and Campus SaVE. Further, victim participation has long been recognized as an essential factor in a successful sexual assault prosecution (Spohn & Tellis, 2014), so mandating reporting for victims who have no interest in cooperating with the criminal justice system is simply a waste of time and resources.

It is paramount that IHEs utilize consented disclosure regarding victim reports to law enforcement or any formal process for that matter. If victims believe that their confidence will not be kept and that they will be compelled to participate in a criminal investigation if they seek Title IX protections, many will stay silent. As such, programs like "You Have Options" represent a potential shift in victim–law enforcement interactions and should be viewed as a current best practice in policing sexual assault. "You Have Options" provides victims with just that—options, choices, control—after sexual assault, an experience that surely removes any sense of options, choice, and control from victims. Law enforcement departments trained in the program allow victims to choose whether they only make a report (victim interview), participate in a partial investigation (victim interview, SAFE exam, witness interview), or participate in a full investigation. Victims also have the option to reduce or increase the "level" of investigation in their case at any point.

Consider Amnesty Policies and the Impact of Honor Codes

A large body of literature has established a relationship between alcohol and sexual assault among college students, with research suggesting that some perpetrators use alcohol to facilitate sexual assault, either by searching for intoxicated targets or attempting to increase a target's level of intoxication (for a review, see Abbey, 2011). Further, evidence suggests that a portion of sexual assaults are facilitated with drugs and/or alcohol without the victim's knowledge (Krebs, Lindquist, Warner, Fisher, & Martin, 2007; Testa, Livingston, & Vanzile-Tamsen, 2003). At the same time, a significant number of college students are between 18 and 20 years old, under the legal age to drink alcohol (National Center for Education Statistics, 2018), and many campuses ban alcohol outright. In addition, many religiously affiliated schools have "honor codes" that prohibit students from drug and alcohol use (as well as premarital sexual contact), and violations may result in severe consequences for students (see Brown, 2016).

Taken together, many college student victims of sexual assault will be assaulted while drinking alcohol illegally or in violation of university policy, and may be in real danger of disciplinary action if they report their assault to campus officials. Bystanders to sexual assault find themselves in a similar quandary. Amnesty policies, therefore, are an important strategy for increasing reports of sexual misconduct to campus officials and law enforcement. Amnesty policies refer to policies that exempt victims or bystanders who experience or witness sexual misconduct while engaged in a campus code of conduct violation (e.g., using alcohol or drugs on campus) from disciplinary action. Amnesty policies aim to increase reporting from victims and/or bystanders who may be hesitant to report because of fear of disciplinary consequences stemming from their own violation of the campus code of conduct. Research demonstrated that in 2015 only 15% of a nationally representative sample of IHEs reported having amnesty policies for drug and/or alcohol code of conduct violations (Richards, 2016); however, some evidence suggests that this trend is changing. For example, California, Maryland, Illinois, New York, Louisiana, and Minnesota have passed legislation implementing amnesty policies in IHEs statewide (Lebioda, 2015; Richards & Kafonek, 2016), while other states—Hawaii and Kansas, for example—have proposed such legislation (Lebioda, 2015). In addition, CASA would require that all IHEs nationwide implement amnesty policies.

Consistently Apply Due Process and Rape Shield Protections

Title IX's central focus is sex-based discrimination that interferes with equal educational opportunities for *all* students. As such, a core element of Title IX is procedural fairness for students involved in alleged violations. Indeed, the 1997 OCR guidance reminds us that "the Constitution guarantees due process to students in public and State-supported schools who are accused of certain types of infractions ... [but] schools should ensure that steps to accord due process rights do not restrict or unnecessarily delay the protections provided by Title IX to the complainant" (p. 15). At the heart of this guidance is the need to strike a *balance* between the rights of the complainant and the respondent. Consequently, balanced discussions of procedural fairness must focus on due process rights for respondents as well as procedural fairness for complainants, which may include policies analogous to **rape shield laws.**

Important elements of procedural fairness include (a) knowing the charges against you, (b) having access to counsel (e.g., an attorney or advisor), (c) having access to the evidence against you, (d) the ability to present and cross-examine witnesses, and (e) an impartial and unbiased hearing. None of these elements is denied to either the accused or the accuser under Title IX guidance (in U.S. Department of Education, 1997, 2001, 2014). For example, OCR guidance (U.S. Department of Education, 2001, 2014) is explicit in that both the complainant and the respondent must be notified of the charges in writing and that the IHE must balance a complainant's right to confidentiality with a respondent's right to due process. According to OCR, any case involving a complainant who chooses to remain unnamed would not be expected to result in disciplinary actions against a respondent (U.S. Department of Education, 2001, 2014). And while the 2001 OCR guidance is silent on the right to counsel (presumably because it is a fundamental due process right), the 2014 guidance explicitly states that if an IHE "permits one party to have lawyers or other advisors at any stage of the proceedings, it must do so equally for both parties" (p. 26), and that whatever role one party's advisor plays in the proceedings, that role must be available to the other party's advisor. In addition, "adequate, reliable, and impartial investigation of complaints, including the opportunity to present witnesses and other evidence" is explicitly stated in both the 2001 (p. 20) and 2014 (p. 26) OCR guidance, with the 2014 guidance extending the explanation to indicate that if one party submits testimony by a third-party expert, the other party also has the right to do so. Regarding the cross-examination of witnesses, the 2001 OCR guidance is silent, but the 2014 guidance indicates that while "OCR does not *require* that a school allow cross-examination of witnesses, including the parties, if they testify at the hearing, if the school allows one party to cross-examine witnesses, it must do so equally for both parties" (U.S. Department of Education, 2014, p. 31). OCR goes on to note that allowing an alleged harasser to directly question an accuser is discouraged given that it might perpetuate the very hostile environment created by sexual harassment that is forbidden under Title IX (U.S. Department of Education, 2001, 2014). Instead, parties may submit questions to a third party such as an advisor, attorney, or IHE hearing officer to be asked on their behalf (U.S.

Department of Education, 2014; see also Rudovsky et al., 2015). While OCR does not *require* that IHEs allow students to appeal decisions, current guidance by OCR (U.S. Department of Education, 2017b) indicates that IHEs have the discretion to offer no appeal, the right to appeal to only the respondent, or to both parties. Prior OCR guidance (U.S. Department of Education, 2014) encouraged IHEs to offer any appellate rights to both parties, and the Clery Act mandates that if IHEs provide an appellate process, it must be afforded to both parties equally.

Likewise, complainants have certain rights under Title IX that ensure they are free from sexual harassment and the associated hostile environment, and these rights extend to investigations and disciplinary hearings. Specifically, complainants should not be required to answer irrelevant questions about their sexual history and/or about partners other than the respondent. Questions about their sexual history with the respondent should be limited to those that directly inform the current allegation. Such limitations were explicitly stated in the now-rescinded 2014 guidance but were not retained in the 2017 Q&A from OCR, and, therefore, are assumedly no longer prohibited. Further, legal scholars from the University of Pennsylvania endorse "reasonable limits [on cross examination], including a ban on irrelevant questions regarding the sexual history and sexual orientation of the complainant; control over unfair, oppressive, or overbearing cross-examination; and even separation of the complainant and accused during the hearing" (Rudovsky et al., 2015, p. 4).

However, research conducted in 2015 examining a nationally representative sample of IHEs found that very few IHEs had written protections in place regarding questions about the accuser's sexual history (Richards, 2016). Richards contends that while the absence of written rules outlawing such questioning does not mean that IHEs do not prohibit them in practice, IHEs should prioritize codifying such victim protections in their written policies in a similar vein as rape shield laws do in the criminal legal system.

Understand the Limitations of Administrative Enforcement

Prior research on incidents of sexual misconduct reported to Title IX coordinators shows that the primary outcome of reports of sexual misconduct to Title IX coordinators involve accommodations to victims, not punishment to alleged perpetrators (Richards, 2018). Specifically, an assessment of all incidents of sexual misconduct at public, private, and independent institutions of higher education in a mid-Atlantic state (n = 1,054) found that 71.63% of victims (n = 755) were referred to counseling, 29.13% (n = 307) were assisted with obtaining no-contact orders against the alleged perpetrator, 20.30% (n = 215) received academic accommodations, and 6.36% (n = 67) were assisted with obtaining alternative housing. Receiving academic and other accommodations were not mutually exclusive such that many victims received more than one type of service. Comparatively, less than 25% of reported incidents resulted in a formal Title IX complaint process (i.e., a formal investigation and disciplinary hearing), less than half of those incidents resulted in a finding of responsibility for violating the school's sexual misconduct policy, and less than half of founded incidents resulted in either a suspension or an expulsion. Thus, overall, few students actually used the campus administrative process, and when they did and there was a finding of responsibility, there was little guarantee that the responsible student would be removed from campus (Richards, 2018).

These findings highlight the limitations of administrative enforcement under Title IX. U.S. Department of Education guidance on Title IX requires that when sexual misconduct becomes so severe and pervasive as to create a hostile environment, it must be mitigated so that the victim is not separated from educational opportunities (1997, 2001). Title IX guidance does not require that those found responsible for perpetrating sexual misconduct be punished; administrative enforcement is not the same as a criminal prosecution. On the other hand, while criminal prosecution aims to punish offenders, it focuses little attention on the well-being of victims (e.g., linking victims to services). It is paramount that these differences are recognized and fully appreciated: Administrative enforcement of Title IX may rarely "feel" like justice for victims of sexual misconduct.

Prevention Is Key: Start Early and Follow Best Practices

Finally, there is a need for widespread education regarding consent, ideally in preschool or early elementary school. Teaching consent—that you have control over your own body and that others' bodies should be respected—is an underutilized tool for preventing both sexual abuse and sexual assault. We must work harder to implement prevention programming early, before unhealthy attitudes become engrained and children and teens unnecessarily experience victimization, while adults are waiting for them to become old enough to learn these vital lessons. As of 2017, while 30 states required "healthy relationship education" in public schools, few schools were required to use evidence-based instruction, and only one state—California—required that such instruction include discussion of "consent" (defined as affirmative, conscious and voluntary agreement to engage in sexual activity (Sexuality Information and Education of the United States, 2017; see chapter 2, however, for a discussion of problems associated with affirmative consent policies).

At the same time, sexual assault prevention programming at IHEs has been mandated since an amendment to the Clery Act in 1992, and in 2013, the Campus SaVE Act specified that prevention programming should include (a) a statement that the IHE prohibits domestic violence, dating violence, sexual assault, and stalking; (b) the definition of domestic violence, dating violence, sexual assault, and stalking; (c) the definition of consent at the IHE (with reference to sexual offenses); (d) "safe and positive" options for bystander intervention that an individual may take to "prevent harm or intervene" in risky situations; and (e) information on risk reduction to recognize signs of abusive behavior and how to avoid potential attacks (Kafonek & Richards, 2017). Several prior meta-analyses have provided reviews of "what works" or "what might work" in sexual assault prevention programming (DeGue, Valle, Holt, Massetti, Matjasko, & Tharp, 2014; Paul & Gray, 2011); however, there has been little examination of whether IHEs adhere to these best practices. The limited existing research on IHEs' use of best practices in evidence-based treatment regarding sexual assault prevention programming indicates that few programs reference the role of alcohol and/or drug use in sexual misconduct (e.g., that would-be perpetrators may target intoxicated victims, that intoxication may limit a partner's ability to consent), include options for bystander intervention, and/or attend to sociocultural differences. Indeed, very few programs undergo any evaluation for efficacy (Kafonek & Richards, 2017). Evidence also suggests that many IHEs rely on online training modules (e.g., HAVEN) (Everfi, 2016; Kafonek & Richards, 2017) that do not include any opportunities for experiential learning, which has been associated with the highest rates of knowledge retention (Potter, Banyard, Stapleton, Demers, Edwards, & Moynihan, 2015).

Conclusion

Since OCR released its first set of guidance on sexual harassment in 1997, huge strides have been made regarding IHEs' responses to sexual misconduct against their students: The majority of IHEs have a Title IX coordinator, a written disciplinary process, prevention programming, and both on- and off-campus resources for interim measures (Richards, 2016). However, not all campuses are created equal in regard to implementing federal mandates related to campus sexual misconduct (Karjane et al., 2002; Richards, 2016). Further, the U.S. Department of Education's recent decision to repeal OCR guidance that included significant steps regarding consistency in the application of Title IX has stoked fear that the pendulum may be swinging back in the other direction and that IHEs may begin to "soften" their stance on Title IX. Further, it seems that much of the argument regarding the failure of Title IX and/or of previous OCR guidance related to Title IX (e.g., the 2011 Dear Colleague Letter, the 2014 Q&A) has been based on cases of the *misapplication of, or failure to comply with, federal mandates* that could and should be rectified through more rigorous monitoring and accountability measures.

Essential elements for administrative enforcement, such as fair and impartial Title IX coordinators and investigations, the availability of victim advocates, and adherence to due process rights, must be consistently applied. Any rolling back of administrative enforcement of Title IX will not bring an end to what the secretary of education has lamented as the "deprivation of rights for many students—both accused students denied fair process and victims denied an adequate resolution of their complaints" (U.S. Department of Education, 2017, pp. 1–2). The concern is that students will simply turn to the civil courts—as they have done in the past—to safeguard their rights under Title IX, often at great expense to their IHE (see Cantalupo, 2014). At the same time, victims seeking perpetrator accountability must recognize the limitations of administrative enforcement. And more effort must be expended in relationship building with both community-based victim services and law enforcement to fill this inevitable "justice gap." Finally, significantly greater attention must be paid to prevention programming, as both the spirit and the letter of federal mandates regarding sexual misconduct highlight the goal of reducing the number of victimizations outright, in addition to mitigating the consequences of victimization when it does occur.

KEY TERMS

Annual security report (ASR): All colleges and universities receiving federal funding must compile and disseminate an annual report detailing their campus's crime statistics for the previous 3 years and the efforts taken to improve campus safety.

Memorandum of understanding (MOU): An agreement between two or more parties expressing intentions regarding roles, responsibilities, and/or procedures for a common activity or activities.

Rape shield laws: State and federal evidence rules that bar certain information about the rape complaint, typically including past sexual behavior and sexual reputation, from the trial.

Sexual harassment: A type of sex discrimination as per OCR that includes unwelcome conduct of a sexual nature including unwelcome sexual advances, requests for sexual favors, and other verbal, nonverbal, or physical conduct of a sexual nature. The EEOC defines sexual harassment as treating someone unfavorably because of that person's sex, which includes unwelcome sexual advances, requests for sexual favors, and other verbal or physical harassment of a sexual nature. Sex harassment can include offensive remarks about a person's sex including making offensive comments about a group of people (e.g., individual who identifies as LGBTQ).

Sexual misconduct: A phrase widely used to describe the behaviors prohibited by Title IX, some of which are criminal in nature (e.g., rape, sexual assault), and others which are illegal, but not criminal in nature (e.g., discrimination).

Title IX of the Education Amendments Act of 1972: Legislation signed into law by President Richard Nixon that prohibits sex discrimination in educational institutions that receive federal funds. This stand-alone legislation fills in the gaps found in Title VII of the Civil Rights Act of 1964 and other legal documents.

DISCUSSION QUESTIONS

1. There have been a number of Title IX-related lawsuits filed in civil court, and many of these suits have been "successful" in that damages have been awarded to plaintiffs. What might be some of the positive and/or negative impacts of these successful lawsuits on IHEs, students, and policies?
2. There are significant shortfalls in the current sexual misconduct prevention programming offered by IHEs. What concepts *should* be included in these programs, who should "teach" them, and in what format(s) should they be delivered?
3. Title IX aims to protect all students' civil rights. What elements in investigating and adjudicating allegations of sexual misconduct are most essential to providing procedural fairness for both complainants and respondents?
4. An old adage states that "an ounce of prevention is worth a pound of cure." In following this conventional wisdom, how might we teach consent to preschoolers, fifth-graders, and first-year high schoolers in a developmentally appropriate way?

References

Abbey, A. (2011). Alcohol's role in sexual violence perpetration: Theoretical explanations, existing evidence, and future directions. *Drug and Alcohol Review, 30*(5), 481–489.

Bachman, R. (1998). The factors related to rape reporting behavior and arrest: New evidence from the National Crime Victimization Survey. *Criminal Justice and Behavior, 25*(1), 8–29.

Brown, S. (2016, April 18). A sex-assault case at Brigham Young puts honor codes in the spotlight. *Chronicle of Higher Education.* Retrieved from https://www.chronicle.com/article/A-Sex-Assault-Case-at-Brigham/236145

Cantor, D., Fisher, B., Chibnall, S., Townsend, R., Lee, H., Bruce, C., & Thomas, G. (2015). *Report on the AAU campus climate survey of sexual assault and sexual misconduct.* Rockville, MD: Westat. Retrieved from https://www.aau.edu/sites/default/files/AAU-Files/Key-Issues/Campus-Safety/AAU-Campus-Climate-Survey-FINAL-10-20-17.pdf

Cantalupo, N. C. (2014). Institution-specific victimization surveys: Addressing legal and practical disincentives to gender-based violence reporting on college campuses. *Trauma, Violence, and Abuse, 15*(3), 227–241.

Campbell, R. (2006). Rape survivors' experiences with the legal and medical systems: Do rape victim advocates make a difference? *Violence Against Women, 12*(1), 30–45.

Clery Center for Security on Campus (2016). *Clery handbook for campus safety and security.* Retrieved from https://www2.ed.gov/admins/lead/safety/handbook.pdf

Crime Awareness and Campus Security Act, 20 U.S.C. § 1092 (f) (1990)

DeGue, S., Valle, L. A., Holt, M. K., Massetti, G. M., Matjasko, J. L., & Tharp, A. T. (2014). A systematic review of primary prevention strategies for sexual violence perpetration. *Aggression and Violent Behavior, 19*(4), 346–362.

DeKeseredy, W. S., & Schwartz, M. D. (1998). *Woman abuse on campus: Results from the Canadian national survey.* Thousand Oaks, CA: SAGE.

Epstein, J., & Langenbahn, S. (1994). *The criminal justice and community response to rape.* Washington, DC: U.S. Department of Justice, National Institute of Justice.

Everfi. (2016). *Sexual assault training for undergraduate students.* Retrieved from: https://everfi.com/higher-education/haven/#different

Fisher, B., Cullen, F., & Turner, M. (2000). *The sexual victimization of college women.* Washington, DC: U.S. Department of Justice, National Institute of Justice. Retrieved from https://www.ncjrs.gov/pdffiles1/nij/182369.pdf

Fisher, B., Daigle, L., & Cullen, F. (2010). *Unsafe in the ivory tower: The sexual victimization of college women.* Thousand Oaks, CA: SAGE.

Fisher, B., Daigle, L., Cullen, F., & Turner, M. (2003). Reporting sexual victimization to the police and others: Results from a national-level study of college women. *Criminal Justice and Behavior, 30*(1), 6–38.

Foundation for Individual Rights in Education. (2017). *Spotlight on due process, 2017.* Retrieved from https://www.thefire.org/due-process-report-2017/

Kafonek, K., & Richards, T.N. (2017). An examination of strategies for the primary prevention of gender-based violence at institutions of higher education: Prevalence and content from a nationally representative sample. *Journal of School Violence, 16*(3), 271–285.

Karjane, H., Fisher, B. S., & Cullen, T. (2002). *Campus sexual assault: How America's institutions of higher education respond* (Final Report, NIJ Grant No. 1999-WA-VX-0008). Newton, MA: Education Development Center. Retrieved from https://www.ncjrs.gov/pdffiles1/nij/grants/196676.pdf

Koss, M. P., Dinero, T. E., Seibel, C. A., & Cox, S. L. (1988). Stranger and acquaintance rape: Are there differences in the victim's experience? *Psychology of Women Quarterly, 12*(1), 1–24.

Krebs, C. P., Lindquist, C. H., Berzofsky, M., Shook-Sa, B., & Peterson, K. (2016). *Campus climate survey validation study final technical report.* (Final Report, NCJRS Document No. 249545). Washington, DC: U.S. Department of Justice.

Krebs, C. P., Lindquist, C. H., Warner, T. D., Fisher, B. S., & Martin, S. L. (2007). *The campus sexual assault (CSA) study* (Final Report, NCJRS Document No. 221153). Washington, DC: U.S. Department of Justice.

Kreighbaum, A. (2017, September 8). DeVos to replace Obama-era sexual assault guidelines. *Inside Higher Education.* Retrieved from https://www.insidehighered.com/news/2017/09/08/devos-says-federal-title-ix-guidelines-have-'failed'-will-seek-public-input-new

Langton, L., Berzofsky, M., Krebs, C. P., & Smiley-McDonald, H. (2012). *Victimizations not reported to the police, 2006-2010* (NCJ 238536). Washington, DC: U.S. Department of Justice Statistics, Office of Justice Programs, Bureau of Justice Statistics. Retrieved from https://www.bjs.gov/content/pub/pdf/vnrp0610.pdf

Lebioda, K. (2015). *Policy matters, a higher education policy brief: State policy proposals to combat campus sexual assault.* Washington, DC: American Association of State Colleges and Universities. Retrieved from https://www.aascu.org/policy/publications/policy-matters/campussexualassault.pdf

Madigan, L., & Gamble, N. (1991). *The second rape: Society's continued betrayal of the victim.* New York, NY: Lexington Books.

Maddox, L., Lee, D., & Barker, C. (2011). Police empathy and victim PTSD as potential factors in rape case attrition. *Journal of Police and Criminal Psychology, 26*(2), 112–117.

Martin, P. Y., & Powell, M. (1994). Accounting for the "second assault": Legal organizations' framing of rape victims. *Law & Social Inquiry, 19*(4), 853–890.

Milne, R., & Bull, R. (2007). *Investigative interviewing: Psychology and practice.* Chichester: Wiley.

National Center for Education Statistics, (2019). Table 304.2: Total fall enrollment in degree-granting post-secondary institutions, by attendance status, sex, and age: Selected years, 1970 through 2017. *Digest of education statistics, 2017.* Washington, D.C.: U.S. Department of Education, (NCES 2018-070).

Paul, L. A., & Gray, M. J. (2011). Sexual assault programming on college campuses: Using social psychological belief and behavior change principles to improve outcomes. *Trauma, Violence, and Abuse, 12*(2) 99–109.

Penney, S. W., Tucker, L., & Lowry, J. W. (2000). *National baseline study on campus sexual assault: Adjudication of sexual assault cases.* College Station, TX: Association for Student Judicial Affairs.

Potter, S. J., Banyard, V. L., Stapleton, J. G., Demers, J. M., Edwards, K. M., & Moynihan, M. M. (2015). It's not just the what but the how: Informing students about campus policies and resources: How they get the message matters. *University of New Hampshire Prevention Innovations Research Center.* Retrieved from https://www.nccpsafety.org/assets/files/library/Infoming_Students_About_Campus_Policies_and_Resources.pdf

Rennison, C. M. (2002). *Rape and sexual assault: Reporting to police and medical attention, 1992-2000* (NCJ 194530). Washington, DC: U.S. Department of Justice, Office of Justice Programs, Bureau of Justice Statistics. Retrieved from https://www.bjs.gov/content/pub/pdf/rsarp00.pdf

Richards, T. N. (2016). An updated review of institutions of higher education's responses to sexual assault results from a nationally representative sample. *Journal of Interpersonal Violence, 34*(10), 1983–2012.

Richards, T.N. (2018). No evidence of "weaponized Title IX" here: An empirical assessment of sexual misconduct reporting, case processing, and outcomes. *Law and Human Behavior, 43*(2), 180–192.

Richards, T.N., & Kafonek, K. (2016). Reviewing state legislative agenda regarding sexual assault in higher education: Proliferation of best practices, and points of caution. *Feminist Criminology, 11*(1), 91–129.

Sexuality Information and Education of the United States. (2017). *State profiles, fiscal year 2017.* Retrieved from https://siecus.org/wp-content/uploads/2018/07/SIECUS-SP-FY17-State-Law-and-Policy-Chart.pdf

Sloan, J., Fisher, B., & Cullen, F. T. (1997). Assessing the Student-Right-to-know and Campus Security Act of 1990: An analysis of victim reporting practices of college and university students. *Crime & Delinquency, 43*(2), 148–168.

Spohn, C. & Tellis, K. (2014). *Policing and prosecuting sexual assault: Inside the criminal justice system.* Boulder, CO: Lynne Rienner Publishers.

Testa, M., Livingston, J. A., VanZile-Tamsen, C., & Frone M. R. (2003). The role of women's substance use in vulnerability to forcible and incapacitated rape. *Journal of Studies on Alcohol, 64*(6), 756–764.

Tjaden, P., & Thoennes, N. (2006). *Extent, nature, and consequences of rape victimization: Findings from the National Violence Against Women Survey* (NCJ 210346). Washington, DC: U.S. Department of Justice, Office of Justice Programs, Bureau of Justice Statistics. Retrieved from https://www.ncjrs.gov/pdffiles1/nij/210346.pdf

Ullman, S. E. (2010). *Talking about sexual assault: Society's response to survivors.* Washington, DC: American Psychological Association.

Rudovsky, D., Bibas, S., Balganesh, S., Berman, M., Burbank, S.B., Fisch, et al. (2015). *Open Letter from members of the University of Pennsylvania Law School Faculty, Sexual assault complaints: Protecting complainants and the accused students at universities.* Retrieved from http://media.philly.com/documents/OpenLetter.pdf

U.S. Department of Education. (1997). *Sexual harassment guidance 1997.* Retrieved from https://www2.ed.gov/about/offices/list/ocr/docs/sexhar01.html

U.S. Department of Education. (2001, January 19). *Revised sexual harassment guidance: Harassment of students by school employees, other students, or third parties.* Retrieved from https://www2.ed.gov/about/offices/list/ocr/docs/shguide.html

U.S. Department of Education. (2011, April 4). *Dear Colleague Letter.* Retrieved from http://www2.ed.gov/about/offices/list/ocr/letters/colleague-201104.pdf

U.S. Department of Education. (2014, April 29). Questions and answers on Title IX and sexual violence. Retrieved from http://www2.ed.gov/about/offices/list/ocr/letters/colleague-201504-title-ix-coordinators.pdf

U.S. Department of Education. (2017a, September 22). *Dear Colleague Letter.* Retrieved from https://www2.ed.gov/about/offices/list/ocr/letters/colleague-title-ix-201709.pdf

U.S. Department of Education, Office for Civil Rights. (2017b, September). Q&A on campus sexual misconduct. Retrieved from https://www2.ed.gov/about/offices/list/ocr/docs/qa-title-ix-201709.pdf

Violence Against Women Reauthorization Act. (2013) Pub. L. No. 113–4. Retrieved from: https://www.gpo.gov/fdsys/pkg/BILLS-113s47enr/pdf/

Washington Post Editorial Board. (2018, September, 13). Due process for sexual assault cases: The Sixth Circuit says the accused have a right to cross examination. *Washington Post.* Retrieved from https://www.wsj.com/articles/due-process-for-sexual-assault-cases-1536881654

Williams, J.E. (1984). Secondary victimization: Confronting public attitudes about rape. *Victimology: An International Journal, 9*(1), 66–81.

Yung, C. R. (2015). Concealing campus sexual assault: An empirical examination. *Psychology, Public Policy, and Law, 21*(1), 11–19.

Index

D

About the Editors

Claire M. Renzetti, PhD, is the Judi Conway Patton Endowed Chair for Studies of Violence Against Women in the Center for Research on Violence Against Women and professor and chair of the Sociology Department at the University of Kentucky. For more than 35 years, her research has focused on the violent victimization experiences of socially and economically marginalized women and girls. She is editor of the international and interdisciplinary journal *Violence Against Women*, editor of the gender and justice book series for the University of California Press, coeditor of the interpersonal violence book series for Oxford University Press, and editor of the family and gender-based violence book series for Cognella. She has written or edited 25 books as well as numerous book chapters and journal articles based on her own research. Her current research includes a federally funded evaluation of a therapeutic horticulture program for battered women at a battered women's shelter; studies related to the problem of domestic sex trafficking, including identifying gaps in the knowledge base and in rigorous and reliable data collection and assisting health care providers and law enforcement in identifying domestic sex trafficking victims; and studies of the effects of religiosity and religious self-regulation on intimate partner violence perpetration and victimization.

Diane R. Follingstad, PhD, ABPP, is the executive director and Women's Circle Endowed Chair of the Center for Research on Violence Against Women and a professor in the Department of Psychiatry at the University of Kentucky. This appointment follows her career as a distinguished professor emeritus in clinical and forensic psychology at the University of South Carolina. She currently holds the diplomate in forensic psychology from the American Board of Forensic Psychology and was awarded fellow status in the Psychology and Law Division of the American Psychological Association. Her quantitative research over 40 years in the area of violence against women has covered issues related to intimate partner violence (e.g., patterns of abuse; physical, sexual, and psychological abuse), physical dating violence (e.g., motivations, model treatment plan for prevention), and factors impacting jury verdicts in cases where battered women killed a partner (e.g., mock juror reactions to clusters of reasons why women remain in abusive relationships, personal aspects of the defendant, jury instructions, issue of retreat). Her research has led to more sophisticated measurement of psychological aggression and abuse, and she has published critiques regarding the problems of measurement in this field. Currently, she heads the campus climate survey research team for the University of Kentucky and runs two federally funded grant projects evaluating the long-term effects on young adults, whether attending institutions of higher education or not, of receiving bystander intervention training in high school and studying the impact of participating in a therapeutic horticulture program on battered women in a shelter. Her research has resulted in publications in almost every major peer-reviewed journal focusing on interpersonal violence as well as book chapters on this topic.

About the Contributors

Kelly Alison Behre directs the University of California, Davis, Family Protection and Legal Assistance Clinic, a clinic providing free civil legal assistance to low-income victims of intimate partner and sexual violence. She previously directed domestic violence law clinics at the West Virginia University College of Law and the University of Alabama School of Law, and she served as a staff attorney at the American Bar Association Commission on Domestic and Sexual Violence and at the Sexual Assault Legal Institute of the Maryland Coalition Against Sexual Assault. Her scholarship focuses on intimate partner violence, sexual assault, and Title IX.

Deborah L. Brake is associate dean for research and faculty development, John E. Murray scholar, and professor of law at the University of Pittsburgh, where she teaches Constitutional Law, Employment Discrimination, and Gender and the Law. She is a nationally recognized scholar on Title IX and author of *Getting in the Game: Title IX and the Women's Sports Revolution* (New York University Press, 2010). She has published numerous book chapters and over 25 law review articles, which have appeared in such publications as *Georgetown Law Journal, William & Mary Law Review, Minnesota Law Review, Ohio State Law Journal, Indiana Law Journal, North Carolina Law Review, Boston University Law Review*, and *Harvard Journal of Law and Gender*. Her scholarship has been cited by the U.S. Supreme Court and she has twice testified before Congress. Before going into academia, she was senior counsel at the National Women's Law Center. She is a graduate of Harvard Law School and Stanford University.

Nancy Chi Cantalupo is an associate professor at Barry University School of Law who has worked against gender-based violence in education as a scholar, administrator, activist, victims' advocate, attorney, and policymaker. A graduate of Georgetown Law and Georgetown University's School of Foreign Service, she has published in the *Harvard Journal of Law and Gender, Wake Forest Law Review, Yale Law Journal Forum, New York Times*, and *Washington Post*, among other venues. Her *pro bono* activities include service on the 2013 VAWA Negotiated Rulemaking Committee, consultations with the Obama-Biden White House Task Force on

Campus Sexual Assault, coauthorship of "Title IX & the Preponderance of the Evidence: A White Paper" (signed by 116 law professors), and leadership of the Big Comment Catalog Project that is in the process of cataloging the more than 124,000 comments filed in response to a recent Notice of Proposed Rulemaking on Title IX.

Melissa Carleton is an Ohio attorney who regularly advises colleges and universities on how to comply with Title IX in a thoughtful manner. She also acts as a neutral investigator in Title IX cases and trains coordinators, investigators, and adjudicators on best practices. Melissa holds a bachelor's degree in music education from The Ohio State University and a juris doctorate from the University of Pennsylvania.

Jaspreet Chahal is the research project manager for the Center for Research on Violence Against Women at the University of Kentucky. She manages Campus Attitudes Toward Safety (CATS), a project developed to provide the university administration with data about campus safety as an internal quality improvement project. The information covers students' perceptions of campus safety, students' knowledge of and inclination to use campus resources, bystander attitudes and behaviors, and students' experience of violent or adverse incidents. Her research interests include violence and victimization on college campuses, cultural factors and vulnerability to sexual violence, and the adverse health outcomes of violence and victimization. She received her M.S. in criminal justice from Eastern Kentucky University and is currently finishing her doctoral degree in criminology, law, and society from George Mason University.

Aya Gruber is a professor at the University of Colorado Law School. Gruber received her law degree from Harvard Law School and graduated *magna cum laude*. She then served as a public defender and a law professor at the University of Iowa and Florida International University. In 2017, she was a visiting professor at Harvard Law School. Gruber's numerous articles focus on feminist criminal law reform and her forthcoming book, *The Feminist War on Crime* (2020), examines the surprising contribution of women's liberation to mass incarceration. Gruber is a member of the American Law Institute and an adviser to its Model Penal Code sexual assault project.

David Karp is professor and director of the Center for Restorative Justice in the School of Leadership and Education Sciences at the University of San Diego. His current scholarship focuses on restorative justice in community and educational settings. For his work on restorative justice, he was the recipient of the 2019 Leadership and Innovation Award from the National Association of Community and Restorative Justice as well as the 2011 Donald D. Gehring Award from the Association for Student Conduct Administration. He has published more than one hundred academic papers and six books, including *The Little Book of Restorative Justice for Colleges and Universities*, *Wounds That Do Not Bind: Victim-Based Perspectives on the Death Penalty*, and *The Community Justice Ideal*. Karp serves on the board of directors for the National Association for Community and Restorative Justice. He has previously served as associate dean of student affairs and professor of sociology at Skidmore College. He received a BA in Peace and Conflict Studies from the University of California, Berkeley, and a PhD in Sociology from the University of Washington.

Mary Koss, PhD, is a regents' professor at the University of Arizona College of Public Health. She published the first national study of sexual assault among college students in 1987. She was the principal investigator of the RESTORE program, the first restorative justice program for sex crimes among adults that was quantitatively evaluated. She was the eighth recipient of the Visionary award from End Violence Against Women International. She has received the award for distinguished contributions to research in public policy (2000) and the award for distinguished contributions to the international advancement of psychology (2017) from the American Psychological Association.

Elise Lopez, DrPH, is the director of the University of Arizona's Consortium on Gender-Based Violence and an assistant professor of practice in the UA College of Public Health. She received the 2016 Abstract of the Year honor from the American Public Health Association Law Section for a coauthored paper on restorative justice responses to campus sexual misconduct. She has been an invited speaker on sexual violence in local, national, and international venues. In 2017, Lopez served as one of two non-attorney liaisons to the American Bar Association's Criminal Justice Section Task Force on College Due Process Rights and Victim Protections.

Christina Mancini, PhD, is an associate professor and assistant chair of criminal justice at Virginia Commonwealth University's Wilder School of Government and Public Affairs. She has published over 35 articles in *Sexual Abuse: A Journal of Research and Treatment*, *Criminology*, *Crime & Delinquency*, the *Journal of Criminal Law and Criminology*, and other crime and policy journals. Her current research examines sex crime policy, public opinion, and offending. She is the author of two books, *Sex Crime, Offenders, and Society: A Critical Look at Sexual Offending and Policy* (2014), and *Campus Crime and Safety* (2015).

Callie Marie Rennison, PhD, is the former director of equity and Title IX coordinator for the University of Colorado Denver and Anschutz Medical campuses. She is a professor in the School of Public Affairs at the University of Colorado Denver, where she has also served as associate dean of faculty affairs. Her research interests include violent victimization with an emphasis on methodology, quantitative analysis, and measurement. Her work has focused on marginalized groups including women, African Americans, American Indians, Latinos, and those living in non-urban areas. In addition, she has examined victim interaction with the criminal justice system and college student victimization.

Tara N. Richards, PhD, is an assistant professor in the School of Criminology and Criminal Justice at the University of Nebraska, Omaha. Her research expertise focuses on sexual assault, intimate partner violence, and child maltreatment. Richards has published more than 50 peer-reviewed journal articles, featured in top journals such *Child Abuse and Neglect*, *Law and Human Behavior*, and *Crime & Delinquency*, and she is the coeditor of the book *Sexual Victimization: Then and Now*. Her research has also been cited in the *Chronicle of Higher Education*, *Inside Higher Education*, and the *Huffington Post*.

Valerie Simons is the associate vice chancellor and Title IX coordinator at the University of Colorado (CU), Boulder. Prior to joining CU in 2014, Simons served as a trial attorney at the U.S. Department of Justice, Civil Rights Division, where she litigated cases involving a variety of civil rights laws including Title IX and consulted with the U.S. Department of Education's Office for Civil Rights on federal compliance issues. While in private practice in Colorado from 2007–2014, she was named a Colorado super lawyer in school and education law. She received her bachelor's degree in political economy from UC Berkeley and her law degree from Georgetown.

Joan Tabachnick has developed educational materials and innovative prevention programs for national, state and local organizations over the past 25 years. Her primary focus is on preventing the perpetration of sexually harmful behaviors, particularly in adolescents and young adults. She created the educational programming for Stop It Now! before starting her own consulting practice. Since then she has been director of NEARI Press, founding cochair of ATSA's prevention committee, and executive director of MASOC, and currently she is a fellow with the Department of Justice, SMART Office.

Regina Tirella is the director of remedial and protective measures and deputy Title IX coordinator in the Office of Institutional Equity and Compliance at the

University of Colorado, Boulder. Tirella has 19 years of experience working in higher education and has vast knowledge in adjudicating conduct in student affairs/housing as the assistant director of residence life, as well as now on the Title IX side. She received her master's degree in student college personnel from Kansas State University and is also NABITA and ATIXA certified.

Jay Wilgus is a lawyer, consultant, and facilitator specializing in student behavior and student conflict. He previously served as director of the Office of Student Conflict Resolution at the University of Michigan and assistant dean of students at the University of Utah. He now serves as principal at Klancy Street, LLC, a specialized law, consulting, and dispute resolution firm with expertise in higher education, including restorative justice applications to student sexual misconduct and research-informed interventions for students found responsible for sexual misconduct. Wilgus holds a master's in dispute resolution from Pepperdine University and a juris doctorate from the University of Utah.

Kristi Wold-McCormick has served as university registrar at the University of Colorado, Boulder since 2014. In her leadership role, she focuses on student data privacy, process improvement, academic policy, inclusion, and academic record innovation. She was previously registrar at North Dakota State University and has held various positions in admissions and enrollment services. She chaired a committee for the American Association of Collegiate Registrars and Admissions Officers (AACRAO) that developed guidance on disciplinary transcript notations. Wold-McCormick earned bachelor's and master's degrees from North Dakota State University and a PhD from the University of North Dakota.